EC2ND 2005

Andrew Blyth (Ed.)

EC2ND 2005

**Proceedings of the First European Conference
on Computer Network Defence**
School of Computing, University of Glamorgan, Wales, UK

 Springer

Andrew Blyth, BSc, MSc, PhD
School of Computing, University of Glamorgan, UK

British Library Cataloguing in Publication Data
A catalogue record for this book is available from the British Library

ISBN-10: 1-84628-311-6   Printed on acid-free paper
ISBN-13: 978-1-84628-311-6

9 8 7 6 5 4 3 2 1

Springer Science+Business Media
springer.com

First EC²ND Conference Chair
Andrew Blyth, University of Glamorgan, UK

Conference Programme Committee
Bob Askwith, Liverpool John Moores University, UK

Phil Brooke, University of Plymouth, UK

Bill J Buchanan, Napier University, UK

Tim Charrot, QinetiQ, UK

Paul Chichester, CESG/GCHQ, UK

Tim Cossali-Francis, DSTL, UK

Steve Furnell, University of Plymouth, UK

Andy Jones, BT, UK

George Kalb, John Hopkins University, USA

Maria Karyda, University of the Aegean, Greece

Socratis Katsikas, University of the Aegean, Greece

Evangelos Markatos, University of Crete, Greece

Madjid Merabta, Liverpool John Moores University, UK

David Parish, Loughborough University, UK

Iain Sutherland, University of Glamorgan, UK

Theodore Tryfonas, University of Glamorgan, UK

Craig Valli, Edith Cowen University, Australia

Matt Warren, Deakin University, Australia

Diego Zamboni, IBM Research, Switzerland

Local Organisers

School of Computing, University of Glamorgan, Wales UK

Andrew Blyth

Caroline Bowen

Theodore Tryfonas

Iain Sutherland

Table of Contents

Section III: Network Protocol Analysis & Cryptographic Applications

Section IV: Intrusion Detection & Prevention

Section V: Software for Security in Networked Environments

SECTION I: Network Defence

Network Penetration Testing

Liwen He[1] and Nikolai Bode[2]

[1] Security Research Centre, BT Group CTO Office, PP4, Admin 2, Antares Building,
BT Adastral Park, Ipswich, IP5 3RE, United Kingdom
liwen.he@bt.com
[2] Corpus Christi College, University of Cambridge,
Cambridge CB2 1RH, United Kingdom
nwfb2@cam.ac.uk

Abstract. Network penetration testing is a way for companies and other organisations to find out about vulnerabilities in their network security before hackers use them to break in. In this paper different types of network penetration tests are classified and the general approach to a test is outlined. Different tools and techniques that are used in each step of the test are introduced. The aim is to give a general overview of the techniques employed in network penetration testing as well as identifying the future trends and further research directions in penetration testing and network security.

1 Introduction

The current IP networks are not sufficiently secure, hackers are able to exploit existing vulnerabilities in the network architecture and obtain unauthorised access to sensitive information and subsequently disrupt network services. For 2003 the estimated cost of lost productivity due to malicious cyber attack activities mounted to $113 billion [1].

There are different approaches to investigate the security of an existing network. For example, *network vulnerability assessments* look at every component of the network, trying to determine a wide variety of weaknesses, *automated vulnerability scanners* can be used for routine checks of a network and lastly *penetration tests* evaluate whether a target network can be cracked in a given amount of time [2]. In penetration tests, *ethical hackers*, are hired to break into networks to expose vulnerabilities, and perform various attacks, for example, obtaining administrative access to mail servers, disabling a specific data centre which are controlled simulations of the actions and techniques that might be used by a malicious hacker.

This paper will be organised as follows. In section 2 the different types of network penetration tests and the general procedure are introduced. Section 4 provides a summary of vulnerabilities, and in section 4 a number of popular hacking tools are discussed. Section 5 highlights some recent development and future tendencies of network penetration testing techniques, while in section 7 conclusions and the further research are presented.

2 Overview of Network Penetration Testing

There are different types of penetration tests with varying approaches to the penetration and the degree of realism of the test. The choice of the type of test is usually made by a utility evaluation for a specific organisation

2.1 Types of Penetration Testing

There are essentially two distinct types of penetration tests: announced or unannounced [3]. *Announced testing* is an attempt to access and retrieve pre-identified flag file(s) or to compromise systems on the client network with the full co-operation and knowledge of the IT staff. Such a test examines the existing security infrastructure and individual systems for possible vulnerabilities. *Unannounced testing* is an attempt to access and retrieve pre-identified flag file(s) or to compromise systems on the client network with the awareness of only the upper levels of management. Such a test examines the organisation's security procedures, the existing security infrastructure and the responsiveness of the staff.

Further we can distinguish between *black box* and *crystal/white box* tests [4]. In a black box test the security consultants have no prior knowledge of the network they are trying to penetrate. This means that the team has to spend a considerable amount of time trying to discover such information. In a crystal box test, the team is given inside information about the target network and may even work with insiders who have privilege information, such as the configuration of the network or the types of hardware and software in use.

2.2 General Testing Procedure

In this section the general process of a penetration test is illustrated with the help of figure 1 [2]. Professional testers have to compromise a network in a given period of time, finding as many weaknesses as possible, so a well-defined methodology to systematically check for known vulnerabilities and pursue potential security holes is critical. The importance of a common methodology is further stressed in [5]. Figure 1 shows the four-step process in a typical penetration test.

3 Summary of Vulnerabilities

This section summarises the possible vulnerabilities for hacker to launch attackers. Every month there are about 20-70 new vulnerabilities published on the Internet. An important resource is the System Administration, Networking and Security (SANS) Institute, ISS, HP Security bulletin, *etc.* Some of the vulnerabilities listed below enable to directly compromise a target system, while others provide information that help to develop attacks.

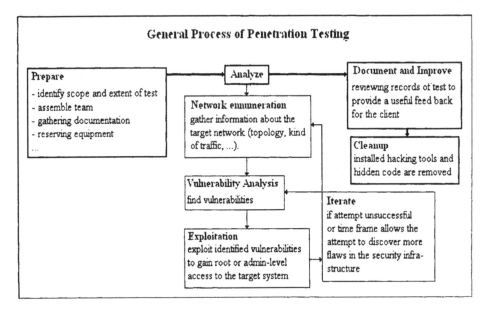

Fig. 1. General Procedure in a penetration test

IP backbone network:

Router OS system (Cisco's IOS and Juniper's JUNOS) vulnerabilities, Cisco, Juniper, etc have internal bug databases requiring a customer login

Name a few vulnerabilities from Cisco router:

- Cisco EIGRP spoofed packet neighbor saturation bug
  (http://www.osvdb.org/displayvuln.php?osvdb_id=18055)
- Cisco IOS CDP Neighbor Announcement DoS –
  (http://www.osvdb.org/displayvuln.php?osvdb_id=1969)

Poor network architecture enables hacker to bypass firewalls and other controls to obtain access to an internal network.

Lack of Monitoring and Intrusion Detection enables hackers to penetrate systems undetected. The hacker can probe the system (e.g. port scans) as long as he wants.

Firewalls:

Firewall identification, scanning through firewalls, application proxy vulnerabilities

Server/host:

Web servers:

Attacking Web authentication, HTTP authentication and digest, session state management, session ID prediction and bruteforcing, password guessing, Web service, WSDL, and Cookie hijacking

Web Server Sample Files are often susceptible to exploits. Hackers exploit the known code contained in them to perform unauthorised functions.

Web Server General Vulnerabilities enable attackers to gain administrative privileges over the server such as Microsoft's IIS, Netscape, Apache, *etc*.

Windows:

Win 9.x: Remote access, Trojan horse, server application vulnerabilities, DoS

Win 2K: Footprinting, NetBIOS-SMB password guessing, remote buffer over-flows, DoS, privilege escalation, grabbing password hashes, keystroke loggers

Win NT: DoS, buffer overflows, sniffer, remote control and back doors, port redirection, disabling auditing and clearing event log, Ports 135-139 for file sharing,

Unix/Linux:

Hacking root account, vulnerabilities mapping, data driven attacks, retrieving /etc/passwd file, Network File System permissions mis-configuration

Application

Application vulnerabilities are general categories referring to specific programming errors or backdoors that allow hackers to penetrate the system:

Common Gateway Interface (CGI): Vulnerable CGI programs normally run with the same privilege as the Web server software.

Default Accounts: Some applications install with default accounts and passwords. If these are not changed, hackers can use their knowledge about them.

Domain Name Service (DNS): Mis-configured DNS servers provide too much information about a network. They may allow zone transfers.

FTP and telnet are both clear text services, if a hacker can gain access to a login prompt, he can use brute force to guess user name and passwords. Also some versions of FTP is vulnerable to some buffer overflows that enable a hacker to execute code on the host or to view files and directory structures.

Remote Procedure Call (RPC) enables a remote system to communicate with others to execute programs. New exploits are being discovered continuously.

Default Services are installed and started when installing an application or even an operating system without the knowledge of the installer.

Simple Mail Transport Protocol (SMTP) has many different vulnerable implementations for example, *Sendmail* installed by default on some UNIX systems. It can be exploited to send spam mail, to extract password files and to invoke DoS attacks.

Remote control, Trojan horse, back doors, worm, Virus and hiding codes:

Discovering remote control software, virtual network computing, attacking MS terminal server, Virus (Nimda, I Love you, Code Red, Chernobyl)

Devices:

Modems: The systems containing rogue modems are often poorly configured and are susceptible to attacks. War dialing enables unauthorised access.

4 Commonly Used Tools

This section introduces a variety of popular penetration test tools that employed the procedure described in last section.

4.1 Network Enumeration

The following tools are primarily used in the network ennumeration phase of a penetration test. They can be classified as discovery tools.

WS_PingProPack (http://www.ipswitch.com/products/ws_ping/index.asp)

Client OS: Windows 98/Me/NT/2000/XP   Target OS: TCP/IP networks

Description: WS_PingProPack wroks as an excellent starting point for any penetration test. It has a very user friendly GUI to obtain information on host names and IP addresses of the target network. It provides whois, finger, ping, DNS, and SNMP information. Additionally WS_PingProPack can be used to search information (such as user's full names and e-mail addresses) available through LDAP and quickly ping an IP address range or host name.

Sam Spade (www.samspade.org)

Client OS: Windows 9x/NT/2000   Target OS: TCP/IP networks

Description: Sam Spade helps with the discovery phase of penetration testing. Sam Spade provides much of the same functionality as WS_Ping Pro-Pack and can perform whois queries, pings, DNS Dig (advanced DNS request), traceroute, finger, zone transfers, SMTP mail relay checking and Web site crawling and mirroring.

Rhino9 Pinger (www.nmrc.org/files/snt/)

Client OS: Windows 9x/NT/2000   Target OS: TCP/IP networks

Description: After obtainning DNS information about an organisation such as domain names and IP blocks, Pinger is used to find active hosts or targets on the target network without being detected. It pings the targets using ICMP ECHO requests and reply. The pinger sends and ICMP ECHO request and the target sends back an ECHO reply.

NetScanTool Pro (http://www.netscantools.com/nstmain.html)

Description: NetScanTool Pro is a software package with multiple solutions for network information discovery, gathering and security testing. It is broadly used in network security/ administration, Internet forensics and law enforcement.

4.2 Vulnerability Analysis

The tools below are vital to find vulnerabilities through identifying the services running on target hosts.

7th Sphere Port Scanner (http://www.megasecurity.org/Scanners.html)

Client OS: Windows 9x/NT/2000   Target OS: TCP/IP networks

Description: 7th Sphere is an excellent tool for scanning a range of ports on a single host and performing banner grabbing. This information offers vital information about the target and the services running on it.

SuperScan (http://www.snapfiles.com/get/superscan.html)

Client OS: Windows 9x/NT/2000   Target OS: TCP/IP networks

Description: SuperScan is a fast and powerful connect-based TCP port scanner, pinger and hostname resolver. It can connect to any discovered open port using user-specified "helper" applications (e.g. Telnet, Web browser, FTP) and assign a custom helper application to any port.

Nmap (www.insecure.org/nmap/)

Client OS: UNIX, Windows NT   Target OS: TCP/IP networks

Description: Nmap is considered to be the premier port scanner available as well as a reliable OS identification tool, it also serve as a ping sweep utility.

Netcat (http://netcat.sourceforge.net/)

Client OS: Windows NT, UNIX   Target OS: TCP/IP hosts

Description: Netcat is a feature-rich network debugging and exploration tool by creating almost any kind of connection using the TCP/IP protocol. It enables user to telnet or obtain command line access on different ports, to create back doors, or to bypass packet-filtering devices.

What's Running (www.woodstone.nu/whats)

Client OS: Windows 9x/NT   Target OS: IP systems

Description: What's running is a banner grabbing program. Once the services running on a target host have been identified via port scanning, this program can be used to investigate a server to see what HTTP/FTP/POP3/SMTP/NNTP software version runs on it. Thus it is easy to understand the associated vulnerabilities.

4.3 Exploitation

The exploitation tools are diversified varying from brute force password crackers to sophisticated remote control tools. A few representative tools are briefly presented.

NetBIOS Auditing Tool (NAT) (www.tux.org/pub/security/secnet/tools/nat10/)

Client OS: Windows NT   Target OS: Windows NT

Description: NAT is a small but well designed tool to launch an automated brute force password attack against systems offering NetBIOS file sharing based on a predefined user list and password list.

Crack/Libcrack (http://www.crypticide.com/users/alecm/)

Platforms: Solaris, Linux, FreeBSD, NetBSD, OSF and Ultrix

Description: Crack 5.0 and **CrackLib v2.7** are designed to crack the passwords of other users (or root) on Unix-like systems.

L0phtCrack (http://www.atstake.com/products/lc/index.html)

Client OS: Windows 9x/NT   Target OS: Windows NT

Description: L0phtCrack is the premier NT password cracker. It can obtain the hashes through many sources (file, network sniffing, registry, etc) stored by the NT operation system and compute NT user passwords from the cryptographic hashes. Also, it has numerous methods of generating password guesses like dictionary, brute force, etc.

BO2k (www.bo2k.com)

Client OS: Windows 98/NT/2000   Target OS: Windows 98/NT/2000

Description: BO2K is the most powerful Windows-based network administration tool and a hacker tool. It facilitates user to gain unauthorised access to target hosts to control the system, network, registry, passwords, file system, and processes.

Nessus (http://www.nessus.org/download/)

Client OS: Windows 98/NT/2000   Target OS: TCP/IP network

Description: Nessus is a remote network security auditor that tests security modules in an attempt to discover vulnerabilities. It is made up of two parts: a server, and a client. The server/daemon, nessusd, is responsible for the attacks, whereas the client, nessus, interferes with the user through nice X11/GTK+ interface.

Ethereal (http://www.ethereal.com/)

Client OS: Unix   Target OS: TCP/IP network

Description: Ethereal is a network traffic analyser/sniffer for Unix-like operating systems. It uses GTK+, a graphical user interface library, and libpcap, a packet capture and filtering library.

Hping2 (http://www.hping.org/)

Client OS: Unix   Target OS: TCP/IP network

Description: Hping2 is a network tool that can send custom ICMP/UDP/TCP packets and display target replies like ping does with ICMP replies. It can be used to test firewall rules, perform spoofed port scanning, test net performance using different protocols, packet size, TOS (type of service), and fragmentation, do path MTU discovery, transfer files, trace route, fingerprint remote OSs, audit a TCP/IP stack, etc.

5 Recent Developments and Future Trends

The penetration test depends heavily on the evolution of the hacking tools used by cyber criminals. The basic structure of a penetration test is quite likely to always be as outlined above (Prepare, Analyse, Documentation and Cleanup). However, the techniques employed and the emphasis are going to change by a great deal depending on the new threats to network security emerging from the development of even more sophisticated hacking tools, the need to reduce costs and the introduction of new types of networks. The following introduces four of these trends that can be identified

5.1 "Semi-automatic" Penetration Tests

Since the quality of a penetration test relies on the knowledge and skill of the testers, it is desired to provide consistency and reduction of costs. Currently "semi-automatic" penetration testing is thought to be the best way to introduce a certain consistent standard without loosing the creativity and flexibility needed.

A product called **CORE IMPACT** developed by Core Security Technologies is a comprehensive penetration testing solution for assessing specific information security threats. It features the CORE IMPACT Rapid Penetration Test (RPT), an industry-first step-by-step automation of the penetration testing process to identify what resources are exposed, and determine if their current security investments are actually detecting and preventing attacks [6]. It provides a framework for a penetration test consisting of seven steps: information gathering, information analysis and planning, vulnerability detection, target penetration, attack/privilege escalation, analysis and reporting, and cleanup.

The ProCheckNet developed by ProCheckUp [7] have a unique artificial intelligence-based approach to penetration testing. ProCheckNet allows itself to be modified either to run in stealth mode or make a lot of noise. It can even act like a hacker and attempt to avoid security devices. It can perfectly mimic a real data exchange using FTP, SMTP, HTTP, POP3, NNTP and Imap, firewalls believe this traffic is normal, and let it through. To get past an intrusion detection system (IDS) the system can use polymorphic code. This encodes URL strings differently to confuse the IDS pattern matching [8].

Kwon, *et. al.* [9] introduces an extensible exploit framework for automation of penetration testing. Their platform implements HackSim, a tool that remotely exploits known buffer-overflow vulnerabilities for Solaris and Windows systems.

5.2 IP backbone networks

IP network is gradually becoming communication infrastructure to deliver converged network services. Direct attacks to IP backbone networks might be more damaging than a local network or server/host. This section focuses on discussing how to find the vulnerabilities information about IP backbone network.

First, keep eyes on the vendors such as Cisco, Juniper, *etc.* They have internal bug databases requiring a customer login.

Second, public available databases such as CVE and OSVDB about network vulnerability are extremely useful. Common Vulnerabilities and Exposures (CVE) (http://www.cve.mitre.org/) is a list of standardised names for vulnerabilities and other information security exposures. It is a dictionary about all publicly known vulnerabilities and security exposures. OSVDB (http://www.osvdb.org/) is an independent and open source database to provide accurate, detailed, current, and unbiased technical information on security vulnerabilities.

Third, there is a Web site (http://www.phenoelit.de/ultimaratio/index.html) teaching researcher how to exploit the vulnerabilities of IOS, Cisco's router OS system.

Fourth, there are a variety of penetration test tools for routing protocol. *The Nemesis Packet Injection suite* [10] is well suited for testing Network IDS, firewalls, IP stacks and other task. Also, it is perfect for crafting and injecting ARP, DNS, ETHERNET, ICMP, IGMP, IP, OSPF, RIP, TCP and UDP packets for *Unix / Windows* systems, can then be used to circumvent network security at the host and network level. *IRPAS, Internetwork Routing Protocol Attack Suite* [11] includes a number of small tools, which can be scripted for larger tests by using the different IP protocols and working with Cisco routing equipment at the protocol level.

5.3 Wireless Networks

The nature of wireless networks makes a whole range of penetration test either much more difficult or completely impossible to execute with a standard, wired network. Wireless networks only know the boundaries of their own signal: streets, parks, nearby buildings, and cars all offer a virtual "port" into your wireless network [12]. Wireless networks lack in the security of the physical layer. Tens of thousands of unauthorised wireless LAN hardware devices called access points (AP) have popped up in enterprise networks nation-wide." [13]. These industry standard devices can be plugged directly into a company's network, even behind a firewall. They then transmit sensitive data that can be easily picked up by a snoop using freeware hacking tools such as AirSnort (http://airsnort.shmoo.com/). And this is just one example for the numerous vulnerabilities of wireless networks. The report [12] describes three steps to penetrate the wireless networks:

- Gaining access to the wireless network protected by WEP2. Using AirSnort passively monitor transmissions across a wireless network and monitoring, derive the encryption key for a WEP-protected network once you have an adequate base of packets. Then finding available servers on the network
- Determining the services on those servers available for connection and exploit using port scanning.
- Exploit a well-known vulnerability to gain unauthorised access to a machine

Steps 2 and 3 are employing the similar testing methods to wired network.

5.4 Integration of Application security with Penetration Test

Through experience researchers have found out that only traditional measures for the protection of networks (such as firewalls) are not sufficient. Traditionally, vulnerability analysis has been focusing on the network or operating system level. Now trends are going towards merging the ability to scan for network vulnerabilities and application-level vulnerabilities together, as there are many attacks against Web application code that will traverse firewalls easily. In addition to building secure Web servers and installing the latest patches, the Web code has also to be secured since insecure application code can undermine even the most secure Web server and firewall configurations [13]. The goal in this merging of network and application vulnerability analysis is the ability to use data found from one level and drive a more focused approach for the other level [14].

6 Conclusions and Further Research

In this paper, the general concept and procedures of penetration test are introduced. This is followed by the detailed description of vulnerabilities from IP backbone network, Firewalls to servers/host and applications/services. Subsequently numerous hacking or auditing tools used for penetration tests are illustrated. Recent development and future trends are identified in the fields of automation and standardisation of penetration tests, IP backbone and wireless network penetration and merge of penetration test and application security.

We have seen that penetration tests are a useful measure to check the sanity of network infrastructure. However, as penetration tests only aim to reveal a small number of vulnerabilities in a given time, they are not sufficient to guarantee a certain degree of network security. This motivates our further research in two key areas.

Singh, *et. al.* [15] propose a new systematic method to obtain statistically valid estimates of security metrics by performing repeated penetration testing of detailed system models. They employ importance sampling techniques with heuristics to help reduce the variance of the estimates, and achieve relative error bounds quickly. They validate this approach by estimating security metrics of a large model with more than 2^1700 possible states.

The Open Source Security Testing Methodology Manual (OSSTMM) [16] has gradually been adopted to be a frequently updated frequently updated international open standard. Its test cases are divided into five major components: information and data controls, personnel security awareness levels, fraud and social engineering control levels, computer and telecommunications networks, wireless devices, physical security access controls, security processes, and physical locations such as buildings, perimeters, and military bases. It is interesting to understand its comparison with several government-endorsed approaches such as UK's CESG IT security health check [17] and the USA's NIST Guideline on network security testing [18].

References

1. http://www.crime-research.org/analytics/501
2. Lam, F., Beekey, M., and Cayo, K.: Can you hack it? Security Management, vol. 47 no. 2, pp. 83-88, Feb 2003.
3. Klevinsky, T.J., Laliberte S., Gupta A.: Hack I.T., Addison – Wesley, December 2004.
4. Geer, D., Harthorne, J.: Penetration Testing: A Duet. Proceedings of the 18th Annual Computer Security Applications Conference (ACSAC'02), pp 185-198.
5. Budiarto, R., Ramadass, S., Samsudin, A., Noor, S.: Development of Penetration Testing Model for Increasing Network Security, Proceedings. 2004 International Conference on Information and Communication Technologies: From Theory to Applications, 19-23 April 2004, IEEE pp 563-4.
6. http://www.coresecurity.com/products/index.php
7. http://www.procheckup.com/
8. http://www.computing.co.uk/networkitweek/software/2058434/procheckup-security-scanner
9. Kwon, O.H., et al: HackSim: an automation of penetration testing for remote buffer overflow vulnerabilities. International Conference on Information Networking, (ICOIN) 2005, LNCS 3391, pp. 652–661, 2005. Springer-Verlag Berlin Heidelberg.
10. Obecian and Grimes, M.: Nemesis Packet Injection suite, http://nemesis.sourceforge.net/.
11. FX, Internetwork Routing Protocol Attack Suite, http://www.phenoelit.de/irpas/.
12. Hassell, J.: Wireless Attacks and Penetration Testing, 14th June, 2004, http://www.securityfocus.com/infocus/1785
13. Midian, P: Perspectives on penetration testing - what's the deal with Web security?, Network Security, Aug. 2002 pp 5-8.
14. Raina, K: Trends in Web Application Security, 27th October, 2004, http://www.securityfocus.com/infocus/1809.
15. Sigh, S., Lyons, J., Nicol, D.M.: Fast model-based penetration testing, Proceedings of the 2004 Winter Simulation Conference, pp. 309-317.
16. http://www.isecom.org/osstmm/
17. http://www.boldonjames.com/downloads/documents/IT%20Security%20Health%20CHECK%20Services.pdf
18. http://csrc.nist.gov/publications/nistpubs/800-42/NIST-SP800-42.pdf

A Taxonomy of Criteria for Evaluating Defence Mechanisms against Flooding DoS Attacks

Jarmo V. E. Mölsä

Communications Laboratory, Helsinki University of Technology,
P.O. Box 3000, FI-02015 TKK, Finland
jarmo.molsa@tkk.fi

Abstract. This paper describes a set of criteria for evaluating defence mechanisms against flooding denial of service (DoS) attacks. Effectiveness and usefulness of a defence mechanism in mitigating a DoS attack depends on many issues which are presented here in the form of a taxonomy. The primary goal of this taxonomy is to help in getting a comprehensive view on both the strengths and weaknesses of a specific defence mechanism. A good defence mechanism should not disturb legitimate traffic when there is no attack, should mitigate the amount of attack traffic well enough, should increase the quality of service (QoS) available to legitimate traffic during an attack, and should use as little resources in this task as possible. In addition, any defence mechanism should be robust against changes in attack characteristics and intentional misuse.

1 Introduction

Flooding denial of service (DoS) attacks [1] cannot be mitigated in any straightforward way. These attacks use brute force to exploit normal behaviour of protocols and services in an excessive manner. As attack traffic looks similar to legitimate traffic it is not possible to simply block all attack traffic, because some legitimate flows will be misclassified as attack flows (false positives), and some attack flows will not be detected at all (false negatives) [2–4]. Another difficulty in mitigating flooding DoS attacks is the collateral damage from using a defence mechanism, such as performance degradation in routers. A defence mechanism may cause collateral damage even if an attack is not present. Defences also increase the complexity of a system, which results in more vulnerabilities available for an attacker to exploit. All these issues should be considered when evaluating effectiveness and usefulness of defence mechanisms against flooding DoS attacks. Distributed DoS (DDoS) attacks using multiple sources at the same time are considered as subtypes of DoS attacks in this paper.

Evaluation of defence mechanisms is typically based on very limited criteria. Sometimes evaluation is carried out under ideal conditions, where there are no false positives and no collateral damage, such as when studying rate-limiting in [5]. Three existing preventive defence mechanisms were compared in [6], and it was found out that they were originally evaluated according to restricted criteria, ignoring the risk of attacks that they cannot solve. In [7] rate-limiting is carried out against any excessive traffic aggregate, regardless of being malicious or benign, but it emphasizes the difficulty in differentiating between innocent and attack traffic. In [8] it is argued that a relatively complex overlay structure to mitigate DoS attacks does not introduce any new vulnerabilities, which is not a reasonable claim. [9] describes a defence against TCP SYN attacks and considers shortly the possibility of false positives and false negatives, but still the final evaluation is based on the easiest test cases. Some commercial products promise to "prevent DoS attacks", which implies that difficult issues in mitigating flooding DoS attacks are forgotten. All these examples show that it is difficult to make an extensive evaluation of a defence mechanism. It should be emphasized here that all well-specified defences have definitely their application areas regardless of a restricted evaluation. The point here is that an extensive evaluation will help to identify the limitations and the best application areas, and to get the best benefit out of a defence mechanism.

An organized approach for evaluating defence mechanisms is missing. As expressed in [6], very little has been done to compare, contrast, and categorize the different ideas related to DoS attacks and defences. A user of a defence mechanism should be able to consider both advantages and disadvantages in an objective way. A taxonomy of DDoS attack and DDoS defence mechanisms is presented in [10]. This taxonomy, however, lacks all evaluation issues.

The main contribution of this paper is to present a taxonomy of criteria for evaluating defence mechanisms against flooding DoS attacks. This taxonomy will point out important issues in evaluating a defence mechanism, which will make it easier to carry out a more realistic evaluation. The taxonomy can be considered as an extension to the taxonomy defined in [10]. Together these two taxonomies will help to understand how attacks and defences operate, and what issues have an effect on the effectiveness and usefulness of defence mechanisms.

2   Taxonomy of Evaluation Criteria

This section presents the taxonomy of criteria for evaluating defence mechanisms against flooding DoS attacks. It contains important issues in estimating the effectiveness and usefulness of a defence. The taxonomy is shown in the Fig. 1.

2.1   Effectiveness

A defence mechanism should be effective in mitigating a flooding DoS attack. This attack time effectiveness, however, is not enough because a defence mechanism should also be effective when there is no attack, i.e. during normal time a defence should disturb legitimate traffic as little as possible.

Normal Time. Some defence mechanisms are active continuously both during normal and attack time. In the taxonomy of DDoS defence mechanisms specified in [10] these are called preventive mechanisms. Normal time effectiveness of a defence mechanism is very important because attacks against a specific target are rather rare after all.

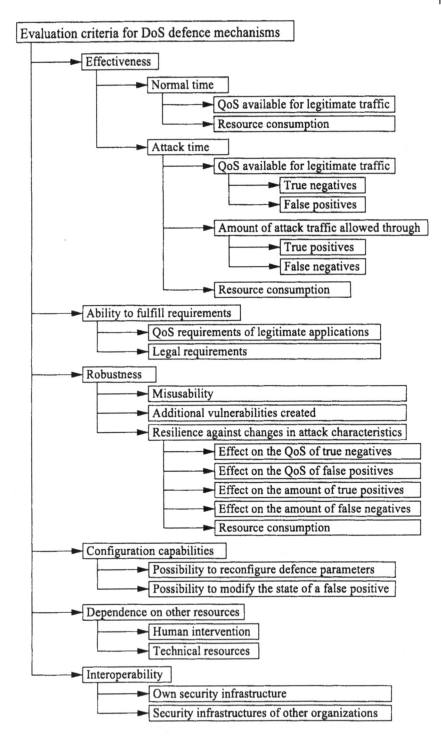

Fig. 1. A taxonomy of criteria for evaluating defence mechanisms against flooding DoS attacks.

Quality of service (QoS) Available for Legitimate Traffic. A preventive defence mechanism can have an effect on the QoS available for legitimate traffic even if there is no attack due to the overhead from running the defence. The term QoS is understood here in a technical way (intrinsic QoS in [11]). QoS experienced by legitimate flows can be deteriorated if a mechanism introduces additional network security devices increasing the transmission latency, new security procedures requiring additional steps for accessing services, new security information increasing the length of legitimate packets etc. An opposite example providing better QoS during normal time is a preventive defence based on resource multiplication [10] which will enhance the QoS experienced by legitimate flows.

QoS degradation during normal time has been analyzed, for example, in [12] which describes a proactive secure overlay service structure (WebSOS) to prevent DDoS attacks against web servers. On average the basic WebSOS increases the end-to-end communication latency between a browser and a web server by a factor of 7 when compared to normal routing used in the current Internet. In the worst-case this latency is increased by a factor of 11 when compared to normal routing. In addition to this permanent increase in latency there is an additional security procedure in WebSOS when initiating an access to a web server. The goal of this initial security procedure is to verify that a human is trying to use the web server. This Completely Automated Public Turing test to tell Computers and Humans Apart (CAPTCHA) increases the time before a user is granted access to a web server.

Resource Consumption. Preventive defence mechanisms will consume resources, such as processing power, memory, and transmission capacity of a network.

For example, if IP packets are encrypted/authenticated, each packet will consume more processing power and memory in nodes initiating or terminating a secured path. Also, the increased packet size will consume more network bandwidth.

Attack Time. The primary goal for any flooding DoS defence mechanism is to limit the volume of malicious traffic during an attack. In addition to preventive mechanisms, also reactive defence mechanisms can be used, but they require a separate detection mechanism. Reactive mechanisms do not generally degrade QoS of legitimate flows during normal time, i.e. when there is no attack. According to the taxonomy of DDoS defences defined in [10] there are four different basic types of reactive defence mechanisms: agent identification (source traceback), rate-limiting, filtering (blocking), and reconfiguration.

QoS Available for Legitimate Traffic. Legitimate traffic is divided in two groups. True negatives are legitimate flows that are classified as legitimate. False positives are those legitimate flows that are classified accidentally as attack flows. Depending on the requirements of the applications used in a network, these two different traffic groups may have similar or different requirements for the QoS. In any case, these both types of legitimate traffic must be considered when evaluating the effectiveness of a defence mechanism.

The QoS available for true negatives is enhanced by preventing part or all of the detected attack traffic from entering a victim network or host. This results in more resources (e.g., network bandwidth or processing power at a server) available for true negatives.

In case of reactive defences, true negatives will experience a short period of time of low QoS at the beginning of an attack. There is an inherent delay between the time when an attack is detected and the corresponding reactive defence begins to mitigate the attack. For example, if the core nodes of the WebSOS overlay network [12] are attacked, the system will heal itself within 10 seconds. This reaction delay should be included in the evaluation of the available QoS during an attack.

The QoS available for false positives, on the other hand, is generally not very high, because these flows cannot be differentiated from attack flows. In other words, both false positives and true positives (attack traffic classified as malicious) are associated with the same QoS level.

If all legitimate traffic, including false positives, require a reasonable QoS even during a flooding DoS attack, both preventive defences (such as resource multiplication) and some of the reactive defences (such as rate-limiting [13] and reconfiguration) can be useful. For example, flooding DoS attacks have mostly failed against the root servers of the Domain Name System (DNS) due to required overprovisioning [14, 15]. Reactive defence mechanisms based on filtering are not suitable, if the QoS of false positives is important.

Amount of Attack Traffic Allowed Through. Attack traffic is divided in two groups. True positives are those attack flows classified as malicious. False negatives are those attack flows classified accidentally as legitimate flows. At least all false negatives are allowed to pass through, and possibly part of the true positives (such as in the case of rate-limiting).

The probabilities for a true positive and a false positive are inter-related [16]. If true positives must be detected with a high probability, then also the probability for a false positive grows. The same holds also between false negatives and true negatives, i.e. if the probability for a false negative must be lowered, then also the probability for a true negative will get lower. In practice this means that the less we allow undetected attack traffic to get in (false negatives), the less we allow legitimate traffic to get in (true negatives). It is not possible to adjust the attack detection so that exactly only legitimate traffic would get in. This fact has been recognized in existing DDoS toolkits which generate attack traffic looking very similar to legitimate traffic [5].

Due to these realities, both true positives and false negatives must be considered in the evaluation of a defence mechanism against flooding DoS attacks. Especially reactive defences do not mitigate the volume of false negatives.

Resource Consumption. Mitigating a detected flooding DoS attack is resource consuming. Limiting the volume of attack traffic may require, for example, several filters for classifying attack flows at routers. There are practical limits on the amount of different filters in routers. If attack traffic is highly variable, it may not be possible to install filters for all detected types of attack traffic due to resource limitations.

At least enough processing power and memory should be available for mitigating an attack at routers and other network security devices.

2.2 Ability to Fulfill Requirements

Different applications have different requirements for QoS. Legislation, standards, specifications, recommendations about best current practices, and other documents may also dictate requirements for the QoS of important applications. All these requirements should be fulfilled as well as possible, even during attack.

QoS Requirements of Legitimate Applications. Using a defence mechanism against a flooding DoS attack increases the level of QoS during attack. To see whether the available QoS is enough, one must compare this available QoS with the requirements of the most important application (or applications) used in a network. There should be a reasonable match between the available and required level of QoS.

Legal Requirements. Legislation or other official rules may require organizations to provide a reasonable resistance to known security vulnerabilities. For example, [17] describes recommended security services and procedures for Internet service providers. DoS attacks found frequently in real-life may have to considered as known security vulnerabilities. Real-life DoS attacks have been investigated, for example, in [1] and [18].

2.3 Robustness

Any defence mechanism should be robust for not opening any new possibilities for carrying out DoS attacks.

Misusability. It is possible to use some defence mechanisms as the ultimate tool for the DoS attack. Such a defence mechanism results in more damage than the original attack itself. Using intelligence in selecting the contents of DoS attack traffic, it may be possible to force a defence mechanism to fail in its most important task.

Additional Vulnerabilities Created. Defence mechanisms increase the complexity of a system and thus result in new vulnerabilities to be exploited by attackers. As attacks can exploit any weaknesses in protocols and services, any additional security protocol, security service, or network security device may provide a possible avenue for carrying out an attack.

Resilience against Changes in Attack Characteristics. Many attacks have varying attack characteristics. Source address validity (how source address spoofing is used), attack rate, possibility of characterization (how easy it is to identify attack packets), persistence of attack sources, and victim type (application, host, resource, network) can be modified on the fly [10].

A defence mechanism should be able to adapt to changes in attack properties. One should also evaluate how varying attack properties affect the QoS of legitimate traffic and the amount of attack traffic allowed to reach a victim.

Frequent changes in attack characteristics may cause excessive resource consumption, for example, by overloading a router when it receives frequent descriptions of attack traffic.

2.4 Configuration Capabilities

Any defence mechanism should incorporate reasonable reconfiguration capabilities. This is required when attack characteristics change, or when a critical false positive is identified.

2.5 Dependence on Other Resources

To operate effectively, a defence mechanism may require extensive human intervention and several other security devices, such as intrusion detection systems. All these dependencies affect the cost-effectiveness of attack detection and response [19].

Human Intervention. If a defence mechanism is dependent on human interaction, this will increase the delays in operating a mechanism. Autonomous defences should be preferred when primary applications cannot tolerate breaks in the availability of services.

Technical Resources. A defence mechanism is more prone to malfunction if it is dependent on availability of other security devices. For example, a reactive defence mechanism is useless without a correctly operating detection system.

A requirement for a large number of other security devices or for a widespread deployment of a distributed defence mechanism has implications on implementation issues. Incremental deployment is needed for these more complex defence systems.

2.6 Interoperability

Defence mechanisms are never separate entities in organizations. A prerequisite for any defence mechanism is that it must fit with an existing security infrastructure of an organization and be able to co-operate with other existing defence mechanisms, such as intrusion detection systems and security management tools. When global or distributed defence infrastructures are used, even higher demands for interoperability exist.

3 Related Work

Only few organized approaches for analyzing denial of service attacks and defence mechanisms have been published in addition to the taxonomy presented in [10].

A framework of criteria for evaluating proactive DoS defence mechanisms is presented in [6] which compares three existing preventive solutions according to the following requirements: incremental deployment, resistance to traffic analysis, resistance to compromised infrastructure routers, and resistance to DoS attack on the infrastructure. In that paper it is expected that attacks are distributed only in a limited fashion, i.e. attack traffic can be mostly distinguished from legitimate traffic. Reactive defences were not considered at all in the paper, and the included set of evaluation criteria omitted many issues included in the taxonomy presented in this paper.

A cost-based framework for analyzing the resistance of cryptographic protocols against DoS attacks is presented in [20]. It provides a formalized mechanism for comparing the costs of a DoS attack for both an attacker and a victim. The goal is to make the cost of carrying out a DoS attack as expensive as possible when compared to the costs of the victim who is required to process attack packets.

The number of attacking source hosts (DDoS agents) is important for initiating source traceback for locating the real source of attack traffic. If there is only one host transmitting attack traffic, source traceback can be a useful reactive defence mechanism against this kind of an attack. The more there are hosts sending attack traffic against a single victim, the more difficult it is to mitigate an attack by using source traceback. A framework for classifying DoS attacks as either single- or multi-source is presented in [18], and it is based on analyzing packet headers, the ramp-up behaviour of attack traffic intensity, and the spectral content analysis of the inter-message time.

4 Conclusion

Evaluation of defence mechanisms against flooding DoS attacks has often concentrated on easy or simple test scenarios, where the possibility to circumvent or defeat a defence mechanism has been either underestimated or completely forgotten. There are no existing papers providing any framework or taxonomy for this important subject.

This paper presented a taxonomy which classifies evaluation criteria for defence mechanisms against flooding DoS attacks. This taxonomy can be treated as an extension to the taxonomy of DDoS attack and DDoS defence mechanisms presented in [10].

The presented taxonomy emphasizes effectiveness when there is no attack, effectiveness during an attack, ability to fulfill requirements on application QoS, robustness against misuse, resilience against changes in attack characteristics, possibility for dynamic configuration especially for removing critical false positives, dependence on technical resources and human interaction, and interoperability with existing security infrastructures.

As evaluation of DoS defence mechanisms is fairly complicated, the presented taxonomy will provide a structured list of things to be considered during an evaluation process.

Acknowledgement

This work was partially funded by the Finnish Defence Forces.

References

1. Moore, D., Voelker, G.M., Savage, S.: Inferring Internet denial-of-service activity. In: Proceedings of the 10th USENIX Security Symposium, Washington, D.C. (2001)
2. Ptacek, T.H., Newsham, T.N.: Insertion, Evasion, and Denial of Service: Eluding Network Intrusion Detection. Secure Networks, Inc. (1998)
3. Durst, R., Champion, T., Witten, B., Miller, E., Spagnuolo, L.: Testing and evaluating computer intrusion detection systems. Communications of the ACM **42** (1999) 53–61
4. Lippmann, R.P., Fried, D.J., Graf, I., Haines, J.W., Kendall, K.R., McClung, D., Weber, D., Webster, S.E., Wyschogrod, D., Cunningham, R.K., Zissman, M.A.: Evaluating intrusion detection systems: The 1998 DARPA off-line intrusion detection evaluation. In: Proceedings of the DARPA Information Survivability Conference and Exposition. (2000)
5. Sterne, D., Djahandari, K., Wilson, B., Babson, B., Schnackenberg, D., Holliday, H., Reid, T.: Autonomic response to distributed Denial of Service attacks. In: Proceedings of Recent Advances in Intrusion Detection, 4th International Symposium, Davis, California (2001) 134–149
6. Mulligan, J.A.: A comparison framework for proactive Internet denial of service solutions. Technical report, Massachusetts Institute of Technology (2005)
7. Mahajan, R., Bellovin, S.M., Floyd, S., Ioannidis, J., Paxson, V., Shenker, S.: Controlling high bandwidth aggregates in the network. ACM SIGCOMM Computer Communication Review **32** (2002) 62–73
8. Adkins, D., Lakshminarayanan, K., Perrig, A., Stoica, I.: Towards a more functional and secure network infrastructure. Technical Report UCB/CSD-03-1242, University of California, Berkeley (2003)
9. Schuba, C.L., Krsul, I.V., Kuhn, M.G., Spafford, E.H., Sundaram, A., Zamboni, D.: Analysis of a Denial of Service attack on TCP. In: Proceedings of the IEEE Symposium on Security and Privacy, Oakland, California (1997) 208–223
10. Mirkovic, J., Reiher, P.: A taxonomy of DDoS attack and DDoS defense mechanisms. ACM SIGCOMM Computer Communication Review **34** (2004) 39–53
11. Gozdecki, J., Jajszczyk, A., Stankiewicz, R.: Quality of service terminology in IP networks. IEEE Commun. Mag. **41** (2003) 153–159
12. Morein, W.G., Stavrou, A., Cook, D.L., Keromytis, A.D., Misra, V., Rubenstein, D.: Using graphic Turing tests to counter automated DDoS attacks against web servers. In: Proceedings of the ACM conference on computer and communications security, Washington, DC, USA (2003) 8–19

13. Mölsä, J.V.E.: Effectiveness of rate-limiting in mitigating flooding DoS attacks. In Hamza, M.H., ed.: Proceedings of the Third IASTED International Conference on Communications, Internet, and Information Technology at St. Thomas, US Virgin Islands, Anaheim, California, USA, ACTA Press (2004) 155–160
14. Vixie, P., Sneeringer, G., Schleifer, M.: Events of 21-Oct-2002. Technical report, ISC/UMD/Cogent (2002)
15. Bush, R., Karrenberg, D., Kosters, M., Plzak, R.: Root name server operational requirements. Request for Comments RFC 2870, Internet Engineering Task Force (2000)
16. Wickens, C.D., Hollands, J.G.: Engineering Psychology and Human Performance. 3 edn. Prentice Hall, Upper Saddle River, New Jersey, USA (2000)
17. Killalea, T.: Recommended Internet Service Provider Security Services and Procedures. RFC 3013 (2000)
18. Hussain, A., Heidemann, J., Papadopoulos, C.: A framework for classifying denial of service attacks. In: Proceedings of ACM SIGCOMM, Karlsruhe, Germany (2003)
19. Lee, W., Fan, W., Miller, M., Stolfo, S.J., Zadok, E.: Toward cost-sensitive modeling for intrusion detection and response. Journal of Computer Security 10 (2002)
20. Meadows, C.: A cost-based framework for analysis of denial of service in networks. Journal of Computer Security 9 (2001) 143–164

Spam Honey Pot Research

An Analysis on a Three-Month University Data Corpus

Liam Meany

School of Electronic Engineering, Dublin City University, Ireland.

meanyl@eeng.dcu.ie

Abstract. Most current anti spam research focuses on defensive technical or legal measures, which deal with spam after it arrives. This paper focuses attention on the initial stages of the spam lifecycle. It deals with researching how spammers harvest e-mail addresses with a view to eliminating the problem at source rather than the current destination method. The paper presents hypotheses regarding harvesting methods based on current research. The hypotheses are tested within a controlled Honey Pot environment located within a university department. The Honey Pot contains 400 e-mail addresses seeded in various Internet locations. The e-mail accounts are checked regularly for new messages to study the amount of spam that arrives. This makes up the statistics that test the hypotheses.

1 Introduction

The simplest way of dealing with spam is to prevent spammers from obtaining e-mail addresses. In theory, this sounds reasonable but difficult to achieve in practice due to the ubiquitous nature of the web. Traditional defensive methods such as Bayesian filters, real-time block lists and legal proceedings etc. continue to limit the problem but have not yet succeeded in eliminating it. Indeed, it is now widely accepted that a magic bullet defensive measure is unlikely to be found without involving a complete redesign of the current e-mail network. Understanding the behaviour of spammers is therefore very important in containing the problem.[1]

Research carried out by CDT[2] and the FTC[3] has found the following three popular Internet activities to be key harvesting grounds for spammers:

1. E-mail postings to websites

---

[1] "Understanding How Spammers Steal Your E-Mail Address Prince", B., Holloway, L., Keller, M. <http://www.ceas.cc/papers-2005/163.pdf>

[2] "Why am I getting all this spam?" Centre for Democracy and Technology, March 2003 <http://www.cdt.org/speech/spam/030319spamreport.shtml>

[3] "Email Address Harvesting: How Spammers Reap What You Sow," FTC Report, Nov. 2002 <http://www.ftc.gov/bcp/conline/pubs/alerts/spamalrt.htm>

2. E-mail postings to newsgroups
3. E-mail postings to mailing lists

These activities also form the hypotheses for this research. However, CDT's e-mail postings were on what they refer to as *"public websites"* namely, *cdt.org, getnetwise.org* and *consumerprivacyguide.org*.[4] These sites are both high profile and well established, so the likelihood of them attracting the attention of spammers is naturally higher than if they were located on less popular sites.

This paper investigates e-mail address postings to lower profile domains, such as those of a university department, to ascertain if spammers are applying similar harvesting methods to those already identified. The Honey Pot began hosting e-mail addresses on July 4th, 2003 and ran until October 6th, 2003. It was located within the School of Electronic Engineering at Dublin City University. The research is unique in that it presents insights on spam harvesting within the university sector.

2 Spam Definition

The IETF's Anti-Spam Research Group, (ASRG),[5] leaves it up to individual organisations to devise and implement their own spam definition. A spam definition is necessary so that all e-mail messages, spam or otherwise, may be judged equally. With the help of existing spam definitions from Spamhaus[6] and MAPS[7] and for the purpose of this research, an e-mail message was classified as spam, if it was sent:

(1) Unsolicited and bulk.
(2) For the benefit of the sender or expense of the recipient.
(3) Where the recipient has not verifiably granted deliberate, explicit, and revocable permission for it to be sent.

3. Technical Background

3.1 Configuration

The Honey Pot concept is presented in Fig 1. It functions simultaneously as a web server, mail server and spam repository. In all, 400 user accounts were setup on it, each forwarding their mail to a central spam repository account. The web server hosts various websites with e-mail addresses. The web and mail server logs are examined daily to provide information on the web and mail traffic to and from the servers.

---

4 Op. Cit. note 2.

5 Anti-Spam Research Group (ASRG). 2003.
<http://asrg.sp.am/about/faq.shtml>

6 Spamhaus, The Spamhaus Project The Definition of Spam. Sept 20th 2003
<http://www.spamhaus.org/definition.html>

7 , Mail Abuse Prevention system. Definition of "spam". Sept 20th 2003
<http://www.mail-abuse.org/standard.html>

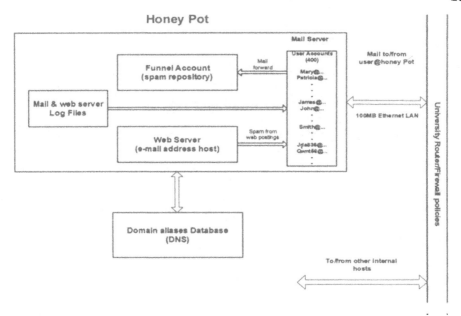

Fig 1. *The Honey Pot concept*

3.2 E-mail Addresses

All 400 e-mail addresses should reflect real and working e-mail addresses. To achieve this, data from the 1990 USA[8] census provides a list of the top 100 first (male & female) and last names of people living in the USA at that time. This list was used to generate each user's account. Also, e-mail addresses with a completely random, alphanumeric makeup were chosen. The format of the e-mail addresses is presented in Table 1.

Address Type	Sample Format
100 first name (male)	joe@ <domain>
100 first name (female)	mary@ <domain>
100 last name	murphy@ <domain>
100 random	vpm726@ <domain>

Table 1. *E-mail Address Format*

It is quite common for an Internet user to place their e-mail address simultaneously in many different Internet locations depending on the activity in which they engage. However, when a spam is later received it is not possible to definitively say exactly what activity generated that particular spam.

---

[8] Government publication. 1990. Most common names in the United States 1990 Census. <http://www.census.gov/genealogy/names/>

For this reason it is necessary to adopt a *one-address-one-posting* concept. This means that each e-mail address has just one posting or a one-to-one relationship with each activity. This is necessary in order to link each spam received to a corresponding e-mail address with 100% certainty.

4. Analysis

4.1 Analysis Overview

Of the three Internet activities in Section 1, two emerged as especially attractive harvesting sources to spammers during this research period. In order of spam quantity received, these are:

#1. Plain text postings to websites
#2. Plain text postings to Newsgroups

This is in keeping with CDT's six month study, which also rank plain text e-mail address postings to Web sites as the primary source for harvesting e-mail addresses with Newsgroup postings ranked second[9].

For the three month analysis period, it may be observed from Table 2, that a slight majority, (51%) of the total spam came from plain text website postings. 49% of the total spam received originated from Newsgroup postings.

Variable	%
WWW	50.71%
Newsgroup	48.37%
Other	0.91%
Total	**100%**

Table 2. *Internet Activity by Category*

4.2 Analysis of Total spam Messages Received

Since the first e-mail addresses were posted on July 4th 2003, a total of 1302 e-mail messages were received to the Honey Pot, of which 984 were spam. The messages were classified as spam in accordance with the working definition.

The remaining 318 legitimate messages were the natural by-product of placing the e-mail addresses in various Newsgroups, mailing lists and websites etc. The line plot of Fig 2 presents the total daily spam received from the period July 7th 2003 to Oct. 6th 2003, the period in which the analysis was allowed to run.

---

[9] Op. Cit. note 2.

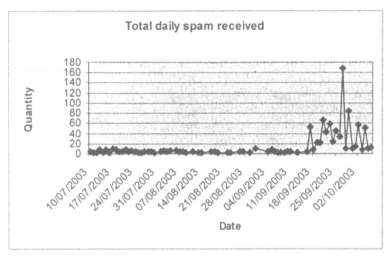

Fig 2.

What is immediately noteworthy from the plot in Fig 2 is that no spam messages were received prior to July10th, although the first e-mails were posted on July 4th. Therefore, a time lapse of six days occurred before the first spam e-mail was received to the Honey Pot. This contrasts with just eight hours from *Broadband Reports*[10] and is perhaps due to the fact that the domain, on which the Honey Pot resides, is less well known than those investigated by them. It would appear therefore, that domain popularity has a role to play in attracting spam.

For the period Aug. 10th to Sept. 16th, a daily quantity of approximately 20 e-mail messages was received. However, after Sept 16th this increased dramatically, reaching a peak of 169 messages on Sept. 27th. By the end of the analysis period on Oct 6th, the Honey Pot was averaging 38 spam e-mails daily. Also, in the 21-day period from Aug. 16th to Oct. 6th a total of 800 e-mail messages were received accounting for 81% of the total spam quantity.

This therefore demonstrates that the longer an e-mail address is visible, in plaintext format, on either Newsgroups or web, the greater the likelihood of it being spammed.

4.3 Newsgroup spam Analysis

The first Newsgroup e-mail addresses were posted on July 8th 2003. From the plot of daily Newsgroup spam received to the Honey Pot in Fig 3, it may be observed that it took a period of just two days before the first account was spammed via a Newsgroup. For the spammer, this represents a very quick turn around from harvesting to spamming and demonstrates that Newsgroups are attractive targets for spammers. Also, the one-to-one relationship between a posting and its corresponding e-mail address is likely to mean the e-mail address is legitimate.

---

[10] Broadband Reports. 2003. Spam and web-visible email addresses
<http://www.dslreports.com/shownews/15234>

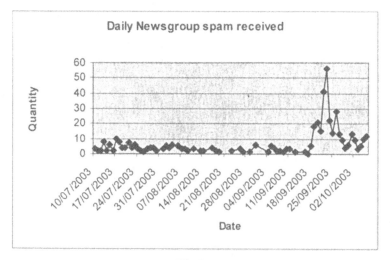

Fig 3.

The plot of Fig 3 also shows an even flow of approximately ten Newsgroups based spams to the Honey Pot for the period July 10th to Sept. 19th. On Sept. 20th, this number began to rise sharply, reaching a peak of 56 on Sept 23rd.

E-mail addresses were posted to a total of forty-nine Newsgroups on different dates. Not all of these Newsgroups generated spam equally, and some none at all. The top four Newsgroups, which generated spam are presented in Table 3.

Newsgroup	%
alt.ads	33.19%
comp.emulators.ms-windows.wine	29.20%
soc.sexuality.general	21.01%
humanities.philosophy.objectivism	10.92%
Other	5.67%
Total	**100%**

Table 3. *Top four spam generating newsgroups*

Newsgroup *alt.ads* attracted the most spam at 33% followed closely by *comp.emulators.ms-windows.wine* at 29%. It may be speculated that this is due to the respective popularities and captive audiences of each group. For example, *alt.ads* is an advertisement based Newsgroup and as such likely to attract many potential customers. Spammers, aware of this, will thus use it to harvest e-mail addresses knowing that there is an increased likelihood it will yield well.

4.4 Website spam Analysis

The first website Honey Pot e-mail addresses were posted on July 4th. However, it took until the 18th of August, a period of forty-five days later, before the first spam was received. A time lag of this order is perhaps not unexpected as spammers will need to locate the web site and then harvest e-mail addresses from it using freely available web crawlers such as *Grub*[11] or those already well established such as *Google*[12] or *AltaVista*[13].

From the recorded web access logs, which were e-mailed to the author daily, it was observed that five crawlers visited the hosted Honey Pot websites. These crawlers are: *Inktomi*,[14] *Grub*, *Google*, *WiseNut*[15] and *AltaVista*.

Outside of these five crawlers, none other was identified, so it may be concluded that wherever the spammer harvested the e-mail addresses, they had to come via one of these crawlers. What is also interesting to note, is the presence of the *Grub* crawler. Of the five visiting, *Grub* is the only one, which allows users install their own client, allowing them to choose specific URLs to crawl. Its very existence therefore, identifies the presence of a suspicious visitor.

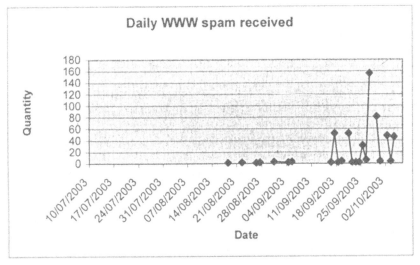

Fig 4.

It may be observed from the plot in Fig 4 that from Aug. 18th to Sept 6th a small quantity of website spam was received to the Honey Pot, with several days producing none at all. However, on Sept. 17th, things began to change, with bursts of spam arriving on an irregular basis. A possible explanation for this might be that a spammer

---

[11] http://www.grub.org

[12] http://www.google.com

[13] http://www.altavista.com

[14] http://www.inktomi.com

[15] http://www.wisenut.com

was testing or probing the website e-mail addresses for validity. Having not received an error message, the spammer thus concludes that this website containing that particular e-mail address is valid and that there is a reasonable chance that all other e-mail addresses located here are too.

Very high peaks and troughs also mark the quantity of spam to the Honey Pot. This contrasts greatly with Newsgroup spam, which tends to be more evenly distributed having lower peak quantities, i.e. 56 as opposed to 169.

Another aspect of website postings, which was noted from the analysis, was that all e-mail addresses with a random, alphanumeric makeup, did not receive any spam. Only those e-mail addresses that contained first (male & female) or last names received spam. This appears to suggest that the harvesting of e-mails from websites involves some form of applied reasoning where spammers will only send spam to e-mail addresses that appear real. This reduces their chances of hitting on a poisoned one.

4.5 Spam Country of Origin

Each e-mail on its way from source to destination can pass through many e-mail servers, each of which will add its own header information. This describes where it received the e-mail and to whom it passed it on. Therefore, header information is very important and can reveal much about an e-mail's origin.

While many of the parameters may be forged, such as: *ToAddress*, *ToName*, and *FromAddress*, it is difficult to forge the unique Internet Protocol (IP) number of the last e-mail server the e-mail passed through on its way to its destination. This is especially true when many relays are involved in an e-mail's path, as headers closest to the destination mailer are unlikely to be forged since they fall outside a spammer's control. In determining the country of origin of each spam e-mail received to the Honey Pot, attention is focused on the header information.

All 984 spam e-mail messages were examined and the results are presented in Table 4 below. In total, 50 countries were involved in sending spam to the Honey Pot. The top four are presented in Table 4 below and account for 71% of the total spam received.

Rank	Country	Spam quantity
1	Nigeria	353
2	USA	157
3	Netherlands	129
4	UK	56
Total		**695**

Table 4. *Top four spam producing countries*

In this project, Nigeria is the worst offender for sending spam, with a total of 353 messages received. All of these messages are of a similar scam nature, trying to solicit the recipient's bank account, or other personal details in order to defraud them. Brightmail, also carried out a study of spam received to their Probe Network from

August 2001 to January 2003. They discovered that during this period scam type e-mails such as these accounted for 5% of the total 30 million received.[16]. This translates to 1.5 million "scam" type messages, using much needed bandwidth.

4.6 Relaying

While not a harvesting technique itself, spammers nonetheless use relaying to disguise themselves from a recipient's e-mail server. This is now of more importance to them as many anti spam measures, [17] incorporate Blacklisting to refuse e-mail from e-mail servers known to be involved in spamming or other black hat activities.

Each of the 984 spam e-mails received to the Honey Pot were examined for evidence of e-mail relaying and the results are presented below in Table 5.

Variable	%
Not Relayed	60.47%
Relayed	39.53%
Total	**100%**

Table 5. *Quantity of spam Relayed*

Almost 40% of the spam received to the Honey Pot was relayed via a third party server. This is a very high percentage and demonstrates that spammers are now engaging this vulnerability more and more in an effort to avoid detection. In particular, it was noted from the Honey Pot that almost all of the Nigerian based spam was not relayed with header forgeries.

The relayed spam did not come from an Open Relay. Open Relays are now closed by default on most current mailer distributions. The relaying observed by this Honey Pot involves spammers making use of an e-mail server's MX table, and not via the original Open Relay method. Many e-mail servers in organisations have a backup e-mail server in the event of a problem with their own such as power failure, etc. This is now a standard procedure to safeguard e-mails and help maintain a robust network.

Spammers are now engaging in this in order to cleverly avoid detection from Realtime Blackhole Lists (RBL), which are an integral component of most current anti spam content filters. Others have also identified this practice [18] it appears to be a relatively new technique used by spammers in avoiding DNS-based spam filtering.

---

[16] Hornung, Jeanne. Jan 2003. "The state of Spam Impact & Solutions" white paper <http://www.brightmail.com/press-vpk.html>

[17] For Example: *SpamAssassin* <http://spamassassin.apache.org/> and *SpamCop* <http://www.spamcop.net/>

[18] Slashdot.org email posting by Cliff. 2003. <http://ask.slashdot.org/askslashdot/03/10/07/1944217.shtml?tid=111&tid=126>

5. Conclusions and Further Research

In keeping with the research carried out by CDT and the FTC, this three month university analysis demonstrates effectively, that Internet users who subscribe to Newsgroups, giving their e-mail address with even one posting, stand a high chance of getting spammed. Furthermore, this research shows that there is a high likelihood that Newsgroup postings will generate spam in the shorter rather than the longer term. This is most likely due to the attraction to of the one-to-one relationship between each posting and its associated e-mail address.

This Honey Pot research also shows that websites are a popular harvesting ground for spammers, especially those of the Nigerian scam category. The research further shows that it takes longer for spam to arrive via this harvesting method than through Newsgroups, most likely due to the effort involved in their harvesting. Users therefore should try to disguise their e-mail addresses as much as possible from web harvesters.

The relaying of e-mails through an e-mail server's MX table has also been shown to be a more sophisticated technique used by spammers in helping them avoid detection from RBL or DNS lookups. As far as can be ascertained, this represents a new and increased level of technical expertise. Further research in this area would reveal the true extent of its use.

E-mail addresses with a random, alphanumeric format did not get spammed during the analysis period. This shows that spammers are selective when deciding on which e-mails to spam, preferring to target those that look legitimate. This would also appear to support the idea that *munging* (spam poisoning) is helping to deter spammers. A longer time period analysis would reveal more regarding the effectiveness of the technique.

A universal spam definition is very important if spam data is to be collated and compared in a meaningful way. Such a definition would benefit the anti spam research community and would also benefit the legal community, where justice may very well depend on such a definition.

The research presented here reflects three months of analysis carried out on a single Honey Pot within a university domain. The research would be greatly enhanced if more, similarly configured but remotely positioned Honey Pots were to combine and share data. Within the university sector, the information gleaned would help to alert staff and students alike on e-mail best practices.

Privacy Protection Mechanism in Grid Computing Environment*

MingChu Li, Hongyan Yao, Cheng Guo and Na Zhang

School of Software
Dalian University of Technology
Dalian 116620, China
li_mingchu@yahoo.com

Abstract. Many users consider their true identities as their privacy, and just wish to pay for the service without exposing their identities, which leads to the problem of the privacy protection in grid environment. The pseudonym management is already well understood in current internet. But up to now, there is no good solution in grid environment. In this paper, we explore whether the current pseudonym management in internet can be applied to grid environment or not, and provide a good solution to solve this issue. Through the analysis of both X.509 format certificates with entity information and the process of entity authentication, we present an approach of how to wrap the privacy information of grid users using alias name schema.

1 Introduction

Computation grid is evolved from the idea of "electricity grid" and its goal is that users can use the infrastructure of computation grid as convenient as the common electricity service. They do not need to care about where the computing power comes from and how it works, all they care about is how to submit their job requests and get the correct results back from grid services. In order to get grid services, users need to provide their information to the service providers. However, a lot of users do not want to expose too much of their personal information while using the services. Thus the problem of privacy protection in grid occurs. The pseudonym management is already well understood in current internet. Up to now, there is no good solution in grid environment. As we know, service providers only provide services to legal users. Thus it is inevitable for users to provide some real information to service providers in order to get the services. On the other hand, in order to guarantee security in grid environment, users are required to provide true personal information for authentication and authority. It shows that if users need some kind of service, they have to give some of their true personal information. However, a lot of users just want to pay for the service without exposing their identities. As a result of tradeoff, users

---

* Supported by National Nature Science Foundation of China under grant no.:90412007

give out no more personal information than services needed. In fact, the key point of the problem is whether the information will be used by trusted parties or by untrusted parties. Also, the service providers are considering whether to give the users privilege based on the information the users offered. That is, more real identifier information, more privileges, and service providers want users to provide more real information in order to improve their services. Hence we have to find good mechanism to protect users' private information. The problem is becoming more and more important as the development of computational grid. As grid services are more complicated than the common internet ones, privacy protection in grid environment is more complicated and needs more attention as grid services will be widely used in future.

Anita Smith and Roger Clarke [4] focuses on this scenario with respect to identifier and certificate authentication, and explores two methods to solve the privacy in the scope of electric media using anonymous deal schema and alias name deal schema, respectively. Anonymous schema is suitable for super market and public services because users' identity is not important. However, the anonymous schema is not suitable for internet service although the privacy is protected, and usually, alias name schema is adopted for electronic services in internet due to the security and privacy protection. For example, when filling some form in internet, we are allowed to fill certain fields with alias name. But some information, such as telephone number or address of the users must be real so that the service providers can be paid and to provide good services. Secure Electronic Transaction (SET) protocol [3] has taken the alias name schema as its application. Naturally, we ask such questions: whether this alias name mechanism can be used in grid environment so that users private information can be protected? Whether we can also give users more privileges using alias name schema or not? What information can be protected by consulting with Certificate Authority (CA)? What information fields in X.509 certificate should not be exposed during the process of using services so that they would not affect the normal grid certificate authentication and authorization? In this paper, we will discuss these problems and provide our corresponding solutions for solving privacy issues in grid after the analysis of both X.509 format certificates and process of mutual authentication.

The other sections of this paper are organized as follows: Section 2 introduces X.509 certificate format and certificate mutual authentication process. In section 3, we analyze the replacement of some field in a certificate with alias name, and this replacement would not bring any bad side-effect on current grid operations. In section 4 we propose a solution model associated with privacy issue in grid, Section 5 summarizes this paper.

2 Certificate format and mutual authentication

In order to better understand our mechanism below, we introduce the X.509 certificate structure and the process of mutual authentication, in this section. Then we will make analysis for alias name schema in our model of privacy protection. Internet security commonly supports the following two kinds of secure services:

(1). Access control service. It is used to prevent all kinds of resources from access without authorization;

(2). Secure communication service. It mainly serves for authentication, non-repudiation, data integrity and data confidentiality. Note that these two kinds of secure services supported by internet can not fully solve the secure problems in grid environment. In addition, the security architecture of grid has to be improved so that it meets grid security requirement due to the dynamic nature of grid and the relation between grid and internet. For example, Globus [1], taking all security factors into account, proposed a Grid Security Infrastructure (GSI) for the abilities of authentication and secure communication in grid. GSI is used to support secure communication between grid entities, authentication, and data confidentiality and message integrity, and to integrate different secure architectures from different secure domains; and to support single sign-on (see [2]). Note that a key point of GSI [2] is to verify respective certificate to confirm the identities of each user and each service. The certificate includes the following information:

a) Subject name, which reflects the true entity.

b) Public key, which belongs to the subject and is used for X.509 authentication.

c) CA identifier, which claims this certificate issued by this CA.

d) Signature of CA, which is used to confirm the certificate's validity.

Next, we briefly describe the process of authentication. Assume that A is the user and B is the service provider. A connects to B and passes B its certificate. After B received A's certificate, B judges the validity of this certificate by verifying CA's signature. If valid, then B transmits A a random message and requires A to return the message encrypted by A's private key. B uses A's public key to decrypt the message from A, and compare it with the original message to see if they are the same. If matched successfully, then B trusts A's identity. Similarly, A can verify B's identity. If A also trusts B, then secure connection between A and B is established. Following the certificate format and authentication process above, we will analyze the alias name schema for our mechanism of privacy protection in next section.

2.1 Analysis of feasibility for alias name schema

In order to design our model of privacy protection in grid environment, we now make analysis for alias name schema following the certificate format and authentication process above. That is, we discuss feasibility using alias name schema in grid in order to protect privacy. We first build a matching table at CA, which records the matching relations between users' subject names and users' alias names (and map alias names into corresponding subject names). If A tells B its alias name instead of true name in the authentication process above, then does this replacement of subject name by alias name influences the normal process of authentication? Further, does this replacement influences authority in grid? If both answers are no, then alias name schema in certificate is applicable. Adoption of alias name in certificate is our fundamental for building our model to deal with privacy problems in grid in the next section. We now discuss the alias name schema. The first step of authentication is to ensure that the certificate is valid and issued by a legal CA. At this stage of confirmation, it may easily be performed by verifying CA's signature. For CA, it checks its signature and responds if the certificate is valid. Note that it is not necessary to connect to CA each time for ensuring whether the current certificate is valid. If CA's identifier information has been registered into a local resource (see Section 3), then the resource can verify its validity accordingly. The second step of authentication is to confirm whether the subject is the true one that the certificate has claimed or not. It mainly relies on whether the subject own the corresponding true private key or not. From this, we can see that the replacement of subject name by alias name does not change the fact that this subject still owns its true private key. Thus, the replacement of subject name by alias name does not influence the process of authentication. The third step of authentication is to establish a secure connection. It is easy to see that the replacement of subject name by alias name does not influence the establishment of secure connection.

Therefore the alias name schema in the process of authentication is feasible. We will detail our mechanism to solve the privacy protection problem in grid in next section by using the alias name schema.

3   New solutions for privacy protection in grid

In this section, using the idea of SET protocol and extending it to grid environment, we propose our model. The new model gives the users more freedom, and permits users to consult with CA to hide some privacy that the users want before they enjoy grid services. As described in Section 2, alias name schema does not influence the result of authentication in grid. Then we want to ask whether it will affect the authorization in grid environment. Now we will analyze it.

Von Welch, Ian Foster, Carl Kesselman, Olle Mulmo, Laura Pearlman and Steven Tuecke [6] describes the proxy certificate authentication and dynamic authorization in grid environment. We say that alias name schema does not affect authorization. Because, for authorization, it is OK as long as it has been verified in the process of authentication mentioned in Section 2, no matter it is true subject name or alias name. Delegation of the rights to a legal entity is what the authorization refers to. In other words, alias name schema does not change the entity identifier but just confuses the verifier whether the subject name in the certificate has been changed. Hence, the verifier is not sure whether the entity information from the subject name is valuable. However, it will not affect users' authorization. So authorization for the entity with alias name is equal to authorization for the entity with true subject name. It is very important that CA must keep a map from subject names to alias names, and do some other maintenance such as keeping the matching table during the user session time and maintaining CRL (Certificate Revocation List), so that, within the session time, both the alias name and its corresponding subject name have the same status. That is, if the user's certificate is invalid, then alias name should appear in the corresponding field of both expired certificate table and CRL.

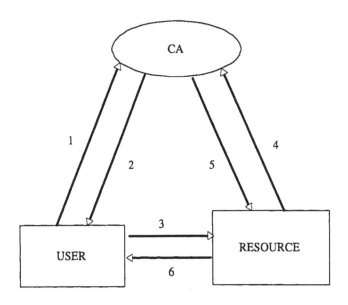

Fig. 1. A model using alias name management

Now, we illustrate our model as in Figure 1, and see how to work among CA, user and resource. Note that we apply the alias name as the substitute of corresponding subject name in this scenario. These steps are described as follows.

Step 1. The user A submits his request to CA for hiding some of his information (such as his subject name) in his certificate. Note that the user can go straight to the resource (i.e., it is not necessary for the user to communicate with CA each time before he gets the grid service) if he does not want to keep any of his information secret.

Step 2. CA will verify the user's certificate. If his certificate is valid, then CA updates the subject name in the user's certificate with alias name and set a mark of using alias name, and records the matching between subject name and alias name (see Table 1) in CA's matching table. After that, CA sends the updated certificate back to the user A.

Step 3. The user A sends the new certificate to the resource B.

Step 4. The resource B sends CA request to confirm A's identity and the validity of A's certificate. Note that the resource B does not have the corresponding CA information or updated CRL. Thus resource B has to ask CA for verification (according to CA identifier in certificate).

Step 5. After CA receives the request from resource B, CA verifies its own signature and takes out the mark from the certificate. CA uses the alias name as subject name to inspect the CRL and to see whether this certificate is expired or not. Then CA responds to the resource B whether this entity A is credible or not.

Step 6. Based on CA's positive reply, the resource B responds to the user A. Thus, the user A's identity is verified. The user A can further use the grid resource after the process of authorization executed by the resource B itself.

Table 1. Matching table between subject names and alias names

Users	Subject name	Alias name
A	A	id1
B	B	id2

Note that if the CA and the updated CRL are known to the resource B, the resource B can locally do the same work as CA did. Also, we need to use the alias name to query CRL for judging whether the certificate has expired or not because the certificate with the alias name may be expired. Once it expired, the subject name and the alias name in certificates would appear at CRL. Note that CA and resources using alias name to query CRL would not affect the query result. So it is very important that we need to make sure that the user who is using the certificate with alias name is the same as the true user who matches the alias name in the matching table of CA. Thus the matching work is very important task in our model. As we know, in order to conveniently manage users' certificates, CA usually adopts some easy identification masks (such as the mask of subject names) as user's LDAP entry (which stores user's certificate information). As a result, the users' individual or organization information from these entry names are not protected. This is not what the users want to see. Our model can overcome this flaw because our model proposes to hide users' privacy information in certificates. On the other hand, we must mention that users need to consult with CA for hiding their privacy information before the grid services are required. Once users' alias names are set, it can not be changed during the time of services. That is, one alias name is used in whole session time. In addition, it seems that anonymous schema is not suitable in grid services, because anonymous schema can not be taken as a carrier who is authorized by resources nor can it promise that all service processes launched by the users are under the control of naming space (see [5]).

4 Conclusions

The original grid intention is that users can use grid services as convenient as using the services of electricity. Because of the specialty of grid services and security, it requires that every user who uses grid service owns his personal certificate and brings it forth as service goes. As a result, it will leads to a lot of problems, for example, the user's identifier information may be exposed and damages the user. This paper explores the privacy protection problem through the analysis of the certificate format and the process of mutual certificate authentication. Although our approach needs to trust CA and consult with CA for hiding information field in certificates, this model can overcome the privacy problem to some extend. As privacy protection problem in grid environment is more important with the development of grid service techniques and the wide application in other fields. We believe that our model will be used more widely and more people will be interested in the problem in the future.

References

1. http://www.globus.org
2. Joshy Joseph and Craig Fellenstein, Grid Computing, IBM Press, 2003.
3. Jin Liang, Ren Shi and Liangmin Wang, Electronic commerce core techniques, Xian University of Electronic Science Press, Agust, 2000.
4. Anita Smith and Roger Clarke, Privacy in electronic media, Computer Law and Security Report, Vol. 16, No. 2, 2000.
5. Subhashini Raghunathan, Armin R. Mikler and Cliff Cozzolino, Secure agent computation: X.509 Proxy Certificates in a multi-lingual agent framework, The Journal of System and Software, January 19, 2004.
6. Von Welch, Ian Foster, Carl Kesselman, Olle Mulmo, Laura Pearlman and Steven Tuecke, X.509 Proxy Certificates for Dynamic Delegation, 3rd Annual PKI Research and Development Workshop, 2004.

Flow Label Filtering Feasibility

Orla McGann and David Malone

1 HEAnet Ltd., Brooklawn House, Shelbourne Road, Ballsbridge, Dublin 4
orla.mcgann@heanet.ie
2 The Hamilton Institute, National University of Ireland Maynooth
david.malone@nuim.ie

Abstract. The IPv6 header has a field called the Flow Label field, which was included to help identify flows of packets, mainly for Quality of Service purposes. We propose using this field, and its randomly generated value, as another piece of state to filter related packets in a TCP connection. This will only be possible if the Flow Label field actually remains constant for the duration of connections and will only be useful if the Flow Label is set in a unpredictable way.

Key words: IPv6, Flow Label, Stateful Firewalling, SYN Cookies

1   Introduction

Stateful packet filtering currently uses a number of parameters in the TCP and IPv4/IPv6 headers to remember the "state" of a connection, in order to process packets entering or leaving the filter more accurately. For example, port numbers or sequence numbers may be examined to make sure the packet is part of a valid TCP connection.

The Flow Label is a 20-bit field that is part of the IPv6 header. It is used by a source to label certain groups of packets for easy identification and handling by routers, mainly to implement Quality of Service (QoS). These groups of packets are called a "flow". We aim to investigate the usefulness of the Flow Label for Stateful Firewalling; that is, as another method of identifying and filtering packets. Can the Flow Label be examined and stored by the firewall? This would introduce an extra piece of state that needs to be correctly guessed in order to blindly inject spoofed packets into the network, thus adding another layer of protection to the firewall.

The IPv4 header has a similar field, the IP ID field, which is used in fragmentation to identify packets that are part of the same datagram. The IP ID field was used to implement the idle scan attack that was popular in the late 1990's. This exploitation was possible due to the sequential allocation of values in the IP ID field[1].

In contrast, the Flow Label is assigned pseudo-randomly from the range 0x00001 – 0xFFFFF to a packet by the source node. It should be chosen randomly so that any set of bits within the Flow Label field are suitable for use as a hash key by routers, for looking up the state associated with the flow. The router, or other devices using the Flow Label, should not depend on this being the case if they want to avoid an algorithmic attack on the hash table using maliciously chosen Flow Labels[2]. The Flow Label 0x000000 (zero) has a special meaning and is reserved to indicate that the packet has not been associated with any flow[3].

In IPv4, flow classifiers are based on the quintuple of source and destination addresses and port numbers, and on the transport layer type. This can be problematic as some of these fields may not always be available; either due to fragmentation or encryption. It is more efficient to base the classifiers solely on the IP header, so that the introduction of newer transport types will not require "flow aware" routers to be updated.

Thus for IPv6, a flow is uniquely identified by the source and destination addresses and the (non-zero) Flow Label. All packets belonging to the same flow should be sent with this same triplet. If there is a Priority label, Hop-by-Hop options header or Routing Header associated with the flow, they must also remain consistent throughout the flow (excluding the Next Header field in the Hop-by-Hop options header and Routing Header obviously). RFC 3697[4] states that the Flow Label is immutable and must be delivered unchanged to the destination node(s).

Routers that do not support the functions of the Flow Label are required to: set the field to zero, when a packet originates locally; pass the field on unchanged, when forwarding a packet; and ignore the field, when receiving a packet. Routers may choose to set up a flow-handling state for any packet, even when one has not been explicitly established by the source of the packet. There is no requirement that all, or even most, packets belong to flows. There may also be multiple concurrent active flows between two hosts, as well as traffic that does not belong to any flow.

In order to establish whether it is possible to use the Flow Label for stateful packet filtering, we must first check to make sure that the Flow Label actually stays constant across the lifetime of a flow in practice. Otherwise requiring a fixed Flow Label at a firewall would block legitimate packets.

2 Examining the Flow Label for consistency

A packet capture program[3] was written to track the IPv6 packets on the network. The program extracted the source and destination addresses; ports; transport type and the Flow Label from the IPv6 and TCP headers of each packet. Then a table of active connections was created for listing each flow; as determined by the quintuple of source and destination addresses, source and destination ports, and transport type and each packet was compared to this table. The program then checked to make sure the Flow Labels matched for each packet in a connection; if they did not, the program logged a message. If

---

[3] The libpcap library is part of the TCPdump program (http://www.tcpdump.org)

there was no such flow, it was added to the table of active connections. The program also deleted ("flushed") any stale flow once the connection had been closed or timed out. This allowed us to see whether the Flow Label was kept constant for the lifetime of a TCP connection.

Initial testing with FreeBSD and Debian Linux using the program showed that a Flow Label of "00000" was set by the local FreeBSD machine when establishing connections to both the FreeBSD and Debian hosts. The KAME IPv6 stack, used by FreeBSD, was supposed to set the Flow Label on TCP connections, so we submitted a small patch to implement this.

```
/* update flowinfo - draft-itojun-ipv6-flowlabel-api-00 */
inp->in6p_flowinfo &= ~IPV6_FLOWLABEL_MASK;
if (inp->in6p_flags & IN6P_AUTOFLOWLABEL)
    inp->in6p_flowinfo |=
        (htonl(ip6_randomflowlabel()) & IPV6_FLOWLABEL_MASK);
```

Further testing showed that Debian Linux always sets a Flow Label of "00000", whether it establishes the flow or it is responding to a connection attempt from another host. A stranger phenomenon was noted on FreeBSD however: a Flow Label was set by the remote machine on the first response packet. But, another different Flow Label was then sent when the transfer of data began. This problem was identified as a problem with FreeBSD's SYN Cookies/SYN Caching implementation, where the Flow Label on the SYN/ACK was uninitialised, and then correctly set once the connection was fully established. We discuss this further in Section 3.

Further tests were run to see if the problem identified by our initial observations was widespread, or just local to particular implementations of IPv6 and operating systems that use TCP optimisations. A long list of IPv6 enabled websites[5] was used to generate TCP flows from various IPv6 enabled platforms and the capture program was used to analyse if the Flow Label was being set consistently.

Table 1 contains a detailed break down of the setting of the Flow Label by the various hosts observed. Of the 1105 hosts that sent TCP packets, 427 of them (38.64%) set the Flow Label to something other than "00000"; but only 84 of these consistently set the Flow Label during the flow. The remaining 343 set the Flow Label once during the three-way handshake and then again once the transfer of data started, as was noted in our initial observations. The remaining 678 hosts (61.36%) set the Flow Label to "00000" consistently. These hosts are most likely using some Linux distribution or OpenBSD. OpenBSD explicitly states in its source code that it leaves the Flow Label field set to zero so that it does not require any state management.

The operating system of the hosts analysed was determined from two tests that were performed on each host. The first test probed each host using the netcat program[6] to collect the banners that are displayed by hosts when they are remotely accessed. The second test checked to see if the hosts responded to

TCP Hosts and the Flow Label	Hosts	%
Hosts with Flow Label set to something other than 0	427	38.64
Hosts with the Flow Label = 0	784	
Hosts consistently setting Flow Label to 0	678	61.36
Hosts who set the Flow Label to 0 and set it again after handshake	106	
Hosts who set the Flow Label (but not necessarily consistently)	321	
Hosts who consistently set the Flow Label (never changes)	84	19.67
Hosts who inconsistently set the flow (incl. setting it to 0)	343	80.33

Table 1. Table of consistency of Flow Label Setting on TCP packets captured for each host

ICMPv6 Node Information solicitations. This is a feature that is currently only implemented in the KAME IPv6 stack[7], which is used by FreeBSD, OpenBSD and NetBSD. These tests served as a crude form of OS finger printing.

In summary, most of the hosts that inconsistently set the Flow Label either used the FreeBSD or NetBSD operating system. Hosts that consistently set the Flow Label to something other than "00000" were mainly running the patched version of FreeBSD or Solaris. Hosts that consistently set the flow label to zero were either using OpenBSD or some version of Linux.

We note two possible biases in these results. Firstly, a FreeBSD machine is always a part of the connections that were captured, as it was used to run our tests. Secondly, all of the connections captured are responses to connections initiated by the machine conducting these tests. No observations are made of how the Flow Label is set by these remote hosts when they initiate connections to other machines. Monitoring the connections at a popular IPv6 web server might produce different results.

In order to discuss what is actually occurring when different Flow Labels are being set during the TCP connections, and how the problem was fixed for FreeBSD, we must discuss SYN Cookies and SYN Caching. A solution to this problem that was later integrated into FreeBSD will also be described.

3 Fixing FreeBSD's SYN Cookie and SYN Cache Implementation

SYN Cookies[8] were devised as a means of alleviating the problem of SYN flooding[9] without the need for major changes to the TCP protocol. They are created by making a MD5 hash[10][4] from a number of parameters that are found in the SYN and ACK packets of the 3-way handshake. These parameters include the source and destination addresses and ports, and the Maximum Segment Size (MSS). A time-based server selected secret is also included in

---
[4] Of course another hashing algorithm could be used, but this is the one originally suggested.

the hash. This Cookie is then sent as the 32-bit TCP initial sequence number (ISN) by the server when responding to new connection requests. When the host receives the ACK for this SYN packet, it can rebuild the MD5 hash from this ACK packet. This removes the need to store the ISN and other information about the connection during the handshake.

The main problem with using SYN Cookies to store connections is that other TCP features, such as TCP options, cannot be used. The server remembers nothing about the connection while waiting for the returning ACK, so options that the originating host sets are lost when the server rebuilds the connection from the information stored in the SYN Cookie. If the ACK received matches the ISN sent, then the SYN Cookies will be the same.

A second method for optimising a TCP implementation to prevent SYN flooding, SYN Caching, was developed by David Borman for BSDi[11]. This was then integrated into FreeBSD by Jonathan Lemon[12]. SYN Caching is similar to the original method of storing connection information in a Protocol Control Block(PCB) structure, but instead a much smaller PCB is allocated which only remembers the key information for the setup of the connection (such as TCP options like window scaling and timestamps). FreeBSD now passes all SYNs it receives through SYN Caching, failing over to SYN Cookies if the SYN Cache is full. So, in FreeBSD traditional TCP connection establishment is now defunct.

It is easy enough to keep the Flow Label constant for a simple TCP implementation, as another variable can just be added to the TCP PCB structure to remember the Flow Label. When TCP optimisations are used to accept connections, these techniques must also keep the Flow Label constant. One simple option would be to set the Flow Label to zero for all such connections, but this is not a rather limited implementation.

The problem we noted previously arose because the code in the FreeBSD kernel did not set the Flow Label correctly for packets generated by the SYN Cache/SYN Cookie code; the Flow Label was not initialised on the SYN/ACK packet. It was only being set when the first packet of data was being ACKed. Instead, whatever junk that was in the memory allocated to the packet was being sent as the Flow Label.

Modifications were made to the kernel code to rectify this problem and were subsequently incorporated into FreeBSD. We will describe these modifications here.

In the SYN Cache case, the Flow Label can be generated either sequentially or randomly and stored as a variable added to the syncache structure (u_int32_t sc_FlowLabel). We are free to choose either for the SYN Cache case. There is less potential for collisions if the Flow Label is set sequentially, but there is potential for abuse, just as with the IPv4 IP ID field, if sequential Flow Labels are used.

In the SYN Cookie case, the cookie is derived from the source and destination IP addresses and ports and the MSS, as well as a random secret, which are then passed through an MD5 hash. From this hash, 25 bits of the resulting output are used for the Cookie, and another 7 bits are used for the window-size. These 32 bits are sent as the ISN. We use an additional 20 bits of the MD5 hash to generate the Flow Label. When the ACK is received, the hash can be recreated, as all the original information from the connection will be returned in the ACK packet, and this can be compared to the original Cookie sent as this is stored in the acknowledgement number as the ISN+1. We can do this because we are free to choose any (random) Flow Label for the SYN Cookie case. It is not possible to choose a sequentially increasing Flow Label. We must use the value generated from the hash because it is always possible to recreate the hash, therefore it is always possible to recreate the Flow Label.

Strictly speaking the Flow Label (and addresses) should uniquely identify a flow, but this is not enforced by KAME. The risk of collisions may be reduced by checking for existing flows with that ID and if one exists, resorting to a zero Flow Label (the use of a zero Flow Label could be encoded in a SYN Cookie in a similar way to that used to store TCP Maximum Segment Size[12]).

Now, with the addition of this code, when the ACK is returned a full PCB is constructed and the Flow Label is copied from the SYN Cache, or from the regenerated cookie, allowing subsequent data packets to be sent using the same Flow Label.

The addition of this code means that FreeBSD now sets the Flow Label at the beginning of a TCP connection, and it remains constant across the lifetime of the connection. Any operating system that implements techniques like SYN Caching or Cookies will need to use similar measures to ensure the Flow Label is consistent across the flow.

While completing the analysis of the packet capture program output, it was observed that on a number of occasions a patched machine did not consistently set the Flow Label. After examining the connections in question, it was established that the Flow Label sometimes changed from its properly set Flow Label value to "00000". These inconsistencies only occurred when the patched machine sent a RST packet in response to receiving a packet that corresponded to a flow that had already been shut down.

RSTs are sent when the host receives packets for a connection it does not know anything about, or when a remote host tries to connect to a port that no service is listening on. Hence, it knows nothing of the state of the connection (or lack thereof) so it does not know what to set the Flow Label to so it sets it to "00000". The FreeBSD machine sent RSTs with a Flow Label of "00000" in response to ACKs that were received after the connection had closed or timed out, so it no longer had the Flow Label state stored.

4 Using the Flow Label for Stateful Filtering

Once the setting of the Flow Label is consistent, either set to "00000" or some other value, it is possible to use this information as another piece of state remembered by the firewall. Consider the scenario where host A sends a SYN packet to host B to initiate a connection with the Flow Label set. The packet filter creates a new state for this connection from the source address, destination addresses, ports and the Flow Label for direction A to B.

Host B sends back a SYN/ACK packet to host A with its own Flow Label set. This is the final piece of state remembered by the packet filter: the Flow Label for direction B to A. Host A sends the final ACK to host B to complete the three way handshake. The firewall checks the Flow Label to make sure it matches the one stored from the original SYN packet. If it does match, the packet is let through. As with normal stateful packet filters, once the packet matches the state stored in the firewall all subsequent packets in the connection are passed through the firewall.

Depending on how strict a firewall wants to be, we suggest a number of actions that can be taken when a packet with an inconsistent Flow Label are seen. It may:

- block packets with a different Flow Label from that recorded.
- replace the stored Flow Label if the Flow Label has changed from 00000 to another value. Then, block packets if the Flow Label changes again.
- Allow the Flow Label to change once, assuming that the label set on the SYN or SYN/ACK (depending on direction) might not have been set correctly. Thereafter, block any packets with a different Flow Label set (for that connection). This might be restricted to the the second packet of the connection.

Flaws in old implementations will cause problems until the patched code for consistent flows propagates. Each of the different strategies proposed to deal with packets from hosts that inconsistently set the Flow Label are problematic in some way.

Obviously, blocking packets that have different Flow Labels set during the same connection is the safest solution. It prevents the possibility of spoofed packets circumventing the the packet filter. On the other hand, there are hosts that inconsistently set the Flow Label at present. There will be a lot of false positives until the patched code propagates, with packets from legitimate hosts being blocked by the filter.

The second option — allowing the Flow Label to change once from "00000" to some other value — provides for the correct handling of packets from un-patched hosts by the packet filter. But, this also means that there is an increased possibility of packets circumventing the packet filter. There is also no provision for packets from hosts running the un-patched version of FreeBSD or NetBSD, where the Flow Label is set to whatever was previously stored in the memory, which may not necessarily be zero.

The final solution proposed covers the correct filtering of packets through the packet filter from all hosts, including packets from un-patched machines. Unfortunately, allowing a change to the Flow Label value stored in state opens up the possibility for attackers to blindly inject packets into the connection by replacing the Flow Label in the final ACK of the 3-way handshake with one of its own choosing, which will block all other legitimate packets from the real host.

It should be noted though, that someone blindly injecting packets into the network and trying to inject their own packets will have to create a packet that matches all the other information stored in state: the source and destination addresses and ports and also be in the expected range of the TCP sequence and acknowledgement fields, which is no mean feat. Carefully checking these fields before accepting a Flow Label change could make these techniques useful while still accommodating unpatched machines.

5 Conclusion

The Flow Label field of the IPv6 header has potential uses other than for QoS. Its use for Stateful Filtering is problematic because of a number of issues in the implementation of the Flow Label in the various IPv6 stacks. Linux and OpenBSD default to setting the Flow Label to "00000", which does not reduce the ability to guess firewall state information. FreeBSD and NetBSD have had flaws in their implementation with the setting of the Flow Label, which would require tweaks to a potential stateful packet filter design.

Once the use of Flow Labels becomes more widely implemented and such implementation problems are fixed, the Flow Label should provide a useful additional piece of state to keep the attackers guessing.

References

1. Salvatore (Antirez) Sanfilippo. Idle scan [online]. http://wiki.hping.org/8. Last visited 26/09/2005.
2. Scott A. Crosby and Dan S. Wallach. Denial of Service via Algorithmic Complexity Attacks. In *USENIX Security 2003*, aug 2003. http://www.cs.rice.edu/~scrosby/hash/CrosbyWallach_UsenixSec2003.pdf.
3. Steve E. Deering and Robert M. Hinden. *RFC 2460: Internet Protocol version Six (IPv6)*, dec 1998. http://www.faqs.org/rfcs/rfc2460.html.
4. Jarno Rajahalme, Alex Conta, Brian E. Carpenter, and Steve E. Deering. *RFC 3697: IPv6 Flow Label Specification*, mar 2004. http://www.faqs.org/rfcs/rfc3697.html.
5. Sander Jonkers. IPv6 Enabled Sites / IPv6 Accessible Sites [online]. http://www.prik.net/list.html. Last visited 23/05/2005.
6. Giovanni Giacobbi. The GNU Netcat – Official homepage [online]. http://netcat.sourceforge.net/. Last visited 28/09/2005.
7. KAME project. Webpage of Kame Project [online]. http://www.kame.org. Last visited 23/05/2005.
8. Dan J. Bernstein. SYN Cookies. http://cr.yp.to/syncookies.html. Last visited 28/09/2005.
9. daemon9. IP-Spoofing Demystified. *Phrack*, 48, sep 1996. http://www.phrack.org/show.php?p=48&a=14.

10. Ronald L. Rivest. *RFC 1321: The MD5 Message-Digest Algorithm*, apr 1992. http://www.faqs.org/rfcs/rfc1321.html.
11. David Borman. TCP-SYN and delayed TCB allocation. http://www.postel.org/pipermail/end2end-interest/2003-May/003118.html. Last visited 23/05/2005.
12. Jonathan Lemon. Resisiting SYN flood DoS attacks with a SYN cache. In *BSD-Con 2002*, feb 2002. http://people.freebsd.org/~jlemon/papers/syncache.pdf.

The Representation and use of Relation Information for the Detection of Threats by Security Information Management Systems

Cyril Onwubiko, Andrew P. Lenaghan, Luke Hebbes and Ron R. Malyan

Networking and Communications Group, Kingston University
Penrhyn Road, Kingston Upon Thames, KT1 2EE, UK
{k0327645; a.lenaghan; l.hebbes; rmalyan}@kingston.ac.uk

Abstract. A graph-based data structure is proposed for security information management systems (SIM) to analyse security event data from varying security sources. The proposed relation information graph-based representation is used to model attack graphs from a simulation-based network environment, which represent security classes in terms of security events and attributes as graph node, and graph edge as temporal relationships. An efficient pattern matching (isomorphism) technique is then utilised to analyse security attack graphs based on matching known security pattern in a database of pattern attack graphs. The graph matching technique decomposes graph data structure into path, and filtering of paths to reduce search space by discarding graphs that do not match.

Attack graphs are used to detect security attacks, and utilised in security information management systems to provide powerful analysis of correlated security event data from heterogeneous network monitoring systems.

Keywords: *computer network attack, attack graph, graph isomorphism, security information management systems*

1   Introduction

There is a growing trend in computer network security threats, vulnerabilities and attacks; with recent computer attacks exhibiting features of coordination and multiplicity[1]. These attacks exploit multiple chains of vulnerabilities to infiltrate computer systems, and act as attack vectors to computer networks and systems. The concern that threats and vulnerabilities in information systems are unavoidable makes their protection essential. However, to suitably protect information systems, there are two requirements: i) appropriate and expressive representation of security attacks and ii) analysis of security attacks - integrated and real-time - that assists security information management systems in decision making.

To analyse security attacks, an approach is to represent audit trail and event logs in a graph-based representation often referred to as an attack graph. Attack graphs show the characteristics, pattern and propagation of an attack. We argue for the use of relation information in the representation of attack graphs that reveal temporal, logical and spatial relationships of security events and attributes that when well-formulated offers insight on how to comprehensively analyse security events to detect security attacks. Attack graphs have been used for detection, defense and forensics when utilized in intrusion detection systems (IDS) [2] and can be utilised in security information management systems to analyse security event data.

There is a growing use of SIM solutions in proactive monitoring of computer networks. SIM solutions through centralised integration, correlation, normalisation and analysis of security event data from varying network security sensors provide an integrated and unified actionable logic for protecting an enterprise network. SIM's centralised integration offers the potential for more flexible and powerful detection of attacks, compared to the use of stand-alone point solutions; however, centralised systems, like SIM, are faced with two major problems:

1) the volume and diversity of security related information; although, relational database management systems (RDBMS) can handle the volume.
2) the analysis offered by the relational database model (querying tables) is limited because the relational information RDBMS's makes use of is usually implicitly in the ordering of the rows in the tables. That is primarily temporally ordered sequences.

We argue that a more expressive graph-based representational scheme is needed that can simultaneously express different types of attributes and relationships between security events including not only temporal but also logical spatial. This richer scheme, however, significantly provides elaborate representation of security event data that helps reveal hiding characteristics of attacks, and therefore assists in seeking for known patterns of attack. Our contributions in this paper to address these issues are as follows:

- We propose a new relation information graph-based representation that describes security events with attributes as graph node, and represent graph edge as temporal relationships, such as time occurrence and "coincidence" of security events.
- We investigate the need for a pattern matching approach in the new scheme (isomorphism); that assists in detecting matching (known) classes of attacks.

In section 2 the motivation behind this research and related work are discussed; section 3 discusses background aspects of this research such as security information management systems and attack graphs, graph theory, graph and subgraph isomorphism; in section 4 we present our implementation and analysis of result and finally, we conclude the discussion with a summary in section 5.

2   Motivation and Related Work

2.1   Motivation

Graphs are a rich and flexible data structure for the representation of objects, object attributes and relationships; while graph matching is a technique utilised extensively in the analysis of real-world applications and problems. The application of graph matching have been used in diverse disciplines such as computer vision, machine learning, pattern recognition [3], case-based reasoning and monitoring of computer networks [4] to successfully manipulate and analyse problems using existing and novel graph algorithms. However, in most practical applications, exact graph matching may not exist, because of distortion, noise or changes in the pattern of propagation of the attacks or threats, as is the case with network attack problems; attack patterns may change due to network re-route, adaptive defence mechanisms and link saturation; so inexact graph matching are employed in the graph matching problem. But, the task of inexact graph matching or subgraph isomorphism in identifying security threats is believed to be in the non-polynomial complete [NP-complete] class of problems, and is therefore computationally expensive to solve using traditional methods.

In an attempt to solve this problem, we applied an efficient graph matching technique that performs *exact* and *inexact* subgraph queries in a database of graphs. The method finds all the occurrences of a template-graph (subgraph) by filtering the database of graphs in a linear time in the size of the database [5].

2.2   Related Work
Attack graph formalism and application have attracted recent research interests, typically in model checking and verification, presenting a general purpose scenario [6, 7]. However, previous contributions did not model attack graphs in terms of relation information with spatio-temporal qualities, as proposed in this work.

3   Background

3.1   Attack Graphs and Security Information Management Systems (SIM)
SIM solutions integrate, correlate, normalise and analyse security event data from varying network security sensors/sources to provide an integrated and unified actionable logic for protecting an enterprise network. It is overwhelming to monitor and manage an enterprise network for an organisation without efficient security information management systems in place; however, the astuteness in SIM solutions are provided by intelligent analysis of security event logs and audit trails coming from numerous security sources (intrusion detection systems, firewalls, security sensors, secure routers, antiviral systems and proxy gateways) that output security logs in different formats. To assist security information management systems better analyse security event data, we used relation information graph-based representation that describe the spatio-temporal features and relationships among the events extracted from security data. The new graph-based data structure represents graph node as a security class, which has security events and attributes; while graph edge is represented in terms of both spatial and temporal relationships, for example, the occurrence of security events, say A and B, is: i) A "coincidental" to B, that is, did the events occur at the same time? ii) A "before" B; iii) A "after" B; iv) A "during" B; v) A "starts" B; vi) A "ends" at B. The security event is the computer or network device compromised during the attack, and the attributes are: a) the type of device, (for example, router, sensor, firewall) b) the classification, where the security event-type had been previously classified, as *critical, major* or *minor* according to an organisation's classification scheme based on the importance of the device to them. The spatial relationships include: i) spatial distance between any two security event-type, (for example, how close are the two attacks, ii) orientation (subnets). The proposed graph-based representation provides temporal and spatial relationships to represent security data and by using suitable graph techniques to manipulate its database, a matching set of attack characteristics and attributes are produced that assists security information management systems to better detect security threats.

Graph-based representation can be utilised to detect network intrusions as it reveals most relationships among events – often passive and subtle – that assists in detecting attack characteristics and attributes; which guarantees:

a) Appropriate representation of event attributes
b) Detailed examination and expression of event characteristics
c) Appropriate consideration of temporal relationship among security events
d) Detailed association of event data object with distinctive attributes
e) Appropriate classification of spatial relationship among security events.

3.2 Graph Theory

Graphs are a data structure for the representation of objects and relationships. In a graph representation, the nodes represent security event or its parts, while the edges represent temporal relationships between events or events parts. There are several graph discussions in literature, for example [8].

DEFINITION 1: A Directed Attributed Graph $M(V, E, \alpha, \beta, V_w, E_w)$ is a digraph with labels assigned to graph set of vertices and edges. $M(V, E, \alpha, \beta, V_w, E_w)$ is a six-tuple, such that:

- V is a finite set of vertices
- $E \subseteq V \times V$ is a finite set of edges
- $\alpha : V \mapsto V_p$ is a labelling function for finite set of vertices
- $\beta : E \mapsto E_p$ is a labelling function for finite set of edge relationships
- V_w is a finite set of vertex labels (numbers), and
- E_w is a finite set of edge labels (numbers)

3.3 Constructing Attack Graphs

Firstly, we formally define *pattern attack graphs (PAG)*, the data structure used to represent all possible attacks on our *detailed network* (DN). We restrict our attention to pattern attack graphs representing worm infection of susceptible computer systems. PAG is a directed attributed graph; i) "directed", because the occurrence of any two security events is temporally related, for instance, say between any two events A and B, we have A "coincidental" to B; A "before" B; A "after" B; A "starts" B, and A "ends" in B; ii) "attributed", because the edge relationship is spatial, and of *number of infection* and *proximity (distance) of infected nodes* (see fig. 2 & 4).

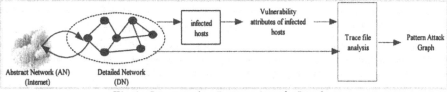

Fig.1: Constructing Pattern Attack Graph

Figure 1 shows how our pattern attack graph is constructed. The simulation models worm infection in *detailed* and *abstract networks* [9]. A detailed network (DN) depicts an enterprise network, such run by an Internet Service Provider (ISP); while the abstract network (AN) mathematically models the Internet using the Kermack-Mckendric SIR model [10]. Output files, *trace file and NAM file* (network animation file) obtained are analysed to generate pattern attack graphs (fig.2 & 4).

REMARK 1: Subgraphs (**Template graphs**): Templates that describe potential threats, or known security violations to be searched in the super graph.

REMARK 2: **Super graph** describes the state of the entire network that is to be searched for occurrences of the template, as in REMARK 1.

DEFINITION 2: A *pattern attack graph* is a directed weighted graph, as in definition 1, given as a six-tuple. $PAG = (V, E, \alpha, \beta, V_p, E_p)$, where:
- V is a finite set of vertices, representing security objects
- $E \subseteq V \times V$ is a finite set of spatial edges between adjacent security objects
- $\alpha : V \mapsto V_p$ is a labelling function generating vertex attributes
- $\beta : E \mapsto E_p$ is a labelling function generating spatial edge attributes
- V_p is a finite set of vertex labels (numbers) representing vertex attributes
- E_p is a finite set of temporal edges between temporally consecutive vertices.

A vertex $(v \in V)$ corresponds to a *security event* and a spatial edge $(e \in E)$ represents a *temporal relationship* between two adjacent vertices (security events). The possible *vertex attributes* (V_p) are *security object type* (for example, router, sensor, server, PC), and *classification* (for example, *critical, major* or *minor*) of corresponding security event. The temporal edge attributes (E_p) indicate relationships between two adjacent security events such as *time occurrence*, (for example, events are "coincidental", "before", "after", "during", "starts", "ends") and the *direction* of the security event (temporally).

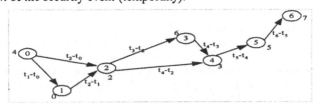

Fig. 2: An example of a descriptive representation of attack graph

Figure 2 shows the nodes infected and the temporal relationship between adjacent nodes (time duration of infection). Graph vertices represent compromised computer nodes, while the edges represent attack duration in time. The numbers in the circle depict iterative graph node (0, 1, 2, ...) while the number outside the circle shows the attribute of security object infected. By definition 1, using figure 2, we have:
- $V = \{0, 1, 2, 3, 4, 5, 6\}$
- $E = \{(0, 1), (0, 2), (1, 2), (2, 3), (2, 4), (3, 4), (4, 5), (5, 6)\}$

- $\alpha : 0 \mapsto 4,\ 1 \mapsto 0,\ 2 \mapsto 2,\ 3 \mapsto 6,\ 4 \mapsto 3,\ 5 \mapsto 5,\ 6 \mapsto 7$

- $\beta : (0,1) \mapsto (t_1 - t_0),\ (0,2) \mapsto (t_2 - t_0),\ (1,2) \mapsto (t_2 - t_1),\ (2,3) \mapsto (t_3 - t_2),\ (2,4) \mapsto (t_4 - t_2),$

  $\dots (3,4) \mapsto (t_4 - t_3),\ (4,5) \mapsto (t_5 - t_4),\ (5,6) \mapsto (t_6 - t_5)$

- $V_p = \{4, 0, 2, 6, 3, 5, 7\}$

- $E_p = \{(t_1 - t_0), (t_2 - t_0), (t_2 - t_1), (t_3 - t_2), (t_4 - t_2), (t_4 - t_3), (t_5 - t_4), (t_6 - t_5)\}$

3.4   Basic concepts in graph matching

In graph matching, however, we determine the similarities in graph representations. In most real world applications there may not always exist perfect (exact) match between graph representations; therefore, a function is required that computes a measure of similarities between two given graph representations, which is the basis of graph matching (see fig. 3).

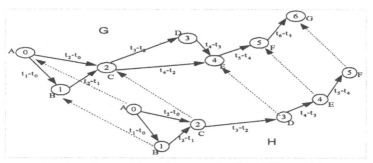

Fig. 3: An example of graph matching of two graphs G and H, matching vertex and preserving edge invariant property.

DEFINITION 3: A subgraph $G_s(V_s, E_s, \alpha_s, \beta_s, V_{ps}, E_{ps})$ of G, $G_s \subseteq G$, is a six-tuple, such that:

$$V_s \subseteq V;\ \ E_s \subseteq E \cap (V_s x V_s);\ \ \alpha_s(v) = \alpha(v) \forall v \in V_s\ \ and\ \ \beta_s(e) = \beta(e) \forall e \in E_s$$

DEFINITION 4: Graph isomorphism: A graph G is isomorphic to a graph H, if there exists a bijective function (mapping) ϕ from the nodes of G to the nodes of H that preserves all labels and structures of the edges. That is:

$$\phi : G \mapsto H, \phi \text{ is a bijective function if:}$$

- $e = (v_1, v_2) \in E(G);\ iff\ e' = (\phi(v_1), \phi(v_2)) \in E(H)\ \ such that\ \ \beta(e) = \beta'(e')$

- $\forall e' = (\phi(v_1), \phi(v_2)) \in E(H),$ there exist $e = (\phi^{-1}(v'_1), \phi^{-1}(v'_2)) \in E(G)$
  such that $\beta(e) = \beta'(e).$

DEFINITION 5: Subgraph isomorphism: A mapping ϕ is a subgraph isomorphism from a graph G to a graph G' if $G' \subseteq G$ such that ϕ is a graph isomorphism from G to G'. That is, $\phi : G \mapsto G'$ such that $(e_1, e_2) \in E(G); iff (\phi(e_1), \phi(e_2)) \in E(G')$

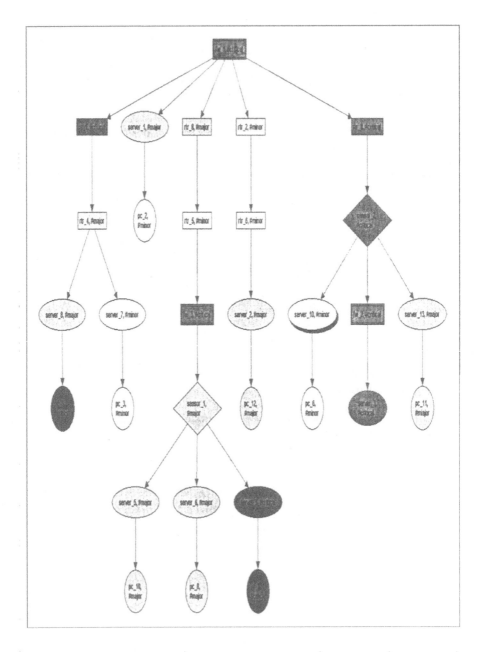

Fig. 4: Visualisation of "attribute" information graph-based representation

Figure 4 shows graph-based representation - constructed according to definition 2. Each graph node indicates a security event. The attributes of the security event are shape and colour, where the shape indicates the type of security event (routers, firewall, PC, sensors), and the colour indicates the classification (critical, major or minor). The temporal attributes are indication of the edge connecting adjacent security events.

4　Experiment and Result Analysis

4.1　Experiment

Our implementation is network simulation-based that successfully analyses computer network attacks, typically, a network worm model, by:
i) Using a Network Simulator (NS) to model network worm infection in an enterprise network for a mid-size organisation; ii) Constructing pattern attack graphs from security event logs and audit trails generated in the form of tracefile and NAMfile from the simulation; iii) Building a database containing pattern attack graphs and iv) Using a subgraph (template) to match the database containing pattern attack graphs for graph similarities of security violation.

The problem of checking for graph similarities in the database is generally referred to as graph matching. Because our template is a subgraph, our pattern attack graph matching problem decomposes to a subgraph isomorphism type.

To use attack graphs to detect a security violation, a template is used to match its occurrences in the super graph (see Remark 2).

GraphGrep is a graph technique employed for both *exact* and *inexact* matching, which uses Glide (*Graph Linear Description*) language to formulate queries. Glide combines the power of XPath [11] for XML documents and Smart [12] for molecules in its formulations. It is pertinent to note that before using GraphGrep for this analysis, we examined two graph matching applications [13, 14], but a constraint is finding an approach suitable for: a) *exact* and *inexact* matching b) performs efficiently in time with the size of the database.

The task of building a database is performed once, which is, to turn each graph in the database into a set of paths – path representation. While the filtering of the database using the subgraph is to reduce the size of the database in space by discarding graphs that clearly do not contain any occurrences of the subgraph. The filtering action compares fingerprints of the database with the fingerprint of the subgraph, and a graph whose fingerprint is one less than the corresponding value in the fingerprint of the subgraph is discarded. The final step is then to perform exact or inexact matching of graph; which looks for all the matching occurrences of the subgraphs in the remaining graphs.

4.2　Analysis of Result

Our experiment was carried out on a database containing 100 pattern attack graphs of security events obtained from our simulation. The graphs in this database contain an average of 55 nodes, although several of these graphs contain nodes up to 70. Our subgraph of known security breach is a graph with 5 nodes (see table 1 & fig.5). From the results, it took 0.58 seconds to inert all the graphs in the database (path representation) and 1.17 seconds (measured in CPU time)[1] to complete the matching (see table 2). The matching outputs graphs that show similarities in the pattern of security violations constructed using our subgraph that reveals computer nodes compromised in the attack and also reveals the sequence of the attack propagation.

Table 1. Result Mechanics:

Number of graphs in DB: 100
Inerting time into DB: 0.58
Total running time: 1.17
nV:5
SQ:0;
Graphs after filtered: 34

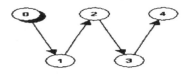

Fig.5: Subgraph (query graph)

Table 2: A sample of the matching results from the Experiment

```
********
4 3 2 1 0
********
```

Graph index: gn0 Subgraph matches: 1
0 4 3 2 1
Graph index: gn1 Subgraph matches: 1
0 4 3 2 1
Graph index: gn2 Subgraph matches: 1
4 5 0 2 1
Graph index: gn3 Subgraph matches: 1
2 0 7 5 1
Graph index: gn4 Subgraph matches: 1
2 0 6 9 1

Graph index: gn5 Subgraph matches: 1
9 7 2 6 1
Graph index: gn7 Subgraph matches: 1
5 12 2 7 1
Graph index: gn8 Subgraph matches: 1
5 2 13 10 1
Graph index: gn9 Subgraph matches: 1
7 2 5 10 1
Graph index: gn11 Subgraph matches: 1
10 8 14 7 1
< ...>

5   Summary

In this paper, we discussed attack graphs, demonstrated the need for its use in the analysis of security event data for security information management systems and proposed a relation information graph-based representation for it. The proposed graph-based representation was employed to model security events; while utilising an efficient graph matching technique to match and analyse the attack graphs using a subgraph (template). The result obtained from the analyses showed that the technique reduced the well-known graph matching problem to a polynomial time through the decomposition of graph structure to set of paths and filtering based on matching fingerprints.

However, with our proposed graph-based representation and the application of an efficient pattern matching technique both assist security information management systems to explicitly and better analyse security event data compared to RDBMS's tables that lack explicit analyse of event attribute and relationships.

---

[1] P4, 3.06GHz CPU

Reference

[1] S. Braynov and M. Jadliwala (2003) "Representation and Analysis of Coordinated Attacks", Proceeding of FMSE'03, Washington DC, USA, October 30, 2003

[2] S. Jha; O. Sheyner and J. Wing (2002) "Two Formal Analyses of Attack Graphs" Proceeding of the 15th IEEE Computer Security Foundations Workshop (CSFW'02), 2002.

[3] W.H. Tsai and K.S. Fu (1979) "Error-correcting isomorphism of attributed relational graphs for pattern recognition", *IEEE Trans. SMC 9*, pp.31-42

[4] P. Shoubridge, M. Krarne and D. Ray (1999) "Detection of abnormal change in dynamic networks" In Proc. *Of IDC'99, Adelaide*, pp.557-562

[5] R. Giugno and D. Shasha (2002) "GraphGrep: A Fast and Universal Method for Querying Graphs" *Proceeding of the International Conference in Pattern recognition (ICPR), Quebec, Canada,* August 2002

[6] C. Philips and L. Swiler (1998) "A graph-based system for network vulnerability analysis", in ACM New Security Paradigms workshop, pp. 71-79, 1998

[7] R. Ritchey and P. Ammann (2001) "Using model checking to analyze network vulnerabilities" *Proceedings of IEEE Symposium on Security and Privacy, pp. 156-165,* 2001

[8] H. Bunke (2000) "Graph Matching: Theoretical Foundations, Algorithms, and Applications, University of Bern, Neubruckstr. 10, CH-3012 Bern, Switzerland

[9] K. Fall and K. Varadhan (2005) "The NS Manual (formerly ns Notes and Documentation)", *The VINT Project, A Collaboration between researchers at UC Berkeley,* LBL, USC/ISI, and Xerox PARC, pp.353

[10] C. Onwubiko, A.P. Lenaghan, L. Hebbes (2005) "An Improved Worm Mitigation Model for Evaluating the Spread of Aggressive Network Worms"; *Proc. of the IEEE - EUROCON 2005 - IEEE Region 8, Belgrade,("to appear in November 21-24, 2005")*

[11] J. Clark and S. DeRose (1999) "Xml Path Language (Xath)"; http://www.w3.org/TR/xpath

[12] C. A. James, D. Weininger, and J. Delany (2000) "Daylight theory manual-Daylight 4.71 Daylight Chemical Information Systems"; http://www.daylight.com [20/09/2005]

[13] Graph Matching Library – GOBLIN: http://www.math.uni-augsburg.de/opt/goblin.html

[14] A toolkit for graph editor and graph algorithms - GRAPHLET: http://infosun.fmi.uni-passau.de/Graphlet/ [20/09/2005]

Intelligent real-time reactive Network Management

Abhishek Jain[1], Guillaume Andreys[2], G. Sivakumar[3]

[1] CSE Department, IT-BHU, India
a.jain@cse06.itbhu.org
[2] INSA, Lyon, France
guillaume.andreys@gmail.com
[3] CSE Department, IIT Mumbai, India
siva@cse.iitb.ac.in

Abstract. A variety of sophisticated tools already exist for monitoring and analyzing various parameters and events in large enterprise networks. However, not only is there the high overhead cost of continuously running these tools, but there is also the need for constant human monitoring and decision making on how to react to various critical events and alarms. Ideally, we would like to have a system that allows the administrator to encode using policy & rules, the knowledge needed to automatically invoke only when needed the right monitoring and analysis tools only on relevant systems. In this paper we propose a framework for achieving the above. Based on this, we have developed a prototype implementation that harnesses existing tools. An illustrative example of intelligent real-time reactive network management achieved using this tool is also described.

1 Introduction

Computer networks are an integral part of enterprise in the current world. Not only are the networks large but they are also complex. Nothing is perfect and even the best designed network have problems. The objective of network administrator is to detect these problems and solve them as soon as possible. The solution is efficient network management that essentially involves collecting information all over the network to detect problems and events; and take adequate decisions. This task is also linked to network security since it is possible to detect security events by network management tools. Various tools exist to perform the above tasks. They can collect data from network hardware through SNMP, analyze network traffic and report all the data at a central point.

Common Problems. The networks generally comprise of hundreds of users at various levels of knowledge and privileges. Since the bandwidth is limited, it needs to be conserved. However, one malicious user can easily limit the bandwidth availability for the entire network. Due to Internet access, a network comprising of various systems with different configurations is exposed to virus and worm attacks, since some computers may not have sufficient protection level. Thus, ignorance or lack of protection at one node can easily compromise the entire network. We do not cover problems like intrusion in this paper.

Existing solutions & drawbacks. There are many existing tools that can perform various network management tasks. An example of such a tool is Ntop[1] which is a network traffic probe that shows the network usage, similar to what the popular "top" UNIX command does. However, most of these widely used tools suffer from the following drawbacks.

- Most of them are designed to perform only a specific task by collecting some specific data and performing basic reaction like an alarm. Thus, any one tool is clearly insufficient to perform all the tasks of network management.
- Those that are not limited to a specific task and rather address various problems in the network generally suffer with the drawback of high resource consumption.
- The frequency of false alert generation is generally high.

Besides, the task of network administrator is made tough due to the following reasons.

- Since one tool generally does not suffice the requirements of a network, the administrator is required to launch various tools manually and take manual decisions based on the data collected.
- Real-time reaction to different anomalies occurring concurrently in the network is difficult due to the manual process.

To eliminate the above problems, we propose a new system consisting of an intelligent framework and a collection of various tools. The aim is to minimize the resource consumption by using a distributed system and a sophisticated layered analysis of the events generated. The user is given the option to write Rules in an XML derived language. These set of rules serve as an intelligence unit for the framework. The choice of tools may be done to suit the network requirements. Thus, the system is sufficiently flexible to meet the requirements of different networks. The intelligent framework takes automatic decisions and performs complex real-time reactions based on data provided by the various tools distributed over the network. This would do away with the administrator's problem of performing the entire process manually. The alerts raised by the system are categorized by a Policy.

The rest of the paper is organized as follows. Section 2 presents our proposed construction. In section 3, we give a prototype implementation of our system with an example. Section 4 analyzes the proposed system on various grounds. We conclude in Section 5.

2 The Proposed Construction

We present our proposed construction in this section.

2.1 Preliminaries

We introduce the term "Framework" as a distributed system comprising of a "Manager" and a group of "Agents" that harnesses various tools to carry out different tasks and provides a consolidated output. Manager and Agents are described later.

The construction of such a framework is described. The principle motivation is an 'intelligent', 'real-time reactive', 'lazy' framework to perform efficient network management. Now we give the definitions of the terms used above.

Intelligent. A system that detects specific events and takes automatic decisions according to a pre-defined set of Rules.

Real-time reactive. A system which performs complex automatic reactions to specific events in real-time.

Lazy. A system which performs a sophisticated layered analysis of events. The detection of the global event (top layer) triggers further analysis in a recursive routine (inner layers).

The above properties are further discussed in Section 3. Since the framework is essentially an administrative body, various tools designed to perform specific tasks are used with the framework to perform efficient network management. The choice of the tools may be made to suit the network. It is discussed further in Section 3.3.1.

2.2 Summary

Setup. The network administrator must have prior knowledge of his network, and the tools->data mapping. He writes a set of set of rules and policy in a predefined language. These rules and policy provide intelligence to the framework.

Operation. Various nodes of interest in the network are monitored constantly. On the detection of an anomaly (first alert, top layer) the framework reacts and launches new tools for further analysis at the relevant nodes. This is performed recursively (complex automatic reactions) until a consolidated final output listing down the source of anomaly and the culprit is obtained. At each layer, the newly launched tools do data collection. The decision making at each step of the protocol is governed by the set of predefined 'rules' by taking the collected data into consideration. An important point to note is that the tools are launched at the relevant nodes only when required. The principle followed is that of Intrusion Detection. The set of predefined rules can be compared with intrusion signatures. The tools required can be classified into (a) High level tools for anomaly detection and (b) Low level tools for detailed analysis. Now we proceed with the detailed description of the system.

2.3 The Framework

The framework comprises of a group of agents and a manager.

64

Agents. They reside on the various hosts that are to be monitored. Typical examples of such hosts are a mail server, a web-proxy, a firewall, etc.

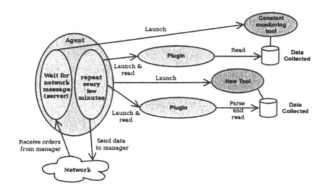

Fig. 1. An Agent in Operation

An agent coordinates the monitoring of the host on which it resides. In this process, it uses various tools that detect events and collect useful data by performing network analysis. It performs two tasks-

- Its first task is to react to a network request sent by the manager and perform a specific action like launching a tool such as a log analyzer.
- Its second task is to collect data from the launched tool. The agent regularly reads the tool's output and eventually sends the data to the manager. To read this output plug-ins may be used. These plug-ins are launched by the agent and they put the collected data in a normalized form, as a list of data name/data value. Thus one can add new tools without having to recompile the agent by simply writing new plug-ins.

Note that the agent possesses no intelligence of its own. The tool to be launched is specified in the message sent by the manager. It merely follows the instructions of the manager. Thus, an agent acts as a mediator between the manager and the tools thus eliminating the need for the manager to interact with the tools directly. Figure 1 depicts these operations.

Manager. It is the control center of the framework. Corresponding to the tasks performed by an agent, the manager performs the following two tasks;

1. It collects data from all the agents and takes decisions for the subsequent actions to be performed.
2. It sends messages to the agents specifying the action to be performed i.e. the tools to be launched.

The manager is divided into two parts. The first part is the 'Server', which awaits an agent's connection and receives the data. The communication protocol between the agent and the manager allows simple transfer of the data from an agent to the manager. Since plug-ins provide a common interface between the agents and the various tools, hence the manager receives the data in a common recognized data name/data value form, independent of the tool which generated it.

The other part is the 'Decision Maker', the heart of the entire system. It takes as input the data received by the Server from an agent, and generates an output. The output may be an order (decision) to an agent specifying the tool to be started or stopped and/or an alarm function to record and display an alarm in the desired way. In order to take the decisions, the decision-maker requires some form of intelligence. This intelligence is provided in the form of a set of 'rules' and a 'policy'. Once a decision is made by the 'Decision maker', subsequent orders can be sent to the agents. Figure 2 depicts the above operations.

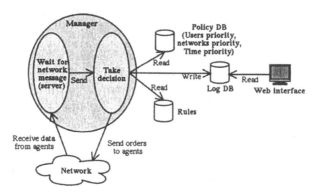

Fig. 2. Manager in action

Now we describe the rules and the policy in detail.

(a) The Rules are used to make a decision tree to specify which tool should be launched / stopped in a particular state of the decision process. The administrator during the system setup writes these rules. The administrator needs to have a prior knowledge of his network, the tools he is using and the tool->data mapping. The rules can be written in a specific language that may be derived from XML, thus simplifying the task of the user. This language would contain specific functions to define the possible decisions and alarms based on the available data and the system policy.

A small example of the rules (written in pseudo-code) may be-

IF ALERT=InBandWidth THEN

IF USER=unknown AND PORT=80 THEN

Decision = Launch WebProxyAnalyzer on WebProxy with parameter IP

A more elaborate example of the rules is given in Section 2.4.

(b) The Policy supplements the set of rules to govern the decision making process. It is some non-network data that influences the decisions and the consequent reactions to be performed. This non-network data may be the user name, the time of the day or the concerned computer. The policy may be defined to give some specific objects higher priority over other similar objects. For example, the administrator may define a policy for different actions to be performed when the user causing the anomaly is an administrator (abnormal behavior can be 'normal') and when the user is a student. It may be defined through a web interface and a database.

3 Prototype Implementation

We have developed a prototype implementation which harnesses existing tools. A detailed description is given in this section.

3.1 Setup

In the prototype implementation, we monitor three hosts to detect the global alert. These hosts are the network firewall, the web proxy running Squid [6] and the mail server running Qmail [7].
Before we proceed to the description of the tools being used, we briefly describe the algorithm used to detect the global alerts.

(a) Aberrant Behavior Detection in Time Series for Network Monitoring (Holt Winters Forecasting Algorithm). Aberrant behavior detection [3] is decomposed into three pieces, each building on its predecessor.

- An algorithm for predicting the values of a time series one time step into the future.

- A measure of deviation between the predicted values and the observed values.

- A mechanism to decide if and when an observed value or sequence of observed values is 'too deviant' from the predicted value(s).

It is an extension of Holt-Winters Forecasting, which supports incremental model updating via exponential smoothing. The algorithm can be tuned with some adaptation parameters. One can choose if more weight should be given to recent observations in the time series than the older ones for prediction of new values. A simple mechanism to detect an anomaly is to check if an observed value of the time series falls outside the confidence band. However, this mechanism often yields a high number of false positives. A more robust mechanism is to use a moving window of a fixed number of observations.

(b) Choice of Tools. The following are the main tools that are being used in the prototype implementation.

MRTG. The Multi Router Traffic Grapher [4] is basically a tool to monitor the traffic load on network links. But it is not limited to monitoring traffic, though. It is possible to monitor any SNMP variable you choose. One can even use an external program to gather the data that should be monitored via MRTG.
We are using it to monitor network-traffic (bandwidth) using SNMP data, web proxy statistics, again using SNMP data and the mail server using an external program to feed data. It is a low resource-consuming tool. We use it as a front-end for RRDTool with aberrant behavior detection to detect the global alerts.

RRDTool. Round Robin Database [5] is a system to store and display time-series data. It stores the data in a very compact way that will not expand over time, and it presents useful graphs by processing the data to enforce a certain data density. It can be used either via simple wrapper scripts (from shell or Perl) or via front-ends that poll network devices and put a friendly user interface on it. We are using RRD for its data storage capabilities and its integration capability with MRTG that acts as it's front-end.

Qmailmrtg. It is C Program [8] that requires multilog and intelligently uses the multi-log (described below) file name time stamp to determine which logs to open and process. It is used to feed the input to MRTG to monitor Qmail statistics on the mail server.

Tcptrack [9]. It is a sniffer that displays information about TCP connections that it sees on a network interface. It passively watches for connections on the network inter-face, keeps track of their state and displays a list of connections in a manner similar to the UNIX 'top' command. It displays source and destination addresses and ports, con-nection state, idle time, and bandwidth usage. We are using it to deduce the source in the case of a bandwidth anomaly.

Multilog. This tool is a log manager. Logs are distributed in small files each having a name consisting of a time-stamp. Thus it makes the task of finding relevant informa-tion in the logs faster and efficient by adding indexed searching. We try to use multi-log [10] for all the logs with the idea of saving resources and minimizing log analysis time.

Besides the above-mentioned tools, various scripts are used as log analyzers.

(c) Rules and Policy. The following pseudo code depicts the Rules and the policy to be used in the decision-making process. Note that it merely serves as an example and other cases are not considered.

```
//We have an alert of bandwidth
  IF ALERT=InBandWidth THEN
//We don't know the concerned service (port)
  IF PORT=unknown THEN
  Decision=Launch TCPTrack on Firewall
  ELSE
//We don't know the user, we have to get it on different
//server depending on the concerned service
  IF USER=unknown AND PORT=80 THEN
  Decision = Launch ProxyUser on ProxyServer with parameter IP
  ELSE IF USER=unknown AND PORT=25 THEN
  Decision = Launch QMailUser on mailserver with parameter IP
//We know the user, we want to send an alarm depending on the
//Policy
  ELSE IF USER is define THEN
  IF Priority(USER)+Priority(IP)+Priority(TIME) > 10 THEN
  Alert(high)
  ELSE
```

Alert(low)
ENDIF
ENDIF
ENDIF
ENDIF

(d) Summary of the entire protocol. The Multi Router Traffic Grapher (MRTG) constantly monitors various hosts like the firewall, web proxy and mail server to collect data and feed into the RRDTool database. A script constantly reads the data from the RRD database at a specified interval to detect an anomaly in case there is one. The detection of the global anomaly raises the first alarm. The manager sends specific messages to relevant agents to launch new tools and scripts to perform further investigation to determine the cause of the anomaly and other details. The agent transfers the data collected to the manager who does further decision-making. The process is continued recursively until the final output is generated.

3.2 Operation

To explain the running system, we consider a specific example of abnormal bandwidth consumption as the global alert.

Here, the network bandwidth through the switch is being monitored using MRTG and RRDTool database with aberrant behavior detection capability. They can be installed on any host on the network to make SNMP requests to the switch.

Figure 4 shows the bandwidth graph generated with MRTG using aberrant behavior detection. The blue line denotes the bandwidth, the red lines form the confidence bands and the yellow lines denote the alerts when the bandwidth goes out of the confidence bands.

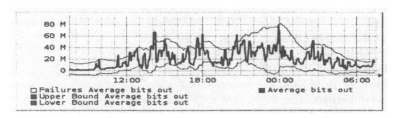

Fig. 3. Graph generated by MRTG-RRDTool depicting the anomaly band

An anomaly is detected on the outgoing bandwidth that is abnormally high. The script that reads the RRDTool database at regular intervals detects this anomaly and reports it to the agent that in turn sends the global alert to the manager.

The following is the message sent by the agent to the manager. Note the general format evident from the example. After the timestamp, the message contains the name of the tool followed by the data name/data value pair.

1088052315 DEBUG : Tool mrtg data, Name : Alert | Value : InBW.
1088052315 DEBUG : Tool mrtg data, Name : FirstFailureTime | Value :

1088051315.

1088052315 DEBUG : Tool mrtg data, Name : LastFailureTime | Value : 1088053315.

The Server part of the manager receives the message and feeds it to the decision-maker as the input. The decision-maker takes the decision that TCPTrack must be launched on the firewall. This message is sent to the agent monitoring the firewall that is running just before the switch. The agent launches TCPTrack on receiving the message.

The following is the message sent by the manager to the agent 'igarbo'. The name of the agent is kept after the name of the firewall.

1088056481 INFO: Decision : on Agent igarbo, Tool TcpTrack should be run

TCPTrack monitors all the connections on the firewall for a specified period of time that may be a few seconds to produce some output data. This output data contains the timestamps followed by the source IP and the destination IP. The destination port number is also present in the output. The agent now runs a script to analyze this output data. The connection that uses the maximum bandwidth during this time of monitoring is determined by the script and reported to the agent.

1088052266 DEBUG : Executing command ./tcptrack -i eth2 dst 10.200.13.50 > tcpoutput

1088052616 DEBUG : Execute plug-in :./maxtcptrack.pl

The agent now sends the source IP and the destination port number to the manager. Here, the source IP is 10.142.148.4 and the destination port number is 80. Note that the general format of the normalized data name/data value pairs as described above is followed.

1088052616 DEBUG : Tool TcpTrack data, Name : IP Value : 10.142.148.4.

1088052616 DEBUG : Tool TcpTrack data, Name : Port Value : 80.

Since the destination port is port 80 (HTTP), the decision-maker takes the decision to launch log analyzer on the web proxy. The message is sent to the web-proxy's agent to execute the log analyzer script. The user logged on the system with IPaddress 10.142.148.4 is to be determined. Here 'netmon' is the name of the proxy host and squid is the web-proxy used.

1088056541 INFO : Receiving message

1088056489:AgentName:igarbo

1088056489:IP:10.107.150.4

1088056489:Port:80

The following is the message sent by the manager to the agent netmon.

1088056544 INFO : Decision : on Agent netmon, Tool SquidUser should be run

The agent now collects data by running the scripts to analyze the squid logs to find the user "badguy" correspond to this IP.

1088056061 INFO : Receiving message 1088056544:SquidUser:run:10.107.150.4 1088055478 1088057478

1088056061 DEBUG: Executing command: ./squiduser.pl /squid/var/logs/access.log 10.107.150.4 1088055478 1088057478

1088056123 DEBUG : Execute plug-in : ./squiduser_plugin.pl

1088056123 DEBUG : User:badguy

The agent sends this information to the manager. In the final step, the manager has got the user name and the IP address. Most importantly, the time is 3pm, a working hour, when users all over the network need the bandwidth. From the policy, we get to know that this IP belongs to a personal computer in a student hostel, and that the user is a student. The priority is high, thus a high alert is sent. The final output contains a detailed report on the alert generated.

Note the role of the policy in the final decision. Had it been night hours when the average bandwidth consumption is generally minimal or had the user been an administrator, the final decision might have been that of no alert or a low alert with a detailed report

4 Discussions and Analysis

We analyze our proposed construction on various grounds.

4.1 Resource Consumption

The proposed construction is a distributed system consisting of a manager and a group of similar agents along with a collection of various tools distributed over different hosts in the network. Constant monitoring is required to be done on some specific hosts to detect the first anomaly. The tools chosen for this purpose are low resource consuming tools. In the running system described in Section 2.4, MRTG and RRDTool performed this task. Once the global anomaly is detected, further analysis is done by taking intelligent decisions. Due to the distributed architecture, the work is divided into different steps which correspond to different layers of analysis, to be performed over various hosts at different points of time. The tools are now launched only on specific hosts as determined by the decision-maker. Besides, only the required tools are chosen to run at a point of time rather than all of them running continuously. Hence a particular tool is launched only when required in a particular situation. All these factors reduce the overall average resource consumption drastically.

4.2. Automatic decision making

The intelligent framework takes automatic decisions in different situations and performs real-time reactions by launching various tools as required in that situation. The set of Rules and Policy together constitute the intelligence unit of the framework. The network administrator is only required to define a system Policy and write a set of Rules in an XML derived language that is relatively easy and flexible. This is done at system startup. The tough and tedious task of taking manual decisions at various stages and launching various tools is no longer required. The system is capable of reacting to various anomalies occurring at the same time. This is in sharp contrast to the tough task to be performed by the administrator to handle various anomalies occurring concurrently in the network.

4.3 Flexibility

One of the biggest problems faced by the network administrators is finding efficient tools that can perform many network management tasks. Most of such existing tools are inefficient by the reasons described in Section 1. The solution is to use a collection of efficient tools that are meant for specific tasks. The system proposed is sufficiently flexible to usage of a variety of tools and addition of new tools whenever required. Besides, the system can be adapted to various network configurations and requirements. Now we discuss the two factors which render the system flexible.

Choice of Tools. A variety of tools may be chosen to supplement the framework. The tools may be chosen to meet the requirements of a particular network. Besides, new tools may be added to the system as and when required by updating the Rules and Policy written earlier at the time of system setup. However, since the framework is only an administrative body and the tools actually perform data collection, proper choice of the tools by the user is very important.

Now we consider various factors that should be considered by the user while choosing the tools to supplement the framework.

1. *Resource consumption.* The tools chosen must be low resource consuming otherwise it would defeat the purpose of the framework. We recommend avoidance of tools like Ntop which are high resource consuming tools.
2. *Work distribution.* A large number of tools may be chosen as per the network requirements. This not only distributes the work but also gives the flexibility of choosing specific tools for specific hosts. The decision making gets complex but more efficient to handle various complex situations. Moreover, different reactions can be made to different anomalies occurring concurrently. This is done by launching different tools to analyze different anomalies. Note that the work distribution also reduces the overall resource consumption.

Rules & Policy. The set of Rules and system Policy together contribute to a lot of important features of the system. Not only do they provide intelligence to the framework, they also lend flexibility to the system. The framework can be adapted to a particular network's requirements by writing the suitable Rules and Policy. The easy option of writing the rules in an XML derived language makes it possible to add new tools dynamically without the need to recompile the manager. Moreover, the use of a normalized and high level language like XML for writing the `Rules' can add the feature of syntax error detection (XML DTD) and preventing errors in a more high level interpretation by doing Rules analysis (using prolog for example). This can be useful to figure out two contradicting rules or others such problems.

4.4. Comparison with Intrusion Detection

One of the principles involved in intrusion detection is to use a set of rules to detect intrusion signature and raise alerts. Our system employs the same basic mechanism by using a set of rules to detect the signatures on events that essentially belong to the category of network management. Such events have been described in Section 1.

4.5. Limitations and Future Work

Since the manager is a central administrative body, it may be targeted specifically to render the entire system inefficient. However, by designing the manager as a distributed body, this can be countered. Besides, no correlation is performed between the collected data. Data correlation could lead to detection of more complex and new events. These inspirations have been taken from OSSIM[2]. We take these considerations for future work.

6 Conclusions

A new solution for efficient network management was proposed. By using a distributed system consisting of an intelligent framework and a collection of tools capable of performing real-time reactions and a layered analysis, the resource consumption is minimized. The principal of intrusion detection is followed. Besides, the system eliminates the network administrator's hard work and is sufficiently flexible to adapt to different network requirements. The proposed system is a complete package for efficient network management.

References

[1]   Ntop, network traffic probe www.ntop.org
[2]   Open Source Security Information Management www.ossim.net
[3]   Aberrant Behavior Detection, LISA 2000 byJake D. Brutlag – WebTV http://www.usenix.org/events/lisa2000/full_papers/brutlag/
[4]   Multi Router Traffic Grapher http://people.ee.ethz.ch/~oetiker/webtools/mrtg/
[5]   Round Robin Database http://people.ee.ethz.ch/~oetiker/webtools/rrdtool
[6]   Squid Proxy server http://www.squid-cache.org
[7]   Qmail Mail server http://www.qmail.org
[8]   QMail-MRTG, MRTG front-end for Qmail http://inter7.com/qmailmrtg7
[9]   TCPTrack, http://www.rhythm.cx/~steve/devel/tcptrack/
[10] Multilog, log tool http://cr.yp.to/daemontools/multilog.html

Security in Passive Optical Network via Wavelength Hopping and Codes cycling techniques

Walid Shawbaki, PhD candidate student

Electrical and Computer Engineering
Iowa State University
7405 Fox Court, NE
Cedar Rapids, IA, 52402 (USA)
shawbaki@iastate.edu

Abstract. Passive Optical Network (PON) provides the answer to increasing demand on bandwidth in access networks; however, PON uses shared fiber link with Broadcast and Select (B&S) type of downstream traffic on single wavelength, which introduces data vulnerability to eavesdropping. This paper proposes an approach to enhance security using slow wavelength hopping and codes cycling in order to make it difficult for eavesdropper to collect good sample for crypto-analysis. Current state of optical transmitters and filters technology does not support high data rate operation in fast hopping mode, and the approach for slow hopping based on encoding each Ethernet frame/packet by single wavelength selected from ONU's specific wavelength sequence generated by mapping ONU's code matrices to network's wavelength grid matrix. Multiple code matrices assignment to single ONU cycled in different order enhances security by reducing probability of tracking the hopping pattern.

Keywords   Optical access network security, Wavelength Hopping, Time Spreading, PON

1. Introduction

The answer to increasing demand on bandwidth in access networks can be satisfied by Passive Optical Network (PON) shown in Figure 1, which has a topology that include an Optical Line Terminal (OLT) located at local Central Office (CO) and Optical Network Units (ONUs) serving K user groups, connected by a Passive Star Coupler (PSC). Existing PON standards such as the International Telecommunication Union-Telecommunication sector ITU-T G983.1 [4] and IEEE 802.ah [6] based on broadband optical access systems that transmit data in downstream direction over single wavelength in Time Division Multiplex (TDM), and a different wavelength in the upstream traffic based on the use of Time Division Multiple Access (TDMA). Downstream traffic is Broadcast & Select (B&S) that is available to all ONUs, which makes it vulnerable to eavesdropping due to shared fiber link. B& S traffic does not fully support privacy and confidentiality where privacy related to identity of users and their activities online while confidentiality related to protection of data against eavesdropping. An ONU operating in promiscuous mode can pick up other ONUs' traffic (plain or encrypted) having all time for eavesdropping undetected. Encryption usually covers payload of the traffic, and in Ethernet based PON, security has never been a strong part of Ethernet networks [1]. Sophistication of attackers and tools endanger privacy in PON, and as with objective of any data security technique, they need to provide Confidentiality, Integrity, and Availability of data [2].

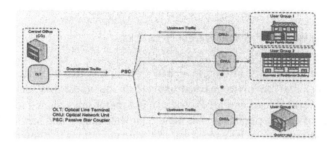

Figure 1: Passive Optical Network (PON) supporting K users groups

Optical Code Division Multiple Access (OCDMA) considered to potentially providing both confidentiality and availability protection by offering some degree of jamming resistance using the OCDMA coding [3]. OCDMA concept is based on coding that consists of time spreading of a single bit into several pulses (called chips) on single wavelength, unfortunately, current state of technology for laser optical components can not meet the per bit high switching speed required for high data rate OCDMA. The approach in this paper uses slower wavelength hopping and relaxes the duration of pulse (chip) to cover transmission of complete Ethernet/packet frame used in indirect modulation of a single wavelength. The duration includes also additional guard band in time for different timing requirements such as round trip delay, tuneability of resources...etc. The goal is to provide secure architecture network that provide methods and techniques to prevent or lessen impact of passive security threats of unauthorized disclosure of information. The rest of the paper organized as follow:

Section 2 expands PON overview in relation to enabling technologies including PON architectures; Section 3 discusses PON security enhancement. Section 4 provides an assessment for the security enhancement, and section 5 provides the conclusion remarks and recommendation.

2. PON and Enabling Technologies

PON traffic in ITU-T G983.1 standard based on Asynchronous Transfer Mode ATM PON (APON) that uses fixed cell frame lengths (56 Cells), while IEEE 802.3ah handles Ethernet (EPONs) traffic. Each ONUs sees traffic only from OLT and peer-to-peer communication passes through the OLT, and only one ONU is allowed to transmit to OLT at any instance. Newly attached and active ONU is detected through downstream transmission discovery messages [6]. OLT sends a GATE flagged message, which is a permission to transmit at a specific time, for a specific duration granted to a node (ONU) by the master OLT. EPON uses fixed lasers, while the approach in this paper implements tunable laser components and Wave

Division Multiplexing (WDM). Several technologies for tunable lasers exist, but parameters such as narrow band of light with small optical line width, in addition to fast responses (tuneability) are some of the expected performance parameters in WDM optical networking operating in the range of1528 nm to 1560 nm.

2.1 Vulnerabilities of Passive Optical Networks

Privacy and confidentiality of data in shared fiber link demands protection against passive attacks that involves eavesdropping online messages data (clear or encrypted). Several threats against PON exist, but major ones related to privacy and confidentiality of data includes eavesdropping, impersonation, and service denial.

External eavesdropping can be carried out in various locations as shown in Figure 2, assuming that Operational and Administration Management (OAM) system does not detect any drop in signal level, or simply by one or more nodes (ONUs) operating in promiscuous mode, which is considered higher threat due to difficulty of detecting such passive attacks. Impersonation in PON can be carried out during Discovery and Report process [6], and vulnerability arise from an ONU hijacking the identity (using other's MAC address) and masquerading as another ONU, which enable transferring the wrong registration frame to OLT during the discovery process [8].

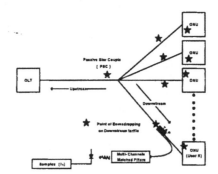

Figure 2: Possible points of attacks (Eavesdropping) on PON

2.2 Cost and assumptions used in the Security enhancements

Higher security level is always associated with higher cost, and justification for cost to be based on the basic rule that security measures need to be in accordance with the assets being protected. Security valued by individuals or organizations in different ways, and value of data against time is another factor, but in general, there must be a balance between security, cost, and usability. Though security must be a prime design consideration, it is not necessarily the overriding one, and benefits to be weighed against costs to achieve a balanced, cost-effective system [10]. The proposed security enhancement in this paper does not substitute for other security measures such as authentication, digital signatures, encryption, or physical security including detection systems and personnel access control to ONUs and OLT locations.

It is also assumed in the approach for security enhancement that access networks as an integral part of whole LAN should be important to all users and there are no collaboration between nodes in order to exchange code matrices. Additional assumption include that eavesdropping at locations shown in Figure 2 carried out with proper tools that are easy to realize using commercially available technologies, and attackers (eavesdroppers) are technologically sophisticated with knowledge about signals being transmitted in PON (i.e types of signals, data rates, type of encoding, structure of codes, synchronization, ...etc). This is based on well-known *Kerckhoffs'* principle in cryptography [9], which essentially states that one should assume that eavesdropper knows everything about cryptographic algorithm except for the key.

3. PON Security Enhancement

The security enhancement is based on wavelength hopping technique, and selection of wavelengths hopping sequence for a specific ONU is provided by mapping two matrices; wavelength grid matrix W_{mn}^{G}, and code matrix C_{mn}^{ks} where m and n in both equal dimension matrices represent number of rows and columns respectively. Wavelength matrix is one of many formatted matrices by simple permutations of ITU-T 694.1 wavelength channels within the matrix. Each format assigned a grid number G. The ONU's specific code matrix is made of 0s and 1s such that all code matrices in the network are orthogonal to each other. A wavelength is selected from wavelength matrix to be part of generated sequence only when corresponding location (i.e m, n) in code matrix includes 1's, and no wavelength is selected for 0's in code matrix. As a minimum for secure operation, each ONU has one code matrix and k designate the specific ONU that has been assigned the specific code matrix. It is possible to assign a set (S_k) of code matrices from the maximum available matrices (S_{max}) for a single ONU depending on security level.

The duration that each wavelength used during transmission of complete frame/packet in the sequence is designated by T_c, and an additional guard time (T_g) to guarantee synchronization in PON is used, which includes the tuning time for laser transmitters/filters $T_\tau \ll T_c$. Each ONU will have minimum of two laser transmitters and two filters. When one laser transmitter (filter) being used at any instant, the other transmitter (filter) will start tuning and getting ready for next wavelength in the sequence. Synchronization scheme must be in place to provide one reference timing for operation of all nodes in PON. The use of multiple laser tuning resources compensates for slow tuning in existing optical components technologies.

3.1 Wavelength Grid Matrix W_{mn}^{G}

The wavelength matrix is constructed from channels in ITU-T G.694.1 standard for Dense (D) WDM Frequency Grid, and the total number of wavelengths channels

(λ_{mn}) is dependant on channel frequency spacing (d) used from a center frequency of 193.1 THz as expressed in (1) below:

$$\lambda_{mn}=193.1+(F)X(d) \tag{1}$$

F can be positive or negative number including 0, and channel spacing (d) can be 12.5 GHz, 25 GHz, 50 GHz, 100 GHZ, or 200GHz. For example, 25GHz channel spacing in (1) provides 200 channels, or 98 channels with 50 GHz channel spacing that are available for hopping within frequency range (wavelength) 191 THz (1529.75 nm) to 195.975 THz (1569.59nm) in both C and L bands. Usually, design with smaller channel spacing needs consideration of fiber non-linearities problems such as Four Wave Mixing (FWM) and Cross Phase Modulations (XPM) that are effective at large distances. Fortunately, PON is limited to less than 50 KM for farthest ONU from OLT, and using Non-Zero Dispersion Shifted Fiber (NZDSF) fiber along with wavelength hopping practically minimizes fiber non-linearities effects in PON.

Wavelength grid matrix shown in (2) is constructed from wavelength channels provided by (1) and has the same dimension as the code matrix.

$$W_{mn}^{G} = \begin{pmatrix} \lambda_{11} & \cdots & \lambda_{1n} \\ \cdot & \cdot & \cdot \\ \lambda_{m1} & \cdot & \lambda_{mn} \end{pmatrix} \tag{2}$$

Permutation of each row in (2) provides different matrix formats with a number (G) assigned to each format, and the maximum number of matrices G_{MAX} that can be generated expressed in (3) below.

$$\text{Maximum wavelength grids} = G_{max} = (n!)^{m} \tag{3}$$

The limitations on m,n are related to availability of enough channels that can practically be generated by (1) from the ITU-T G694.1 grid. For prime number P=m=n =13, 169 wavelength channels will be needed for hopping, $G_{max}= (13!)^{13}=$ $2.1166X10^{127}$ wavelength matrices. All wavelengths (λ_{mn}) in (3) are unique and no repetition, and using each wavelength matrix as a key, G_{max} provide good source of keys for secure operation. It is possible to have an hourly change of wavelength matrix in network and available G_{max} keys will last for 2.416×10^{123} years of operation before any key reused. Only one wavelength matrix used and mapped to all ONUs' code matrices at any instance of PON operation.

3.2   ONU's specific Wavelength Sequence λ_{mn}^{ks} generation

The code matrix C_{mn}^{ks} expressed in (4) is unique for each k ONU, and a_{mn} elements take the value of 1 where a wavelength will be selected, and 0 with no wavelength is selected when mapped to the wavelength grid matrix in (2).

$$C_{mn}^{ks} = \begin{pmatrix} a_{11} & a_{12} & . & a_{n1} \\ a_{21} & a_{22} & . & a_{2n} \\ . & . & . & . \\ a_{m1} & . & . & a_{mn} \end{pmatrix} \tag{4}$$

Mapping between (2) and (4) provides Wavelength sequences (λ_{mn}^{ks}) expressed in (5).

$$\lambda_{mn}^{ks} = a_{mn} \odot W_{mn}^{G} \tag{5}$$

Where $\odot$ denotes AND operation or indexing in matrix language, and the same order of wavelengths sequence generated in (5) used for tuning laser transmitters (filters) in the fixed duration T_c. Each wavelength indirectly modulated by complete single frame/packet, and both OLT and ONUs have the capability of generation and reception of wavelength sequences in (5). Upstream or downstream traffic ca be accommodated in each ONU operating in half-duplex or bidirectional manner where multiple ONUs simultaneous communication to OLT will depend on OLT's available laser resources. Synchronization of transmission necessitates no overlaps between sequences in network produced by OLT and ONUs such that each sequence is used from start to end within the time frame allocated for complete wavelength sequence ($m(T_c+T_g)$). This approach fully uses WDM techniques to support large simultaneous transmission in PON and the absence of optical amplifiers (passive) and short distances remove the constraints on the number of simultaneous users online in a WDM system due to fiber nonlinearities [13].

3.3   Code Matrix C_{mn}^{ks} Construction

In access networks, Multiple Access interference (MAI) needs to be avoided, or at least controlled, which is a function usually assigned to Medium Access Control (MAC). Multiple code matrices assignment (S_k) to each ONU based on security level is possible, but total assigned code matrices cannot exceed total available code matrices set (S_{max}). Several coding schemes are available and the main purpose is to provide orthogonal or pseudo-orthogonal codes to avoid or reduce MAI. C_{mn}^{ks} Code matrix is two dimensional (2-D) and the use of Time Spreading/Wavelength Hopping codes appear to be the most promising code types for generating code spaces that are large enough to prevent successful brute force code search attacks [3]. One important requirement is that code matrices must have good 2-D correlation properties that include both cross correlation (X_c), which represents the degree of mutual interference between two code matrices, and auto correlation (A_c), which facilitates detection of desired signal and determines how well detection at intended receiver (detector) in the presence of mutual inference [11],[12]. Optimum design always calls for maximum cross correlation value to be as small as possible in order to support many simultaneous users [11]. The method for construction of the code matrices will follow a procedure well presented in [13] that uses Time Spreading and Wavelength Hopping with some modification to suite code matrices formats. Two approaches will be used, Symmetric, and Asymmetric Time Spreading/Wavelength Hopping.

3.3.1   Symmetric Time Spreading/Wavelength Hopping

The symmetric 2-D Time Spreading/Wavelength Hopping code matrix has dimensions m=n where m, n are numbers of rows and columns respectively. The process of deciding the values of a_{mn} (0 or1) in the code matrix in (4) uses linear congruent operator in prime sequence for pulse placement [11], as shown in (6):

$$a_{mn}=(s.m)\bmod(P), \quad s=1,2,3,...p, \quad m=1,2,3,...p \qquad (6)$$

Where s represents set number out of all possible S_{max} code matrices. The maximum code matrices (S_{max}) for symmetric case with m=n=P is expressed in (7) as:

$$S_{max}= n(m-1)=P(P-1) \quad \text{because m=n=P for symmetric case} \qquad (7)$$

The symmetric case exhibits zero side-lobes (perfect needle-shaped) and cross-correlation is at most one, truly excellent correlation characteristics [13].

3.3.2   Asymmetric Time Spreading/Wavelength Hopping

Asymmetric Time Spreading/Wavelength Hopping uses different dimensions for code and wavelength matrices (m≠n). Two prime numbers used, one for spreading (P_s) and other for hopping (P_h) with an over colored system used where more wavelengths available than code size for spreading ($P_h> P_s$) in order to avoid wavelength reuse. Asymmetric case reported to have correlation problems and it was recommended in [11], [13], and [14] to use extended quadratic congruence (eqc) sequences to improve correlation and increase cardinality. Codes construction for the spreading using EQC expressed in (8) below:

$$a_{mn}= (s*(m*(m-1)/2)\bmod(P_s); \quad m=1,2,3,....., P_s, \quad s=1,2,3,....., P_s-1 \qquad (8)$$

Equation (8) determines the place of pulse within a row of code matrix C_{mn}^{ks} that has a dimension of n = (2P_s-1) columns and m = (P_s) rows. The use of eqc for spreading and prime for hopping, asymmetric Time Spreading /Wavelength Hopping is referred to in [13] as eqc/prime, and cardinality expressed in (9) as:

$$S_{max}=P_h (P_h-1) (P_s-1) \qquad (9)$$

Using overcolored system has a better autocorrelation where side-lobes are nonexistent and the sequences exhibit perfect, needle-shaped autocorrelation function [13].

4. Assessment of Security Enhancement in PON

In this paper, security improvement assessment achieved is made by making it difficult for an eavesdropper to sample useful traffic data useful in crypto analysis. The probably of capturing correct wavelength sequence generated in (5) is a metric that can be used for evaluating this security enhancement against exhaustive search to break the keys. The probability that an eavesdropper actually captures correct wavelength sequence that belongs to ONU_k is designated by $P(\lambda_c^k)$, and depends on knowing correct wavelength grid matrix used by the network out of $Gmax=(n!)^m$, and knowing the code matrix out of the many available as expressed in (9). $P(\lambda_c^k)$ is shown in (10) for the case of symmetric Time spreading/Wave length hopping, and it is shown that with the use of different sequencing order of assigned ONUs code matrices provide the best security enhancement through reduction of the probability of capturing complete wavelength sequence. The assumption made that traffic with destination to ONU_k embedded among all ONUs traffic and wavelength sequences that belong to other U users online, which actually provide protection to all. Assuming that ONU_k is issued only one code matrix, $P(\lambda^k_c)$ is expresses in (10).

$$P(\lambda^k_c)=(1/(n!)^m)(1/ S_{max}))(1/U) \qquad (10)$$

In order to examine the security improvement by assigning more than one code matrix (S_k) out of the maximum available code matrices in (9) with the order of execution of those multiple code matrices cycling in (S_k) is pre-arranged between OLT and the specific ONU. The order of sequencing (S_k) can be one of the $(S_k!)$ possible sequence and considered as an additional secret key shared between OLT and ONU, the relation in (10) can be expressed as in (11) for using multiple codes S_k per ONU as shown below:

$$P(\lambda^k_c)=(1/(n!)^m))(1/U)((S_{max}- S_k)!/ S_{max}!)(1/ S_k!) \qquad (11)$$

The computation above were based only on probabilities without consideration to using other parameters such as Signal to Noise Ratio (SNR) for example, even though intelligent network design can implement SNR as part of the protection by having SNR low enough for the system to function properly, and make it difficult for eavesdropper to get good samples [3].

The effects of multiple codes assignment to each ONUs and codes cycling can be seen in Figure 3 where with more codes assigned to single ONU, the security is enhanced. Note that also that Figure 3 has a 1 to 1 spreading to hopping ratio, and lower curve uses one code matrix/ONU, and is not related to the number of code matrices shown in the horizontal access, but was added for illustration only as noted in Figure 3. The one code per ONU in lower curve shows slight improvement due to higher time spreading and hopping only and was placed on the same chart for comparison purpose, while the upper two curves represents more than one code matrix per ONU. The use of multiple code matrices with different cycling order selected from $S_k!$ provides the best security as shown in the upper curves in Figure 3. Even with this improvement in security, PON needs to have additional measures that can include frequent change (i.e. hourly) of wavelength grid matrix, and OLT/ONUs coordination to transmit encrypted dummy data when the number of users online drops below certain level in order to avoid exploiting a single user wavelength sequences that are generated in (5).

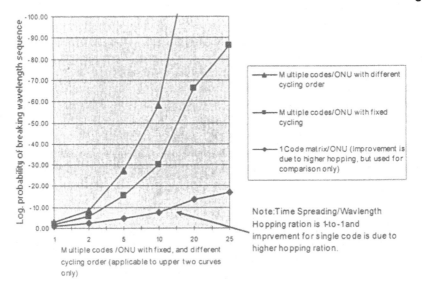

Figure 3: Logarithmic scale of capturing wavelength sequence against codes cycling in the symmetric time spreading /wavelength hopping.

5. Conclusion Remarks and recommendations

PON provides the advantages of meeting demand on bandwidth, low cost, and increased distance of service, but sharing the fiber links between all users is a security concern to all users on the network. The proposed security enhancement in this paper provides the foundation for using multiple security levels for ONUs simply by having multiple code matrices cycled in pre arranged different order between OLT and ONU. The order of cycling can be considered as a shared secret between ONU and OLT, in addition to network wavelength matrix, and ONU code matrix. The technology for implementation of this slow wavelength hopping is available today, and cost factor, analysis of the value of the data against time, and sensitivity of data are factors considered in trade studies for implementation of the approach for security enhancement in this paper.

References

1   Glen Kramer and Gerry Pesavento," Ethernet Passive Optical Network (EPON): Building a Next-Generation Optical Access Network",IEEE Communications Magazine, February 2002.

2   Charles P. Pfleeger, " Security in Computing", $2P^{nd}P$ edition, 1997. Printice-Hall , Inc, 1 Lake Street, Upper Saddle River, NJ 07458. PP 9.

3   Thomas H. Shake," Security Performance of Optical CDMA Against Eavesdropping", JOURNAL OF LIGHTWAVE TECHNOLOGY, VOL. 23, NO. 2, FEBRUARY 2005.

4   International Telecommunication Union-Telecommunication Standardization sector (ITU-T), G9831 standard, "Broadband optical access systems based on Passive Optical Networks (PON)", October, 1998.

5   International Telecommunication Union-Telecommunication Standardization sector (ITU-T), G984.1 standard, "Gigabit-capable Passive Optical Networks (GPON)", March 2003.

6   IEEE Standard for Information technology, IEEE Std 802.3ah.-2004, IEEE Computer Society

7   Muriel Medard, Douglas Marquis, Richard A. Barry, and Steven G. Finn," Security Issues in All Optical Network", IEEE Network May/June 1997.

8   Swapnil Bhatia and Radim Barto·," Performance of the IEEE 802.3 EPON Registration Scheme Under High Load" , Department of Computer Science, University of New Hampshire, Durham, NH 03824, USA, Society of Photo-Optical Instrumentation Engineers, 2004.

9   Douglas R. Stinson, " Cryptography: Theory and Practice", Second Edition, CHAPMAN & HALL/CRC, CRC Press LLC, 2000 N.W Corporate Blvd, Boca Raton, FL 33431

10 Karen J. Profet, Charles H. Lavine, Kraig R. Meyer, "The Risk of Trust vs the Cost of Assurance- Trades in the Implementation of a Secure LAN", IEEE Proceedings. On Aerospace Applications Conference, 1994.

11 Guu-Chang Yang, Wing C. Kwong, " Prime Codes with applications to CDMA Optical and Wireless Network", Artech House mobile communication series, ISBN1-58053-073-7, 2002. PP 44,.247.

12 Fan R.K Chung, JAWAD A. Salehi, "Optical Orthogonal Codes: Design, Analysis, and Application". IEEE Transaction on Information Theory, Vol 35, No 3, May 1989.

13 L. Tancevski, Ian Andonvic, " Hybrid Wavelength Hopping/ Time Spreading Schemes for use in Massive Optical Network with Increase Security", IEEE Journal of lightwave technology, VOL 14,No 12, December 1996..

14 S. V. Maric, " New Family Of Algebraically Designed Optical Orthogonal Codes For Use In CDMA Fibre-Optic Networks", Electronics Letters, $18P^{th}P$ March 1993 Vol. 29 NO. 6.

A Model of Deploying Deception in a Computer Network Operations (CNO) Environment

Zafar Kazmi, Stilianos Vidalis

School of Computing, University of Glamorgan
United Kingdom
zkazmi@glam.ac.uk , *svidalis@glam.ac.uk*

Abstract. The concept of deception has been practised in human conflicts ever since they existed, but its application to an information security environment could only be witnessed in the early 1990s onwards. Since then, different deception techniques have also been introduced to the Computer Network Operations (CNO) environment, in order to achieve desired outcome(s). In the recent years, a number of researchers have investigated in different deception techniques used in computer based networks but more consideration is needed in exploring the strategic deception in a Computer Network Defence (CND) environment. To date, there are no models available that would allow strategic deception in a CNO environment and therefore building such model would be a great achievement. This paper aims to establish an understanding of the role of deception in a CNO environment and will also discuss a draft concept of a deception model that will allow strategic deception in a CNO environment.

1 Introduction

Over the last decade, the increased use of computer systems and the swift boost of the Internet were accompanied by the equal growth of computer security threats and incidents. Both, the technology and the threats related to these technologies are becoming more and more complex and therefore use of targeted deception can be advantageous in a computer systems security environment. Therefore, information and computer systems face a wide variety of threats which can result in significant damage to an organisation's vital infrastructure.

The range of threats varies from threats to data integrity resulting from unintentional errors and omissions, to threats to system confidentiality, integrity and availability from malicious intruders attempting to compromise a system. Awareness of the threats and vulnerabilities of a particular system allows the selection of the most effective security measures for that system. This includes building a strong network defence by employing physical, procedural and personnel security measures as well as deploying electronics security measures such as Firewalls, Anti-Viruses, Intrusion Detection Systems (IDSs), Access Control Lists (ACLs), deployment of deceptive techniques, etc.

Furthermore, network defence is also put in place to deal with other types of attacks such as service interruption, interception of sensitive email or data transmitted and use of computer's resources. In specific, network defence is about taking measures that should reduce the likelihood of intruders breaking into an organisation's critical computer network and causing damage by reading or stealing confidential data or even modifying it in order to sabotage that organisation. Here, an organisation can be an independent establishment, or a group of government officials, or the actual government of a country, that ensures the security and stability of the critical information infrastructure of their organisation or country.

2 A Review of Concepts and Terminology

2.1 Deception

The basic concept of deception is an ancient one, existing in nature, but the application of different deception techniques in a computer network security and information security environment emerged in the early 1990's. In specific, deception is an act of deceiving or misleading and can also be defined as *"the problematic distinction between appearance and reality"* (Rue 1994).

The deception used in military operations is defined in the United States Joint Doctrine for Military Deception as:

"Actions executed to deliberately mislead adversary military decision makers as to friendly military capabilities, intentions, and operations, thereby causing the adversary to take specific actions that will contribute to the accomplishment of the friendly mission" (JCS, 1996).

Deception can be considered as the creation and invocation of both offensive and defensive environments and can be employed for attacking an adversary's perception of what is actually occurring. Furthermore, deception can be applied to enhance an operation, exaggerate, minimise, or distort the enemy/opponent's perception of capabilities and intentions, to mask deficiencies, and to otherwise cause a desired outcome where conventional military activities and security measures were unable to achieve the desired result (Cohen & Lambert, 2001).

The deployment of effective deception can also be an important element of information and computer based system's security. In the past, different deception techniques have been introduced to play their role in information security and to secure a computer based network. For instance, deployment of Honeypots and Honeynets as shown in figure 1 (Spitzner 2003), in a computer based network can lead to the discovery of an attacker's movements and allow the network to be secured against the attacker's next offensive move and strategies.

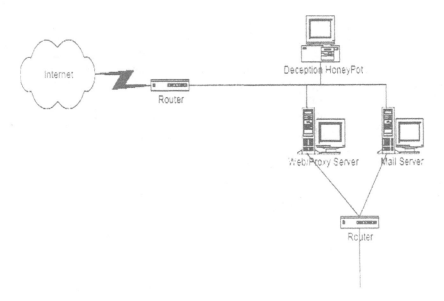

Fig. 1. Typical Honeypot Deployment (Spitzner, 2003)

In specific, Honeypots are systems designed to be appeared as fully functioning elements of the infrastructure, placed at an appropriate location on the network where all inbound and outbound traffic is captured and monitored, providing a secure and controlled environment to allow attackers to access them (Gupta, 2003), (Spitzner, 2003).

2.2 Critical Information Infrastructure (CII)

All critical infrastructures including transportation, finance, water, electric power, public telephone network, the Internet, and terrestrial and satellite wireless networks for a variety of information management, communications, and control functions are increasingly dependent on the evolving Information Infrastructure of a country.

Similarly, an organisation has its own CII including financial controls, information systems, computer network systems, etc. and therefore, security of an organisation's information infrastructure (II) is vital. Here, it is essential to mention that the CII can be seen as the subset of the II as shown in figure 2. It would therefore be a good idea to investigate information infrastructure before actually exploring the CII.

In specific, *II is an integrated system comprising of computing, communications, and the actual information stored within the system as well as the people who use and operate this technology* (Busuttil & Warren, 2003).

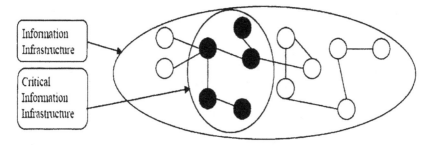

Fig. 2. The relationship between II & CII (Busuttil & Warren, 2003)

CII on the other hand, consists of the minimum amount of human and technological entities within the information infrastructure which needs to be in fully functioning state for an organisation to have information based supports for its business activities (Busuttil & Warren, 2003). Here it is important to mention that the protection of both II and CII includes securing and defending the basic facilities services, information systems itself and more importantly securing the actual elements needed to ensure successful operation of an organisation's information systems.

2.3 Computer Network Operations (CNO)

Computer Network Operations (CNO) can be defined as a combination of Computer Network Attack (CNA), Computer Network Defence (CND) and Computer Network Exploitation (CNE). It would therefore be adequate to gain initial understanding of CNA, CND & CNE, in order to appreciate the concept of CNO:

Computer Network Attack (CNA) can be described as the *"Operations carried out using computer hardware or software, or conducted through computers or computer networks, with the intended objective or likely effect of disrupting, denying, degrading, or destroying information resident in computers and computer networks, or the computers and networks themselves"* (United States Joint Forces Command Glossary, Undated).

The Computer Network Defence (CND) on the other hand, is *"the measures taken to protect and defend information, computers, and networks from intrusion, exploitation, disruption, denial, degradation, or destruction"* (United States Joint Forces Command Glossary, Undated).

Finally, the Computer network exploitation (CNE) can be defined as *"the intelligence collection and enabling operations to gather data from target adversary automated information systems (AIS) or networks"* (United States Joint Forces Command Glossary, Undated).

3 The Role of Deception in Computer Networks

Deception is acknowledged as of being an ancient art (Campen & Dearth, 1998). Through deception we can manage our adversary's perception and disrupt his decision-making processes. These processes feed into his (the adversary's) defensive INFOSEC processes which when disrupted will allow the success of our offensive NETOPS (Waltz, 1998) that will ensure out information superiority. In specific, *"Information superiority is the capability to collect, process, and disseminate an uninterrupted flow of information while exploiting or denying an adversary's ability to do the same."* (Waltz, 1998)

The purpose of deception is to surprise the adversary. If the threat agent is in a state of surprise the outcome can be twofold: either the defenders have time to react and deploy the necessary countermeasures (or finely tune the existing ones), or the threat agent will call off the attack and return to the information gathering process in order to re-examine his plan of action.

Technology has allowed for an increased capability for information gathering, but perceptions and the nature of decision-making have a common vulnerability: the human factor (Mitnick & Simon, 2002). Humans sit behind monitors, typing and/or communicating commands. Humans are in charge of automated procedures and can shut them down if they perceive that something is wrong and that the computer reactions do not make sense; and in the context of a computer network environment humans are tasked with administering the systems and networks.

An indicative list of the responsibilities of network administrators are summarised in the following:
- Design a network which is logical & efficient
- Deploy large numbers of machines which can be easily upgraded later
- Decide what services are needed
- Plan and implement adequate security
- Provide a comfortable environment for users and keep them happy
- Develop ways of fixing errors and problems which occur
- Keep track of, and understand how to use, technology

By designing a logical network though, the administrator makes the life of the threat agents easier, as they can follow the same logic and enumerate the infrastructure. Deception can be used to hide the real computers amongst the false. By having easily upgradeable computers the administrator possibly introduces a critical threat against his infrastructure. Should the upgrade procedures get compromised then threat agents will be able to launch catastrophic active attacks. Again deception can be used to masquerade the procedures and/or produce confusion about what is real. Some would argue that you can never have enough security, a statement that has been argued from the threat and risk assessment professionals. System users are probably the bigger vulnerability of that system as they are susceptible to social engineering attacks (Mitnick & Simon, 2002).

4 Existing Research & Future Work

To date, there are no deception models available which would lead to the strategic deployment of deception in a CNO environment. Similarly, there are no methodologies or models available that would allow targeted deception in a CND environment which may enhance the ability of an organisation's CII, in order to survive a CNA.

Existing frameworks (e.g. Cohen, Undated), do not offer effective and suitable deployment of different deceptive techniques for a specified CNO operation. Similarly, other models, such as the cognitive model for exposition of human deception and counter-deception by Lambert (Lambert, 1987), is quite generic and does not allow targeted deception in a CNO environment. This model is based on developing a basic understanding of human deception which would then lead to a comprehensive development of framework for organising deception principles and examples. Hence a methodological construct to assist in the planning and deployment of deception as part of CND could add value to the defensive organisation of computer networks. In the following paragraphs we outline concepts that could later serve as components of a methodological construct for deploying deception with a computer network environment.

Planning for a targeted deception operation can be outlined as a backwards process. This means that the desired end-result would become a starting point and would then derive the actual target and achievement. Figure 4 below outlines the planning process for preparing and deploying deception.

The starting point for implementing such an approach would be to outline the targets that an organisation may aim to achieve. There are a number of different targets that an organisation may intend to achieve including the defence of its CII against an intruder looking to compromise the organisation's CND.

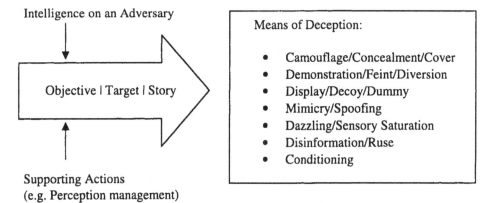

Fig. 3. Deception Planning Process (Gerwehr and Glenn, 2003, p.26)

Similarly, the information gathering process would also play an important role in development of a methodology in discussion. Furthermore, it can be predicted that the initial part of the developed model would be based on collecting information about the intruders / attackers. The following deception techniques could be useful when it comes to gathering information of an attacker with an intention of attacking an organisation's CII by defeating its CND:

☐ Concealment or hiding
☐ Camouflage (hiding movements from the intruder by artificial means)
☐ False and planted information (Misinforming "letting the intruder have the information that may hurt the intruder and may lead to learn attacker's next move")
☐ Displays ("techniques to make the enemy see what is not actually there")
☐ Ruses ("tricks, such as displays that use enemy equipment and procedures")
☐ Insight ("deceiving the attacker by out thinking him")

4.1 Deception Model Development

The concept of proposed deception model is in its early stages and a draft of the model is presented in this paper. Based on research and proceeding literature review, the author initially came up with an idea of designing a deception model which would comprise of four stages (Specification, Design, Implementation & Development, and Evaluation) based on three basic levels of deception (Strategic, Tactical and Operational).

The only problem with this initial thought was the Evaluation Stage of the proposed model, as carrying out evaluation would need another separate level within the proposed model. For this purpose, another level was added to the proposed deception model.

At this point, the author started to build a draft of the proposed model and this resulted in an understanding that the proposed model will initially have the following four different stages based on three levels of deception and an added level named Level 4 (shown in figure 4):

1. Specification Stage - **Strategic Level**
2. Design Stage - **Tactical Level**
3. Implementation and Development Stage - **Operational Level**
4. Evaluation Stage - **Level 4**

These stages are based on the initial concept of three basic levels of deception namely, Strategic Level, Tactical Level, and Operational Level. Additionally, another level is introduced for the purpose of this model named Level 4 (see figure 5). Basically, the Specification Stage of the proposed model will be based on Strategic Level of Deception, Design Stage of the model will be based on the Tactical Level of Deception, and Implementation and Development Stage will be based on Operational Level of deception. Finally, Evaluation of the proposed Model will be carried out during the stage 4 (Evaluation Stage) of the model.

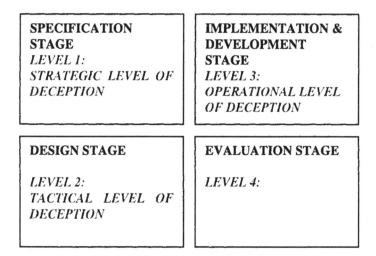

Fig. 4. Proposed Deception Model Stages based on 3 basic Levels of Deception & an Additional Level

The proposed model will also have four different phases namely, Infrastructure Analysis, Information Gathering, Information Assessment, and Deception Planning (shown in figure 5).

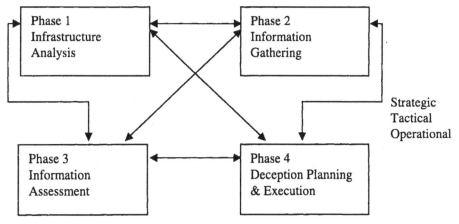

Fig. 5. Proposed Deception Model Phases based on 3 Levels of Deception

The next step was to start populating these phases of the proposed model, with a number of processors. As a result, the following processors were introduced to four different phases of the proposed model:

Phase 1: Infrastructure Analysis

1. Business Analysis (nature of business & related threats)
2. Stakeholder Identification
3. Asset Identification (prioritising the assets / effects on dependants due to the that)
4. Vulnerability Identification
5. Threat Agent Identification
6. Boundary Identification

Phase 2: Information Gathering

1. Perception Operations
2. Asset/Infrastructure Monitoring
3. Vulnerability Monitoring
4. Threat Agent Monitoring

Phase 3: Information Assessment

1. Intelligence Validity Assessment
2. Threat Agent Assessment
3. Vulnerability Assessment
4. Damage Assessment
5. Boundary Assessment
6. Operations Threat Assessment
7. Operation Assessment

Phase 4: Deception Planning

1. Reaction Planning (this will allow us to have an understanding of what needs to be done/modified in order to achieve our goals. This can then be fed in either or all 4 processors below which will also determine how to fix the problems/issues).

- □ PYSOPS Planning
- □ INFOSEC Planning
- □ OPSEC Planning
- □ NETOPS Planning

2. Deception Planning (The output of the above 4 can then be fed here in order to achieve our goal

Moving on, the final milestone to achieve for this research would be to carryout the evaluation upon completion of the first 3 levels of the proposed deception model. For this purpose, the Level 4 (Evaluation Stage) will have following processes:

Evaluation Stage

1. Operations Threats Monitoring
2. Operations Monitoring
3. Operations Threat Assessment
4. Operation Assessment

As this model is in its early development stages, a large amount of development is expected to be carried out in the future, including: defining all four Levels, Stages, and Phases. The definitions will not be the actual generic definition but would actually be tailored to suit the needs of this proposed deception model. The next task would be to define all processes within each phase and more importantly the activities of these processes. At that point, it would be ideal to describe the relationship between all four Stages of the model and also how each Phase may change during different levels of Deception. This would also enable us to outline rules and guidelines of whether a user can move from one Stage to another within this model. For instance, if one could go back to Design Stage if they were in Implementation & Development Stage and if so then on what conditions/limitations.

Finally, it is important to mention that each process will have a number of activities and each activity will have a number of inputs and outputs depending on the actual processes. This will become apparent once the Stages and Phases of the proposed model are more populated, as a result of the future work.

5 Conclusions

Deception can be considered as a vital element of both information security and computer based systems security and therefore can play an increasingly important role to achieve desired objectives when deployed in a CNO environment.

Although, a number of information and computer systems security related frameworks are available out there but the organisations do not have enough guidance in the field of CND and CII protection. Furthermore, there are no models available that would enable an organisation to employ strategic deception in order to increase the security of its CND. This could be due to the fact that deployment of deception in a CND is still in its infancy and a lot of research can still be carried out to achieve a milestone in this area of CNO.

Furthermore, the increasing importance of network defence in the field of this high-tech CNO environment has resulted in an understanding that a key objective in network security should be to improve defences through the use of deception proactively against a target such as an intruder aiming to target the network defence of an organisation's CII by compromising its CND. It would therefore be beneficial to design a model that would enable us to deploy strategic deception in a CNO environment.

References

1. Busuttil, T. & Warren, M. (2003). A Review of critical Information Infrastructure Protection within IT Security Guidelines, 4th Australian Information warfare and IT security Conference 2003.

2. Campen, A. D. and D. H. Dearth (1998). Cyberwar 2.0: Myths, Mysteries and Reality. Fairfax, Virginia, AFCEA International Press

3. Cohen, F & Lambert, D. (2001). A Framework for Deception, [online], http://all.net/journal/deception/Framework/Framework.html

4. Gerwehr, S. & Glenn, R. W. (2003). Unweaving the Web: Deception and Adoption in Future Urban Operations, Rand, Santa Monica.

5. Gupta, N. (2003). Improving the Effectiveness of Deceptive Honeynets through an Empirical Learning Approach, [online], http://www.infosecwriters.com/text_resources/pdf/Gupta_Honeynets.pdf

6. JCS. (1996). Joint Doctrine for Military Deception, Joint Pub 3-58, [online], http://www.fas.org/irp/doddir/dod/jp3_58.pdf

7. Lambert, D. (1987). A Cognitive Model for Exposition of Human Deception and Counterdeception), [online], http://jps.lanl.gov/vol1_iss1/5Cognitive_Model_of_Deception.pdf

8. Mitnick, K. D. & Simon, W. L. (2002). The Art of Deception. Indianapolis, USA, Wiley Publishing

9. Rue, L. (1994). By The Grace ff Guile: The Role of Deception in Natural History and Human Affairs. New York: Oxford University Press.

10. Spitzner, L. (2003). Honeypots - Tracking Hackers. Boston: Pearson Education Inc.

11. (United States Joint Forces Command Glossary, Undated). [online], http://www.jfcom.mil/about/glossary.htm

12. Waltz, E. (1998). Information Warfare. Norwood, USA, Artech House

SECTION II: Wireless & Ad Hoc Network Security

Taxonomy of Attacks on Wireless Sensor Networks

Song Han[1], Elizabeth Chang[1], Li Gao[1], and Tharam Dillon[2]

[1] School of Information Systems,
Curtin Business School,
Curtin University of Technology, GPO Box U1987,
Perth WA 6845, Australia

[2] Faculty of Information Technology,
University of Technology Sydney,
PO Box 123, Broadway NSW 2007, Australia

Abstract. Along with sensor networks popularly utilized in the practical applications, to design optimistic security mechanisms is becoming a big challenge within the wireless sensor networks. As a result, it is imperative to propose a taxonomy of attacks on wireless sensor networks, since good security mechanism should address the attacks on wireless sensor networks. This paper presents the first work of the taxonomy of attacks on wireless sensor networks in a systematic way. This will help researchers in the area of wireless sensor networks to better understand wireless sensor network security and design more optimistic security countermeasures for wireless sensor networks.

1 Introduction

A sensor network [1] is composed of a large number of sensor nodes with limited power, computation capability, and storage/communication capability. This characteristic induces that wireless sensor networks are liable to be attacked by outside adversaries or inside compromised sensor nodes. A number of sensor network systems have been proposed [2], [3], [8], [9], [10], [11], [13], [14]. However, most of the proposed sensor network systems with security mechanism are located in the area B as shown in Fig 1. It is still an open problem to design more optimistic wireless sensor network security mechanisms that: (1) can address various attacks, and (2) have good tradeoff between security and performance within the wireless sensor networks.

So far, various attacks and the corresponding security mechanisms for sensor networks have been studied [4], [5], [6], [7], [9], [12], [15]. Perrig et al. reported a number of attacks on sensor networks in [4]; while their classification does not cover all the existing attacks on sensor networks. Avancha et al. reported several attacks on wireless sensor networks in [5]; but they did not analyze those attacks from optimal criteria. Li et al. proposed a number of attacks on sensor networks in [9]. As location-based services become more prevalent, the localization infrastructure will become the target of malicious attacks. These attacks will not be conventional security threats, but rather threats that adversely affect the ability of localization schemes to provide trustworthy location information. Their paper [9] identifies a list of attacks that are unique to localization algorithms. Since these attacks are diverse in nature, and there may be many unforeseen attacks that can bypass traditional security countermeasures. Wood et al. also classified a number of attacks on sensor networks [15]. They only focused on the denial-of-service attacks on wireless sensor networks.

However, no work has been done to classify various attacks on wireless sensor networks in a systematic way. As we know, it will be helpful to researchers in the realm of sensor networks if a systematic taxonomy of attacks on wireless sensor networks is presented, since better understanding of attacks would help to better understand the principles of wireless sensor networks, and to further design more optimistic security countermeasures for wireless sensor networks. Based on this point, our paper presents the first attempt to classify various attacks on wireless sensor networks in a systematic way.

The proposed taxonomy of attacks on wireless sensor networks is complete in the following sense: the taxonomy covers known attacks and those which have not yet appeared but are realistic potential threats that would affect current security mechanisms for sensor networks. We do not claim that the taxonomy is as detailed as possible. Many classes could be divided into several deeper levels. Also, new attack approach may appear, thus adding new classes to the ones we propose.

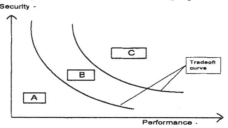

Fig 1. The tradeoff between Security and Performance of sensor network systems. Most of the existing sensor network systems stay within the area B located between two tradeoff curves as above. An open problem is to design new sensor network systems which can stay in the area C, since it denotes the more optimistic tradeoff between Security and Performance.

Our goal is to select a number of important features of attacks on wireless sensor networks that might help to design innovative solutions which are located in the area C in Fig 1, and to use these features as taxonomy criteria. In this sense, we do not claim that the proposed taxonomy divides attacks in an exclusive manner.

The organization of the rest of the paper is as follows: Section 2 reviews the characteristics and the communication architecture of sensor networks. Section 3 presents the taxonomy of attacks on wireless sensor networks. The taxonomy criteria will be given in Section 4. Section 5 concludes this paper.

2 Background

Sensor network is an emerging wireless computing technology for monitoring a variety of environments in scientific, military, medical, or other critical applications. In detail, the sensor networks can be applied to ocean and wildlife monitoring, manufacturing machinery performance monitoring, building safety and earthquake monitoring, and many military applications. An even wider spectrum of future applications is likely to follow, including the monitoring of highway traffic, pollution, wildfires, building security, water quality, and even people's heart rates. A major benefit of these systems is that they perform in-network processing to reduce large streams of raw data into useful aggregated information. Protecting it all is critical. Because sensor networks pose unique challenges, traditional security techniques used in traditional networks cannot be applied directly. The characteristics and the communication architecture of sensor networks are as follows:

2.1 Characteristics of Sensor Networks

A sensor network design is influenced by many factors, which include:
(1) The sensor network topology can change very frequently.
(2) The sensor nodes are densely deployed.
(3) The sensor nodes mainly use a broadcast communication paradigm.
(4) The number of sensor nodes can be several orders of magnitude.
(5) The sensor nodes are limited in power, computational capabilities, and memory.
(6) The sensor nodes in a sensor network may not have global identification.

These factors are important because they serve as a guideline to design a desirable protocol or an algorithm for sensor networks.

2.2 Communication Architecture of Sensor Networks

The sensor nodes are usually scattered in a sensor field. Each of these scattered sensor nodes has the capabilities to collect data and route data back to the sink and the end users. The communication architecture consists of the application layer, transport layer, network layer, data link layer, and physical layer.

Depending on the sensing tasks, different types of application software can be built and used on the application layer. The transport layer helps to maintain the flow of data if the sensor networks application requires it. The network layer takes care of routing the data supplied by the transport layer. Since the environment is noisy and sensor nodes can be mobile, the MAC protocol must be power aware and able to minimize collision with neighbors' broadcast. The physical layer addresses the needs of a simple but robust modulation, transmission and receiving techniques.

3   Taxonomy of Attacks on Sensor Networks

There are several existing taxonomys of the attacks on sensor networks, for example [2], [5], [15]. However, the existing taxonomys only focus on some special attacks on sensor networks. It is necessary to propose a sound taxonomy which contains various attacks with respect to the different purpose, behavior and target. That will help researchers to better understand the principles of attacks on sensor networks, and further design more optimistic security countermeasures for sensor networks. In this section, we will classify the various attacks on sensor networks in a systematic way. To the best of our knowledge, this is the first work that systematically studies and classifies various attacks on sensor networks. One of the new attacks is the Policy Attack, which has not yet been studied by the researchers in the area of sensor networks.

3.1 Communication Attacks

Communication attacks on sensor networks can be classified as the following three different types according to the attack behavior: replay attack, denial of service attack, and Sybil attack.

(1) Replay Attacks

(1.11) Run external attacks (replay of messages from outside the current run of the communication): it includes two different interleavings: (a1) message is directed to other than the intended node, and (a2) intended principal receives message, but message is delayed.

(1.12) Run internal attacks (replay of messages from inside the current run of the communication): it also includes two different interleavings: (a1) message is directed to other than the intended node, and (a2) intended principal receives message, but message is delayed.

(2) Denial-of-Service (DOS) Attacks

A denial of service attack is characterized by an explicit attempt to prevent the legitimate use of a service. Another kind of definition for denial-of-service attack is proposed by Wood and Stankovic [15] as "any event that diminishes or eliminates a network's capacity to perform its expected function." In this subsection, we only concentrate on the denial-of-service attack on the communication within the sensor networks. This kind of attacks is classified as follows:

(2.11) General DOS Attacks

(a) Jamming Attack: A standard DOS attack on wireless sensor networks is simply to jam a node or set of nodes. Jamming, in this case, is simply the transmission of a radio signal that interferes with the radio frequencies being used by the sensor network. The jamming attack can result in no messages are able to be sent or received.

(b) Collision Attack: An attacker may simply intentionally violate the communication protocol, and continually transmit messages in an attempt to generate collisions. Such collisions would require the retransmission of any packet affected by the collision.

(c) Routing ill-directing Attack: A malicious node may take advantage of a multi-hop network by simply refusing to route messages. This will render the intended node no receiving the packet.

(d) Flooding Attack: A malicious node may send many connection requests to a susceptible node. In this case, resources must be allocated to handle the connection request. Eventually a node's resources will be exhausted, thus rendering the node useless.

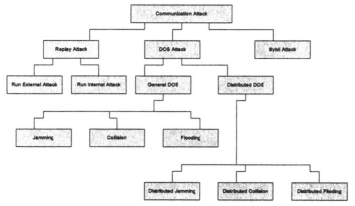

Fig. 2. Taxonomy of the Communication Attacks on Sensor Networks

(2.12)   Distributed DOS Attacks

A distributed DOS attack deploys multiple attacking entities to attain the aim of the general DOS attack. In the area of sensor networks, we consider the distributed DOS in the scenario as the above four different general DOS attack.

(a) A set of attackers simply jam a node or set of nodes.

(b) A set of attackers simply intentionally violate the communication protocol, and continually transmit messages in an attempt to generate collisions.

(c) A set of colluding nodes take advantage of a multihop network by simply refusing to route messages.

(d) A set of colluding nodes send many connection requests to a susceptible node in a way that it renders the node useless.

(3) Sybil Attacks

The Sybil attack is defined as a "malicious device illegitimately taking on multiple identities " [2]. The Sybil attack is effective against routing algorithms, data aggregation, voting, fair resource allocation and foiling misbehavior detection. Regardless of the target (voting, routing, aggregation), the Sybil attack involves utilizing multiple identities. For instance, in a sensor network voting scheme, the Sybil attack might utilize multiple identities to generate additional "votes." Similarly, to attack the routing protocol, the Sybil attack would rely on a malicious node taking on the identity of multiple nodes, and thus routing multiple paths through a single malicious node.

3.2 Attacks against Privacy

Sensor networks have also thrust privacy concerns to the forefront. The most obvious risk is that ubiquitous sensor technology might allow ill-intentioned individuals to deploy secret surveillance networks for spying on unaware victims. Employers might spy on their employees; shop owners might spy on customers; neighbors might spy on each other; and law enforcement agencies might spy on public places. This is certainly a valid concern; historically, as surveillance technology has become cheaper and more effective, it has increasingly been implicated in privacy abuses. Technology trends suggest the problem will only get worse with time. As devices get smaller, they will be easier to conceal; as devices get cheaper, surveillance networks will be more affordable.

The main privacy problem is not that sensor networks enable the collection of information. In fact, much information from sensor networks may be collected through direct site surveillance. The classical attacks against sensor privacy include:

(1)   Eavesdropping: Through taping the information, the attacker could easily discover the communication contents. When the traffic conveys the control information about the sensor network configuration, which contains potentially more detailed information than accessible through the location server, the eavesdropping can act effectively against the privacy protection.

	Attack Name	Attack Details
Attacks against	Eavesdropping	'Taping' information
	Impersonating	Impersonating the victim sensor

Privacy		node
	Traffic Analysis	Examining the pattern of sensor node activities

Table 1. Taxonomy of Attacks against Privacy of Sensor Nodes

(2) Impersonating Attack: The attacker can insert the forged node or compromise the nodes to hide in the sensor network. After that, the forged node can impersonate the original victim sensor node to receive the packets, then misroute the packets, e.g. forward the packets to the nodes conducting the privacy analysis.

(3) Traffic analysis is the term used for the process of inferring information about the communications of an encrypted target sensor network. Although unable to read the encrypted message contents, the attacker examines the externals - which station is sending messages, to whom messages are sent, and the patterns of activity. Sometimes, the identities of the correspondents are contained in unencrypted message headers, while at other times they can be inferred by direction finding techniques on radio signals. Patterns of activity can also be used to deduce the target's alert status. Wireless sensor networks are typically composed of many low-power sensors communicating with a few relatively robust and powerful base stations. By the traffic analysis, the attacker can simultaneously utilize monitor and eavesdropping to identify some sensor nodes that are of special roles or activities [5], [11].

3.3 Sensor-Node-Targeted Attacks

The sensor-node-targeted attack is a method that the attacker intentionally captures or destructs one or more sensor nodes. The details are:

(1) Sensor Node Capture:

This attack is mainly used in military applications. A sensor node captured by the enemy troops may be reverse-engineered and become an instrument for mounting counterattacks.

(2) Sensor Node Destruction:

The attack damages the sensor node permanently in such a way that the damage is irreversible. Some application examples include destructing sensor nodes, extracting cryptographic secrets of the sensor node, modifying the internal codes in the sensor node. The effects of these attacks can be dramatic: a compromised sensor node in an airport surveillance system may pose serious threats to flight safety.

	Attack Name	Attack Details
Sensor-Node-Targeted Attacks	Sensor Node Capture	The captured sensor node becomes an instrument for mounting counter-attack
	Sensor Node Destruction	Destructing sensor nodes
		Extracting cryptographic secrecy
		Modifying the internal codes

Table 2. Taxonomy of Sensor Node-targeted Attack

3.4 Power Consumption Attacks

The attacker can inflict sleep torture on an energy constrained sensor node by engaging in it in unnecessary communication work to quickly drain its battery power. Depriving the power of a few crucial sensor nodes may lead to the communication breakdown of the entire network. Other researchers ever classified the power consumption attack as one of the denial-of-service attacks [15]. However, we separate it as one of the main attacks on sensor networks, since the denial-of-service attack in our paper is studied within the communication attacks.

3.5 Policy Attacks

This attack has not yet been discussed in the research realm of sensor networks. However, the security and privacy policy is imperative, since the policy basically influences the setup principles of the sensor networks. Therefore, it is important to study the policy attacks in the area of sensor networks.

If a sensor node or an outside attacker can obtain resources without producing a record of the misuse, the attacker is safe from any sanction. Attacks of this kind exploit "holes" in auditing policies, or actively disrupt the auditing mechanism. Policy attacks can be classified as

(1) Excuse attack: If the sensor network policy is overly generous to recovering sensor nodes that recently crashed or damaged by not requiring them to prove they are maintaining their quota, a malicious node may exploit this attack by repeatedly claiming to have been crashed/damaged.

(2) Newbie-picking attack: In some cases, a sensor network may require that new nodes pay their dues by requiring them to give information (e.g. information gained from other networks) to the sensor network for some period of time before they can consume any shared resources. If this policy is not carefully designed, a veteran node could move from one newbie node to another, leeching their information without being required to give any information back.

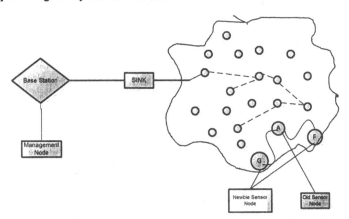

Fig. 3. The Newbie-picking Attack. In this figure, A is an old sensor node. G and P are two newbie sensor nodes that are just arriving at the sensor field. The sensor node A manages to exploit G and P, and obtains their information without giving any information of itself back to the newbie sensor nodes G and P.

3.6 Cryptographic Attacks on Key Management

Apart from the above listed attacks that may hinder the key management of sensor networks sound, the following adversarial actions will also danger the key management within sensor networks: brute force, dictionary attack, and monitoring attack [16].

104

4 Criteria of the Proposed Taxonomy

In this section we provide the criteria for the proposed taxonomy of attacks on sensor networks. The details are in the following Table 3.

	Taxonomy	Taxonomy Criteria
Class 1	Communication Attacks	Behavior
Class 2	Attacks against Privacy	Privacy
Class 3	Sensor-Node-Targeted Attacks	Targeted node
Class 4	Power Consumption Attacks	Power
Class 5	Policy Attacks	Policy hole
Class 6	Cryptographic Attacks on Key Management	Secret Key of sensor node

Table 3. The taxonomy of attacks on sensor networks and the corresponding taxonomy criteria.

5 Conclusions

This paper proposed the first taxonomy of attacks on wireless sensor networks. We expect the proposed taxonomy of attacks on wireless sensor networks will offer a foundation to analyze and better understand the mechanism of attacks on wireless sensor networks. As a result, it will help researchers to design more qualified security mechanisms to prevent as well as react to the attacks induced on wireless sensor networks.

Acknowledgment

The authors would present theirs thanks to the anonymous reviewers. This work is supported by the Curtin Research Fellowship and ARC Funding within the Centre for Extended Enterprises and Business Intelligence and School of Information Systems at Curtin Business School, Curtin University of Technology.

References

1. Akyildiz, Ian F., Su, W., Sankarasubramaniam, Y., Cayirci, E.: A Survey on Sensor Networks. IEEE. Communication Magazine. (2002) 102–114.
2. Newsome, J., Shi, R., Song, D., Perrig, A.: The Sybil attack in sensor networks: analysis & defenses. In 3rd International Symposium on Information Processing in Sensor Networks (IPSN 2004), April 2004.
3. Du, W., Deng, J., Han, Y., Chen, S., and Varshney, P.: A Key Management Scheme for Wireless Sensor Networks Using Deployment Knowledge. IEEE INFOCOM, 2004.
4. Perrig, W., Stankovic, J., Wagner, D.: Security in Wireless Sensor Networks. Communication of The ACM, Vol. 47, No. 6. (2004) 53–57.
5. Avancha, S., Undercoffer, J., Joshi, A., Pinkston, J.: Security for Sensor Networks, in Wireless Sensor Networks, C. S. Raghavendra, Krishna M. Sivalingam and Taieb Znati (Eds), Kluwer Academic Publishers, May 2004.
6. Hu, N., Smith, R. K., Bradford, P. G.: Security for fixed sensor networks. ACM Southeast Regional Conference 2004: 212-213.

7. Yang, H., Ye, F., Yuan, Y., Lu, S., Arbaugh, W.: Toward resilient security in wireless sensor networks. Proc. of ACM Sym. on Mobile ad hoc networking and computing, (2005) 34-45.

8. Chan, H., Perrig, A., and Song, D.: Random Key Predistribution Schemes for Sensor Networks. In Proc. IEEE Symposium on Security and Privacy, 2003.

9. Li, Z., Trappe, W., Zhang, Y., and Nath, B.: Robust Statistical Methods for Securing Wireless Localization in Sensor Networks. In Proc. International Symposium on Information Processing in Sensor Networks (IPSN), 2005.

10. Ye, F., Lu, S., and Zhang, L.: Gradient broadcast: A robust data delivery protocol for large scale sensor networks. ACM WINET, March 2005.

11. Deng, J., Han, R., Mishra, S.: Intrusion Tolerance and Anti-Traffic Analysis Strategies For Wireless Sensor Networks, Proc. of Int. Conf. on Dependable Systems and Networks, 2004.

12. Olariu, S., Xu, Q. W.: Information assurance in wireless sensor networks, IEEE Symposium on Parallel and Distributed Processing, IPDPS 2005.

13. Perrig, A., Szewczyk, R., Wen, V., Culler, D., Tygar, J. D.: SPINS: Security protocols for sensor networks. The 7th Annual International Conference on Mobile Computing and Networks, Rome Italy, June 2001.

14. Zhu, S., Setia, S., Jajodia, S., Ning, P.: An Interleaved Hop-by-Hop Authentication Scheme for Filtering False Data in Sensor Networks. IEEE Sym.Security & Privacy, 2004.

15. Wood, A. D., Stankovic, J. A.: Denial of Service in sensor networks. Computer 35(10): 54-62, 2002.

16. Merkow, M., Breiththaupt, J.: Information security: principles and practices. Prentice Hall Press, 2005.

A Lightweight Identity Authentication Mechanism for Self-Organizing Wireless Sensor Networks

Joon Heo[1], Choong Seon Hong[2]

School of Electronics and Information, Kyung Hee Univerity
1 Seocheon, Giheung, Yongin, Gyeonggi 449-701 KOREA
heojoon@khu.ac.kr[1] *, cshong@khu.ac.kr*[2]

Abstract. Rapid technological advances are being made toward developing self-organizing wireless sensor network. The essential purpose of such system is to sense the environment and inform users. Security and privacy protection are of extreme importance for many of the proposed applications of wireless sensor networks (WSNs). However, security in sensor networks is complicated by the lack of tamper-resistant hardware (to keep per-node costs low). In addition, sensor nodes have limited storage and computational resource. This paper proposes a lightweight identity authentication mechanism at the link layer for data frame in WSNs. With the proposed mechanism there are only n-bits for authentication, which can greatly reduce overhead. Statistical method and simulation results indicate that our mechanism is successful in handling MAC layer attack.

Keywords: self-organizing WSNs, lightweight authentication, synchronization algorithm, attack detection

1 Introduction

Self-organization refers to ability of the system to achieve the necessary structures without requiring human intervention, particularly by specially trained installers and operators. Self-organization is a critical attribute needed to achieve the wide use and applicability of wireless sensor networks. Sensor networking has become an exciting and important technology in recent years. It provides an economical solution to many challenging problems such as traffic monitoring and building safety monitoring. Security and privacy protection are of extreme importance for many of the proposed applications of WSNs. The major challenges in tackling wireless sensor networks security include: power conservation for mobile sensors, cooperation among heterogeneous sensors, flexibility in the security level to match the application needs, scalability, self organizing and self

This work was supported by MIC and ITRC Project. Dr.C.S.Hong is the corresponding author.

learning capabilities of sensor, trust and security decisions for the application, keeping the mobility and volatility transparent, and yet protecting the network from external and internal intrusions. In a nutshell there are three factors that we have to consider energy, computation and communication [9]. Due to resource scarcity (battery power, memory, and processing power) of sensor, securing sensor networks is quite different from traditional schemes that generally involve management and safe keeping of a small number of private management and safe keeping of a small number of private and public key [10]. Disclosing a key with each packet requires too much energy [11]. Storing one-way chain of secret keys along a message route requires considerable memory and computation of the nodes on that route [12]. The key management using a trusted third party requires an engineered solution that makes it unsuitable for sensor network application. Although the asymmetric key cryptography does not require a trusted sever, key revocation becomes a bottleneck as it involves an authority maintaining a list of revoked keys on a server or requesting the public key directly from the owner [13]. In this paper, we propose a lightweight identity authentication at the link layer for data frame in WSNs. Unlike traditional authentication mechanism, the proposed mechanism determines the legitimacy of a sender by continuously checking a series of data frames transmitted by the sender. The major purpose of the proposed mechanism is to detect an attack in an error-prone wireless environment. When the sink detects an attack, some protection or anti-attack approaches for each type attack can be triggered. The proposed mechanism identifies the attack by using a statistical way and provides access control. The goals of our lightweight authentication mechanism are the following:

· *Secure and useful*: an attacker should with low probability be able to gain access to the network.

· *Cheap*: by presenting an optimized n-bits identity authentication method for resource-constrained environments like wireless sensor networks, a cheap and efficient access control procedure is obtained.

· *Robust*: due to loss channels in wireless communications a synchronization algorithm is required for the generated random authentication stream in the sink and the sensor node.

This paper is organized as follows. Section 2 includes security related properties in WSNs. Section 3 describes the proposed mechanism for identity authentication. Section 4 provides the statistical method. Finally, we give some concluding remarks.

2 Security-Related Properties in WSNs

WSNs share several important properties with traditional wireless networks, most notably with mobile ad hoc networks. Both types of networks rely on wireless communication, ad hoc network deployment and setup, and constant changes in the network topology. Many security solutions proposed for wireless networks can be applied in WSNs; however, several unique characteristics of WSNs require new security mechanism. In this section two characteristics specific to WSNs are discussed[7].

· *Limited resources*. Sensor network nodes are designed to be compact and therefore are limited by size, energy, computational power, and storage. The limited resources limit the types of security algorithms and protocols that can be implemented. Security solutions for WSNs operate in a solution space defined by the trade-off between resource spent on security and the achieved protection.

· *In − network processing*. Communication between the nodes in a WSN consumes most of the available energy, much less than sensing and computation do. For that reason, WSNs perform localized processing and data aggregation. An optimal security architecture for this type of communication is one in which a group key is shared among the nodes in an immediate neighborhood. However, in an environment in which the nodes can be captured, the confidentiality offered by the shared symmetric keys is easily compromised.

3 Proposed Mechanism

The proposed security mechanism is designed to provide a lightweight identity authentication at the link layer for data frame in WSNs. The main idea is to compute an identical random identity authentication stream in the sink and the sensor node, and then only add n-bits from this stream into the MAC-layer data frame for identity authentication. Unlike traditional authentication mechanism, the proposed mechanism determines the legitimacy of a sender by continuously checking a series of data frames transmitted by the sender. Ideally, since the attacker does not have the shared key, the probability for the attacker to guess continuously i times of n-bits is as small as $(2^n)^{-i}$. With the proposed mechanism there are only n-bits for identity authentication, which can greatly reduce overhead and thus preserves the scarce wireless bandwidth resource.

3.1 *Authbit set* and *Set number*

As shown in Figure 1, at the beginning, the sink and the sensor node create a random bit stream called the *Authbit*. The length of stream is l-bits where $l = 2^m$. Since the sink and the sensor node have the same shared key and stream generator, the constructed *Authbit* streams are the same[3][4].Shared key between the sink and the node may be provided by the key distribution mechanism, but are out of scope of this paper. And then, the sink and the sensor node create

a_1	a_2	a_3	a_4	a_5	••••	a_{l-3}	a_{l-2}	a_{l-1}	a_l
1	0	0	1	1	••••	0	0	1	1

Fig.1. n-bits *Authbit* stream

110

Authbit sets and Set numbers as shown in Figure 2.

· $S_k = \{a_{k+1}, a_{k+2}, \ldots, a_{k+n-1}, a_{k+n}\}$, where $n > 1$

· $Ck = a_k * 2^{m-1} + a_{k+1} * 2^{m-2} + \ldots + a_{k+m-2} * 2^1 + a_{k+m-1} * 2^0$

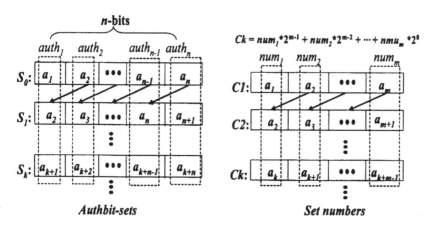

Fig.2. *Authbit sets* and *Set numbers* generation mechanism

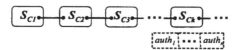

Fig.3. The authentication chain of *Authbit sets*

For example, if the sink and the node use the *Authbit* stream of Fiture 1, $S_0 = \{1,0,0\}$, $S_1 = \{0,0,1\}$ and $S_2 = \{0,1,1\}$ where $n=3$. Also, $C1 = a_1 * 2^3 + a_2 * 2^2 + a_3 * 2^1 + a_4 * 2^0 = 9$ and $C2=3$ where $l = 2^m = 16$. Finally, the *Authbit* set and the *Set number* will be used making the same chain for authentication of data frame between the sink and the sensor node as shown in Figure 3.

3.2 Synchronization and Fault tolerance using the *Set pointer*

Conceptually, both the sink and the sensor node have a pointer pointing to the *Authbit set* for the next outgoing data frame. Ideally, both the sink and the node will have their pointer pointing at exactly the same *Authbit set* and advance synchronously. Initially, the sink and the node pointers are synchronized. The sensor node sends each data frame with n-bits and bits value is equal to the values of the *Set pointer* (P_x). When the sink receives a frame successfully, the sink checks the bits value of the data frame. The synchronization and fault tolerance of *Set pointer* explained above can partially be described with the following Figure 4 and Figure 5.

Algorithm : synchronization and fault tolerance

// Sink receive data frame with *Authbit set* $\{S_{ck}\}_{node}$

if $\{S_{ck}\}_{node} == \{S_{ck}\}_{sink}$ then

P_x++

else if $\{S_{ck}\}_{node} \neq \{S_{ck}\}_{sink}$ then

$P_x = P_{x-d}$

Sink → sensor node: frame {failed, retransmission from S_{ck-d}}

Fig.4. Psudo code of synchronization algorithm

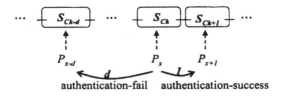

authentication-fail   authentication-success

Fig.5. Synchronization and fault tolerance using the *Set pointer* (P_x)

4   Statistical method and Simulation

The main objective of this authentication mechanism is to determine whether the sending node is an attacker or not. We have analyzed the proposed authentication mechanism and have devised a method to find out the authenticity of a sensor node as a probability value. First let us assume that the sensor node is an attack i.e. it does not know the *Authbit set* chain. According to Geometric Random Variable, the probability of continuously success of attacks can be given as shown Figure 6. Also if the sensor node's *Authbit set* doesn't match the sink's *Authbit set*, this means there are two possibilities either (a) there are no synchronization between the sink and the sensor node *Set pointer* (P_x) or

112

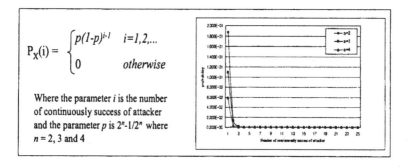

$$P_X(i) = \begin{cases} p(1-p)^{i-1} & i=1,2,... \\ 0 & otherwise \end{cases}$$

Where the parameter i is the number of continuously success of attacker and the parameter p is $2^n\text{-}1/2^n$ where $n = 2, 3$ and 4

Fig.6. Probability of continuously success of attacks

(b) the sending node is an illegitimate node. In an error-prone wireless network, data frames are 'frequently' lost due to wireless error. In [4], authors proposed a lightweight authentication protocol for access control in WLAN. They have devised a statistical method to determine the probability of a station being an attacker. We expanded the statistical method of their paper to support to our mechanism. We know that in a perfect channel, where there are no losses, a legitimate device will not have any synchronization with its receiver. However, in an error-prone wireless network, a receiver cannot differentiate between non-synchronization due to attacker and non-synchronization due to wireless losses. Hence, we devise a statistical method to determine the probability of a node being an attacker. Let the number of data frames from P_1 to P_t be t, let the number of synchronization done by node and sink be s, and let the data frame loss rate be r, where r ($0 \leq r \leq 1$). We have the following theorem.

[Theorem(where using n-bits authentication stream)]
For a sending node D, assum the prior probability of node D to be an attacker is $\frac{1}{2^n}$, i.e., P(D=*attacker*) $= \frac{1}{2^n}$ and P(D=*legitimate*) $= \frac{2^n-1}{2^n}$, the probability of this device D being an attacker is one when the number of synchronization is s, P(D=*attacker* | t, s), is given by

$$P(D = attacker|t,s) = \frac{2^{-t}}{2^{-t} + (2^n - 1) * r^s(1 - r)^{t-s}} \tag{1}$$

[Proof]
We know P (D=*legitimate* | t, s) = 1- P(D=*attacker* | t, s).
According to Bayer's Formula, we have
P(D=*attacker*|t,s) =

$$\frac{P(t, s|D = attacker) * P(D = attacker)}{P(t, s|D = atta.) * P(D = atta.) + P(t, s|D = legi.) * P(D = legi.)}$$

$$= \frac{P(t, s|D = attacker)}{P(t, s|D = attacker) + (2^n - 1) * P(t, s|D = legitimate)} \tag{2}$$

First let us assume that the sending device is an attacker; also it does not know the authentication chain of *Authbitsets*. In this case, the probability of $P(t,s \mid D=attacker)$ can be given as follows:

$$P(t, s|D = attacker) = \binom{t}{s} * 2^{-t} \tag{3}$$

Now let us consider the case where the sending node is a legitimate node. We have the probability of the number of synchronization s where the acknowledgment frame loss rate is r :

$$P(t, s|D = legitimate) = \binom{t}{s} * r^s (1 - r)^{t-s} \tag{4}$$

Combing (2), (3) and (4), it is easy to derive (1), i.e.,

$$P(D = attacker|t, s) = \frac{2^{-t}}{2^{-t} + (2^n - 1) * r^s (1 - r)^{t-s}} \tag{5}$$

Figure 7 shows the probability of a sending device being a legitimate one. We have $t=10$. The analysis is for $r=10\%$, 20% and 30%.

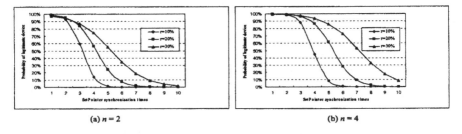

(a) $n = 2$ (b) $n = 4$

Fig.7. Probability of legitimate sender where $n=2$ and $n=4$

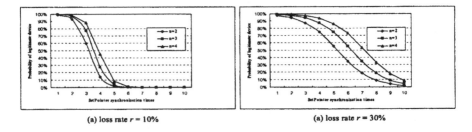

(a) loss rate $r = 10\%$ (a) loss rate $r = 30\%$

Fig.8. Probability of legitimate sender where $r=10\%$ and $r=30\%$

Figure 8 shows the probability of a sending device being a legitimate one. We have $t=10$. The analysis is for $n=2$, 3 and 4.

5   Conclusion

In this paper, we have presented a lightweight identity authentication protocol for data frame in wireless sensor networks. The proposed mechanism inserts identity authentication bits from a data frame known only to the two communicating stations. With the proposed mechanism there are only n-bits for identity authentication, which can greatly reduce overhead and thus preserves the scarce wireless bandwidth resource. The major purpose of the proposed mechanism is to detect an attack in an error-prone wireless environment. When the coordinator detects an attack, some protection or anti-attack approaches for each type attack can be triggered. We plan to foster our solution in the evolutionary computing systems through further development.

References

1. "Wireless Medium Access Control and Physical Layer Specification for Low-Rate Wireless Personal Area Networks", IEEE Standard, 802.15.4-2003, May 2003.
2. N. Sastry, D. Wagner, "Security Consideration for IEEE 802.15.4 Networks", WiSe'04, Proceeding, pp.32-42, 2004.
3. Henric Johnson, Arne Nilsson, Judy Fu, S.Felix Wu, Albert Chen and He Huang, "SOLA: A One-bit Identity Authentication Protocol for Access Control in IEEE 802.11", In Proceedings of IEEE GLOBECOM 2002.
4. Haoli Wang, Aravind Velayuthan, Yong Guan, "A Lightweight Authentication Protocol for Access Control in IEEE 802.11", In Proceedings of IEEE GLOBECOM 2003.
5. Fan Zhao, Yongjoo Shin, S. Felix Wu, Henric Johnson, Arne Nilsson, "RBWA: An Efficient Random-Bit Window-based Authentication Protocol", In Proceedings of IEEE GLOBECOM 2003.
6. Jose A. Gutierrez, Edgar H. Callaway Jr, Raymond L. Barrett Jr, "Low-Rate Wireless Personal Area Networks", IEEE Std 802.15.4.
7. Mohammad Ilyas, Imad Mahgoub, "Handbook of Sensor Networks: Compact Wireless and Wired Sensing Systems" CRC PRESS, 2004.
8. J.R. Douceur, "The sybil attack", In IPTPS, pp.215-260, 2002.
9. Agah. Afrand, Das, S.K., Basu, K.," A game theory based approach for security in wireless sensor networks", Performance, Computing, and Communications, 2004, pp. 259 - 263.
10. A. Menezes, P. Oorschot, S. Vanstone, "Handbook of Applied Cryptography", CRC Press, 1997.
11. A. Perrig, R. Szewczyk, V. Wen, D. Culler, D. Tygar, "SPINS: Security Protocols for Sensor Networks", ACM MobiCom, pp. 189-199, July 2001.
12. A. Perrig, J.D. Tygar, "Secure Broadcast Communication in Wired and Wireless Networks", Kluwer Academic Publisher, 2003.
13. S. Capkun, L. Buttyan, J.P. Hubaux, "Self-Organized Public Key Management for Mobile Ad hoc Networks", MobiHoc 2002.

Modelling the Spread of Computer Worms in Vehicular Ad Hoc Networks

Maziar Nekovee

Mobility Research Centre, BT Group
Polaris 134, Adastral Park, Martlesham, Suffolk IP5 3RE, UK

Abstract. Vehicular ad hoc networks (VANET) are likely to become
one of the most relevant forms of mobile ad hoc networks (MANET).
An important challenge in large scale deployment of these networks is
securing them against potential cyberattacks. An attack scenario with
potentially catastrophic consequences is the outbreak of a worm epidemic
in these networks, which can start by infecting the onboard computer of
a single vehicle and spreads through the whole network by transmission
from vehicle to vehicle. In this paper we investigate the outbreak of
worm epidemics in highway traffic by means of modelling and large-scale
simulations. Our study combines a realistic model of node movements
in VANET with a velocity-dependent shadow-fading model of wireless
links between VANET nodes, and takes into account the full topology
of the resulting ad hoc networks . We perform stochastic simulations of
worm spreading under various traffic conditions, both in the absence and
in the presence of preemptive immunization and an interactive patching
process.

1   Introduction

Vehicular ad hoc networks (VANET) are created by vehicles equipped with short
and medium range wireless communication. Communication is possible between
vehicles within each other's radio range, and with fixed gateways along the road.
The ability of vehicles to communicate directly with each other via wireless links
and form ad hoc networks is opening up a plethora of exciting applications [1–3].
These include safety applications, real-time traffic monitoring and management
and broadband wireless access for automobile users, to name a few. Creating
high-speed, highly scalable and secure vehicular networks presents a formidable
research challenge. This is due to a combination of the highly dynamic nature of
VANET, the relatively high speeds involved and the potentially very large scale
of these networks. In the last few years researchers have intensively investigated
many aspects of vehicular communications, and much progress has been made
[4, 5].

Surprisingly, very few groups have addressed the security threats to VANET
[6], and in particular those resulting from cyberattccks by viruses and other form
of malicious software (malware). While the infection of a car's computer system

by a virus can have potentially severe consequences and have raised recent concerns among automobile makers [7], the interlinking of cars into large scale ad hoc networks is opening up the possibility of much more dangerous cyberattacks by computer worms. Unlike viruses, which attach parasitically to a normal program, worms are stand-alone automated malware which propagate thorough a network without any human intervention. In recent years they have emerged as one of the most prominent threats to the security of computer networks [10]. A worm attack on VANET may interfere with critical applications such as engine control and safety warning systems hence resulting in serious congestion on the road networks and large-scale accidents. While there has been much research on the dynamics of worm spreading on the Internet [10, 9, 11], there has been, to our knowledge, very few studies of worm epidemics in mobile ad hoc network in general [12] and vehicular ad hoc networks in particular [13]. Such studies are critical for assessing the risks associated with worm attacks on VANET, and devising effective counter measures and techniques for their detection and mitigation.

In this paper we investigate worm epidemics in VANET by means of modelling and large-scale simulations. Our study combines a realistic microscopic model of the highly correlated node movements in VANET with a velocity-dependent shadow-fading model of wireless links between VANET nodes. Furthermore, in our simulations we take into account the full topology of the resulting ad hoc networks created by vehicles. These ingredients are crucial in providing a correct description of worm dynamics in vehicular ad hoc networks. We describe an stochastic model for worm propagation in the resulting networks, and perform large-scale simulations of worm epidemics under various traffic conditions, both in the absence and in the presence of preemptive immunization and an interactive patching process. Our study shows that worm epidemics in VANET are characterized by an initial linear growth rate which is much slower than the exponential growth observed in worm attacks on fixed networks [10], and predicted by classical epidemiological models. Furthermore, both the spreading rate of a worm and its success in infecting a VANET depend strongly on vehicular mobility patterns and traffic conditions.

The rest of this paper is organized as follows. In section 2 we describe our models of node mobility, wireless communication channel, and worm spreading in vehicular ad hoc networks. In section 3 we use these models to perform stochastic simulations studies of worm propagation in vehicular networks for a range of traffic conditions in highways, and for different worm attack scenarios. We close this paper in section 4 with conclusions.

2 System Models

2.1 Vehicular mobility

The movement of nodes in vehicular ad hoc networks is constrained by the underlying road network, and is dictated by the highly complex phenomena of traffic flow. The available mobility models for MANET, such as random walk and random waypoint model are fundamentally inappropriate to describe the motion of nodes in VANET. Fortunately modelling vehicular traffic has been the subject of much research, and advanced models of traffic are available [14]. Such models can be classified into macroscopic and microscopic models. In macroscopic models traffic is treated as an incompressible fluid, characterized by average density ρ (cars/km), average velocity V (km/h) and average traffic flow $Q = \rho V$. In microscopic models, on the other hand, each car is treated individually and its motion in time and space is described using the so-called car-following models which incorporate the behaviour of drivers in traffic through simple parameterized distance and velocity-dependent interactions between adjacent cars.

In our study we use the intelligent driver model (IDM), which provides a middle ground between high-fidelity but rather complex microscopic models and macroscopic fluid models of vehicular traffic [18]. It has been shown that IDM is capable of reproducing both quantitatively and qualitatively the phenomenology of vehicular traffic. We consider only the steady-state version of IDM and will focus on vehicular traffic in highways. The traffic flow in a given lane of a highway is is then characterized by the mean equilibrium gap S between two adjacent cars, the mean vehicular velocity V, and the mean vehicle density ρ. In the stationary state regime these quantities are related to each other through the following set of equations [18]:

$$S(V) = (S_0 + VT)\left[1 - \left(\frac{V}{V_0}\right)^{\delta}\right]^{-1/2}, \tag{1}$$

and

$$\rho = \frac{1}{l+S}. \tag{2}$$

In the above equations S_0, δ and V_0 are IDM model parameters [18], T is the so-called time headway and l is the car length.

2.2 Channel model

Consider two fixed nodes i and j located at a distance r_{ij} from each other, and assume that node i transmits a radio signal with power p_r, and node j receives this signal with power p_t. In a shadow fading environment the corresponding signal attenuation at node j is modeled as [16]

$$\beta(r_{ij}) = \beta_1(r_{ij}) + \beta_2 \tag{3}$$

where β_1 is a deterministic distance dependent component given by

$$\beta_1 = \alpha log \frac{|r_i - r_j|}{1m} \, dB, \tag{4}$$

where α is the pathloss exponent, with $2 \leq \alpha \leq 4$. Furthermore, β_2 is a random component which, using a log normal shadow fading model, has a normal probability distribution with zero mean and variance σ. The above model only captures distance and fading based attenuation in the wireless channel but does not incorporate the impact of the relative velocity of two communicating nodes. Recent performance measurements for 802.11 based wireless LAN performance in vehicular traffic scenarios [15] show that the link quality has a strong dependence on relative velocity of communicating vehicles. It is therefore important to take this factor into account when modelling inter-vehicular communication, in particular in highways were relative velocity difference of 200 km/h or more can be reached. Following [17] we model this effect by adding a velocity-dependent deterministic component to β_1

$$\tilde{\beta}_1(r_{ij}, v_{ij}) = \beta_1(r_{ij}) - v_1(1 - e^{-v_{ij}/v_o}),$$ (5)

where v_{ij} is the absolute value of the velocity difference between nodes i and j. The above model produces a reasonable fit to recent empirical measurements of the velocity dependence of signal-to-noise ratio [15, 17].

For a given p_t and p_r node i and j can communicate via a direct link if the power attenuation is less than a threshold β_{th}. Using the above normal distribution for β_2, the probability that two nodes can establish a link is given by

$$p_{ij} = = \int_{-\infty}^{\beta_{th} - \tilde{\beta}_1} \exp(-\frac{\beta_2}{2\sigma^2}) d\beta_2$$
$$= \frac{1}{2} + \frac{1}{2}\text{erf}\left(\frac{\beta_{th} - \tilde{\beta}_1(r_{ij}, v_{ij})}{\sqrt{2}\sigma}\right)$$ (6)

2.3 Worm propagation model

Several previous studies have analyzed and modeled the propagation of computer worms on the Internet [10, 9, 11]. Most contemporary Internet worms work as follows. When a computer worm is fired into the Internet, it scans the IP address in an attempt to find a vulnerable machine to infect. When it finds a vulnerable machine it then sends a probe to infect this host. The newly infected host then begins running the worm and tries to infect other machines. A patch, which repairs the security holes of the machine, is used to defend against worms. When an infected or vulnerable machine is patched against a known worm, it becomes immune to that worm. There are several different scanning mechanisms that worms deploy. Two main mechanisms are random scanning and local subnet scanning. In random scanning an infected computer scans the entire IP address space and select its targets randomly from this space. In local scanning the worm scans the nearby targets (e.g. machines on the same subnet) with a higher probability. Many recent worms, such as codeRed v2 have used localized scanning.

Both of the above mechanisms rely on point-to-point IP routing for the propagation of worms, either as UDP or TCP packets. However, due to well-known problems with point-to-point routing in VANET [4, 5] such mechanisms will be highly inefficient in a VANET environment, as most probes sent from an infected vehicle may never arrive at their destination due to frequent network fragmentations. A much more efficient mechanism for disseminating packets through a VANET is multihop forwarding in which a packet propagates along the road by broadcast transmissions from vehicle to vehicle. We assume therefore that worms targeting VANET will utilize multihop forwarding as their method of propagation. With respect to an attacking worm we assume that nodes in a VANET can be in one of the following three states: vulnerable, infected, or immune. Infected nodes try to transmit the worm to their nearest neighbors at every possible opportunity. Vulnerable nodes can become infected at a rate λ when they receive a transmission containing a copy of the worm from an infected neighbor. Finally immune nodes are either immunized prior to the worm attack (this could be the case when a known worm attacks the network) or get patched interactively during the attack at a rate δ.

Finally, the temporal characteristics of the underlying system such as processing and communication delays are likely to have a significant effect on the propagation of worms. In the current study we model the processing time required by worm to complete the infection of a node as a constant value of one clock tick, and assume that the transmission time can be considered instantaneous (or at least is much smaller than the processing time).

3 Simulation studies

In our simulation studies we considered the propagation of a worm in a vehicular ad hoc network consisting of cars moving in a 10km highway corridor, with one lane in each direction. We characterize traffic conditions on the highway by mean-velocity of vehicles and, for simplicity, we assume this velocity to have the same magnitude in both directions. For each velocity the corresponding mean inter-vehicle spacing, S and density per lane, ρ are obtained from Eq. (1-2). For a given density we distribute vehicles randomly and uniformly in each lane, ensuring that there is no overlap between two adjacent vehicles (i.e. the intervehicular distance is always larger than l.) Once vehicles are distributed in this manner, we create an instant of the corresponding ad hoc network by creating a link between any two vehicles i and j with a probability p_{ij}, as given by Eq. (6). The worm spreading dynamics is then simulated on top of this network.

We note that in reality even in equilibrium traffic conditions a vehicular ad hoc network has a highly dynamic connection topology, with links between vehicles being created and broken all the time. However, under equilibrium conditions we expect the timescale at which the topology of the network changes to be much longer than the timescale of virus propagation. This justifies our approach in using 'frozen networks' to study the spreading of viruses in these networks.

The simulations performed in this and the following section were performed using $\alpha = 2$, $\sigma = 2$ and $\beta_{th} = 40$. This results in an effective transmission range of 250 m for each vehicle. Furthermore, in all simulations of worm epidemics the infection rate was fixed at $\lambda = 1$.

3.1 The spreading of unknown worms

First we consider the spread of a an unknown worm in VANET. In this case none of the nodes is immune against the worm and we also assume that there is no mechanism for interactive immunization of nodes.

We infect a random vehicle in the network with the worm and simulate its propagation in VANET under a range of traffic conditions. In order to obtain results which are statistically significant all simulations reported were performed starting from 10 randomly chosen (and different) initial infected vehicles and for each initial infected node the results were averaged over at least 50 simulation runs.

Figure 1 display the propagation of the worm in VANET for several values of mean velocity in the highway, ranging from free flow of cars ($V = 90$ km/h) to congested traffic ($V = 0$ km/h). For comparison we have also plotted the analytical result obtained from the classical susceptible-infected (SI) epidemiologic model for the $V = 0$ km/h case (thick solid line). It can be seen that for all values of V the propagation rate of the worm is initially linear in time, and is significantly slower than the exponential rate predicted by classical epidemiological model [8]. Furthermore, the propagation rate decreases with increasing velocity and, with respect to the final size of the infection, two velocity regimes can be observed. At low velocities and up to $V = 60$ km/h a worm is able to infect the whole network. At higher velocities, however, the network becomes fragmented into many isolated clusters. Thus any virus outbreak from a single car can only infect the cluster to which it belongs. We note that in reality the difference between the two velocity regimes is less sharp than obtained from our simulations since fast moving vehicles, or those moving in opposite directions maybe able to carry the worm between isolated clusters.

Our result is consistent with the findings in [12] which show that epidemiological models greatly overestimate the spreading rate of worms in MANET. On the other hand they refute the findings in a preliminary study of worm spreading in VANET [13]. In this study the authors characterize a VANET only by its average connectivity, instead of full topology. Consequently their simulations are unable to mimic the localized process of worm spreading in these networks which results in a linear initial growth of the epidemic.

3.2 Preemptive immunization

Next we consider attacks by a known worm on VANET and investigate the impact of preemptive immunization on the success of such attacks. Clearly, it is often not the case that all nodes are patched against a known worm and the important question that arises is what fraction of nodes should be immunized in order to effectively prevent the worm from infecting the whole network. To answer this question we performed a set of simulations in which a certain fraction

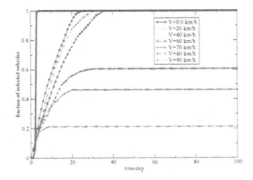

Fig. 1. Dynamics of worm spreading in a 10 km stretch of highway is displayed for a range of mean velocities.

of nodes in the network were selected at random to be immunized prior to infecting another randomly chosen node with the worm. In Fig. 2 results of these simulations are shown for $V = 0$ (congested traffic, top panel) and $V = 40$ km/h, respectively.

It can be seen that in congested traffic pre-emptive immunization is unable to significantly slow down the spread of the worm even when up to 30% of the nodes were immunized prior to the attack. This is due to the fact that under such conditions the average fanout per node is very high, and thus a relatively high number of nodes need to be immunized in order to slow down the spreading of the worm through the network.

3.3 Interactive immunization

Finally we consider the scenario where nodes are patched against the worm in real-time while the worm is spreading in the network. These patches can be downloaded onto VANET nodes by roadside to vehicle communications using, for example, WiFi access points or via a 3G link. Once a node downloads a patch it can send copies to other VANET nodes using multihop forwarding. In the following we shall assume that nodes can be patched at a given rate δ through one or a combination of the above mechanisms, without considering the patching mechanism itself in detail.

Figure 3 (left panel) shows, as an example, the results of our simulations of worm spreading in VANET, where the mean node velocity is set at 40 km/h. It can be seen that while patching does not have a significant impact on the initial spreading rate, it mitigates very effectively a large scale spread of the worm in the network. Even when nodes are immunized at a relatively low rate of $\delta = 0.025$, the maximum fraction of infected nodes is reduced to $\sim 40\%$. Further details of the impact of patching can be seen in Fig. 3 (right panel)

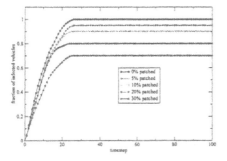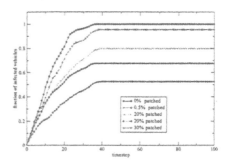

Fig. 2. Worm spreading dynamics in the presence of preemptive random immunization is shown for congested traffic (left panel) and for a tarffic condition charcterized by mean vehicular velocity set at $V = 40$.

where the maximum fraction of infected nodes is plotted versus the patching rate, for VANETs with different mean node velocities. Interactive patching is most effective at higher velocities where the average fanout of VANET nodes is lower. This is in particular the case at low patching rates. For example with $\delta = 0.025$ the worm can infect only 40% when mean velocity is 60 km/h whereas it infects over 60% of the nodes under congested traffic conditions.

4   Conclusions

In this paper we investigated the outbreak of worm epidemics in vehicular ad hoc networks by means of modelling and simulations. We also investigated the effects of preemptive immunization and interactive patching on preventing such worm epidemics. Focusing on highway traffic scenarios we find that that the spreading rate of a worm depends strongly on the mean velocity of vehicles and reaches its highest value in congested traffic, where each car has a very high fanout. In all traffic conditions considered, however, the initial spreading rate is much slower than the exponential spreading rate that has been observed in worm attacks on the Internet. Classical epidemiological models also predict an exponential growth rate and are therefore inadequate for describing worm propagation in VANET. Our study shows that interactive patching, even at a relatively slow rate, can greatly reduce the fraction of vehicles that the worm can infect. On the other hand, preemptive patching is only effective at high velocity conditions. Our results provide quantitative input for devising techniques and algorithms for detection and mitigation of worm epidemics in VANET.

In the present study we did not take into account the limited bandwidth available to VANET nodes and the contention mechanisms for access to radio

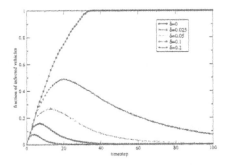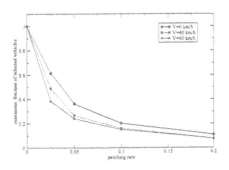

Fig. 3. Left panel shows worm spreading with interactive patching is shown for different patching rates. Right panel shows maximum fraction of infected vehicles is plotted as a function of patching rate is shown at different traffic conditions

channels. We expect these factors to further slow down the rate of worm propagation seen in our simulations. We plan to investigate these effects, and the resulting denial-of-service attcks which may follow as a consequence, in a future study.

References

1. I. Chisaliat and N. Shahmehri. A peer-to-peer approach to vehicular communication for the support of traffic safety applications, in ITSC IEEE, 2002; Safer traffic: Interview with R. Mietzner from Softlab/BMW Group, Eurescome Message, Issue 1, 2005.
2. Drive-thru Internet: IEEE 802.11b for Automobile Users. www.drive-thru-internet.org/index.html
3. Fleetnet www.et2.tu-harburg.du/fleetnet/index.html
4. J. Blum, A. Eskandarian and L. Hoffmman, Challenges of Intervehicle ad hoc networks, IEEE Trans. Intelligent Transportation Systems, Vol. 5, No 4, December 2004.
5. L. Briesmeister, l. Schafters, and G. Hommel, Disseminating messages among highly mobile hosts based on inter-vehicle communication, IEEE Intelligent Vehicle Symposium, Dearbon, MI, Oct 2000.
6. J-P Hubaux, S. Capkun and J. Luo, Security aspects of inter-vehicle communications, IEEE Security & Privacy Magazine, Vol. 2, No. 3, pp 49-55; M. Raya and J-P Hubaux, The security of vehicular networks, Proceedings of STR2005.
7. See, e.g., T. Zeller Jr. and N. Mayersohn, Can a virus hithc a ride in your car?, The New York Times, March 13, 2005; Car computer systems at risk of viruses, CNN technology, August 1, 2005.
8. D. J. Daley and j. Gani, Epidemic modelling: An introduction, Cambridge University Press, 1999.

9. D. Moore and C. Shannon, Code-Red: A case study on the spread of victims of Internet worms, in Proceedings of the 2002 SIGCOMM Internet Measurement Workshop, Marseille, France, pp. 273-248, 2003.

10. T. M. Chen and J-M Robert, Worm epidemics in high-speed networks, IEEE Computer, pp 48-53, June 2004.

11. Z. Chen, L. Gao and K. Kwiat, Modeling the spread of active worms, in Proceedinsg of IEE INFOCOM 2003.

12. R. G. Cole, N. Phamdo, M. Rajab and A. Terzis, Requirements on worm mitigation technologies in MANETS, Proceedings of PADS'05, 2005.

13. S. Khayam and H. Radha, Analyzing the spread of active worms over VANET, Proceedinsg of VANET2004.

14. D. Helbing. Traffic and related self-driven many-particle sytems, Rev. Mod. Phys., Vol. 73 pp. 1067-1141, 2001.

15. J. P.Singh, N. Bambos, B. Srinivassan and D. Clawin, Wireless LAN performance under varied stress conditions in vehicular traffic scenarios, proceedings of Vehicular Technology Conference, Vol. 2, 24-28, 2002.

16. C. Bettstetter and C. Hartmann, Connectivity of wireless multihop networks in a shadow fading environment, Proceedings of MSWIM'03, San Diego, USA, 2003.

17. M. L. Sim, M. Nekovee and Y. F. Ko, Throughput analysis of WiFi based broadband access for mobile users on highways, Proceedings of IEEE MICC/ICON 2005, Kuala Lampur, Malaysia, 2005.

18. M. Treiber, A. Hennecke and D. Helbing, Congested traffic states in empirical observations and microscopic simulations, Phys. Rev. B, Vol. 62, 1805, 2000.

WILY ATTACKERS SEEK WIRELESS NETWORKS IN PERTH, WESTERN AUSTRALIA FOR EASY TARGETS

Suen Yek

School of Computer and Information Science, Edith Cowan University
Perth,Western Australia

syek@student.ecu.edu.au

Abstract. Four rounds of passive wireless packet sniffing were conducted in Perth, Western Australia over two years to determine the nature of wireless network activity occurring in the area and to identify the basic security weaknesses. Trends in the gathered information are discussed in this paper with focus on the application of the Wired Equivalent Privacy and masking of the network name, which are the only security weaknesses detectable by the passive packet sniffer used. The results show that while the detected wireless uptake is growing, mitigation of these basic security weaknesses are declining. Although these results do not conclude on the level of security used in the detected wireless networks, this research highlights the proliferation of opportunities for wily attackers to compromise exposed corporate networks.

Keywords   wireless local area network security, Kismet passive packet sniffing, wireless security options, information broadcasting, masking network presence

1. Introduction

Wireless Local Area Networks (WLANs) are an attractive solution for providing mobile and transparent facilities to the corporate environment. The security options available to protect confidential information in transmission include various forms of encryption and controlling the broadcasting power of the antenna in use. However, these security solutions can be undermined by an attacker with a competing wireless device that gathers information from the airwaves known as packet sniffing. This capability gives opportunity to an attacker to break encrypted passwords and retrieve confidential information [1,2,3] Other hostile attacks include hijacking a wireless connection from legitimate users to collect confidential information, disrupting availability of the wireless services to users, and falsely authenticating to the wireless network, circumventing security to access facilities on the wired network [4].

The detrimental potential of these attacks stress the consequences for unsecured or weakly configured entry points to the corporate network. This paper reports on an empirical study into the exposure of two basic security weaknesses detected in wireless networks. The first is the excessive or redundant broadcasting of network information that can be gathered well out of the physical environment of the corporate users. The second is failure to hide or mask the network's presence in the airwaves so that rogue antennas are not able to eavesdrop from far and undetectable locations.

In Australia, the Australian Communications Authority (ACA) [5] permits a maximum of 4 watts of power to be radiated from an antenna to multiple devices in a point-to-multipoint connection. This amount of power is capable of sending wireless transmissions for up to 26 Kms given a line of sight [6]. Furthermore, narrow beam or high-gain antennas can be constructed or purchased for point-to-point connections, which are permitted up to 10 watts of power. These antennas are capable of reaching over 64 Kms and tuning in to wireless transmissions from remote locations. The ease for an attacker to intercept an organisation's sensitive information surreptitiously is therefore a realistic concern.

The exposure of the basic security weaknesses was observed from collected information in wireless scans using packet sniffing conducted in the Perth Central Business District (CBD) in Western Australia over a two-year period. The passive packet sniffing tool Kismet [7] was used, which captures wireless packets containing network information that organisations were willingly broadcasting into the open airwaves. There was no attempt made to identify or penetrate networks implementing Wi-Fi Protected Access (WPA), Extensible Authentication Protocol (EAP), and Virtual Private Networks (VPNs) as this would breach the Telecommunications Act in Australia [5].

The implications of the collected results show what an attacker could gather, and with further malicious intent, could proceed to target organisations that have not mitigated these basic security weaknesses. Consequently, the detected results in this study show the proliferation of attractive targets for attackers to exploit the confidentiality, integrity, and availability of an organisation's information [8].

2. Method

The scans were conducted in January and August of 2003 [9] and 2004 [10] in the morning and afternoon to account for networks used partially throughout the day. The distance travelled for each scan was approximately 26 Kms and was completed in around one and a half hours. The route incorporated the Perth CBD and several adjacent commercial areas, which was chosen as it yielded a high potential concentration of WLAN deployment and activity. The wireless device that was used for scanning was an IBM ThinkPad, 800MHz Pentium III with a Cabletron/Orinoco

RoamAbout 802.11 Direct Sequence (DS) Peripheral Component (PC) Card, and a Wireless Network Interface Card (WNIC) with a Hermes chipset that supports promiscuous capture using Kismet [7]. At the time, the current version of Kismet 3.0.1 was installed on the laptop, which creates readable files of the network information it collected.

The information that Kismet detects includes the name of the network called a Service Set Identifier (SSID); the Basic Service Set Identifier (BSSID) containing the MAC address of the detected transmitting device; the wireless channel in use of the network; the frequency and wireless protocol used; indication of an infrastructure of ad-hoc type of network; and the status of WEP as a Y/N. Although this information relates to rudimentary network settings, it is sufficient for an attacker to profile an organisation's network and determine if any hardware, software, or protocol weaknesses exist.

Kismet is able to enumerate this information by cycling through the available wireless channels, which in Australia are 1-11 in a promiscuous mode, allowing for non-traceable captures of wireless packets. The tool listens for wireless activity occurring over the 2.4 GigaHertz (GHz) electromagnetic radio frequency spectrum, which the 802.11b and 802.11g protocols operate in. At present, the popularity of wireless devices implementing these protocols are more prevalent than other protocols such as 802.11a and 802.11i, which served to define the scope of this study.

Additional functionality that made Kismet the tool of choice for conducting the research included the tool's ability to detect network names that were masked, and identify the masked name through packet analysis. Other wireless scanning tools include Netstumbler [11], which does not operate in a promiscuous mode, and instead, sends probing wireless packets and does not detect masked networks. Wellenreiter [12] has similar capabilities to Kismet, except for the un-masking feature, and Airsnort [2] passively sniffs wireless transmissions and can recover WEP keys if enough packets are captured.

Kismet was able to detect sufficient information to enumerate the earlier identified basic security weaknesses, which were broadcasting of the network's information outside the physical area of the organisation, and failure to hide the network's presence in the airwaves. It is possible that these capabilities were intended for some of the detected wireless networks; however, the inherent weaknesses still apply and thus, do not offset the conclusions drawn on the security of the detected networks in this study.

3. Results of Broadcasting Beyond the Corporate Environment

The first set of results in Table 1 shows the average number of detected networks over the four rounds of scans conducted. These networks include infrastructure networks that utilise an Access Point (AP) as a gateway for wireless clients to access wired services, and probes from ad-hoc networks where clients connect in a peer-to-peer manner. The results show a growth of detectable networks since January 2003, although the proportion of growth appears to be declining.

Table 1. Average number of networks detected [13]

	Average number of networks detected	% Growth
Round 1 Jan '03	172	n/a
Round 2 Aug '03	315	83%
Round 3 Jan '04	443	41%
Round 4 Aug '04	692	56%

Figure 1 illustrates the number of unique networks that were detected over each scan and Table 2 shows the percentage of growth from each round. Kismet labelled the unique networks as infrastructure, ad-hoc, turbocell and probes. Networks that are identified as turbocell are actually wireless repeaters. Probes can be either a probe request, which is a wireless packet that is sent to search or probe for a network to join; or a probe response, which is sent by a wireless device to a wireless client. Neither are network types, although Kismet identified them as unique networks as shown in the following results.

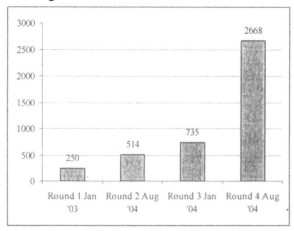

Fig. 1. Total number of unique networks detected [13]

Table 2. Increase in number of unique networks detected over each scan [13]

	Increase in number of unique networks detected	% Growth
Round 1 Jan '03	n/a	n/a
Round 2 Aug '03	255	98%
Round 3 Jan '04	221	43%
Round 4 Aug '04	1933	263%

The significant surge of unique networks detected in round 4 August 2004, shown in Table 2 may be explained through the dissection of probing packets and infrastructure networks from the total amount of unique networks discovered. Figure 2 shows the total number of unique probe requests and response packets enumerated from the total number of unique networks detected in Figure 1. The apparent increase in round 4 August 2004 is due to a 386% growth of detected probing packets, as shown in Table 3.

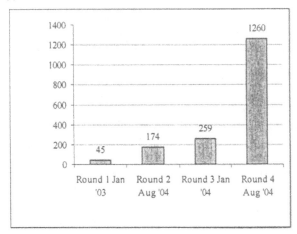

Fig. 2. Total number of unique probe requests and responses [13]

Table 3. Increase in number of unique probe requests and responses [13]

	Increase in number of unique probe requests and responses	% Growth
Round 1 Jan '03	n/a	n/a
Round 2 Aug '03	170	378%
Round 3 Jan '04	85	49%
Round 4 Aug '04	1001	386%

A possible explanation for the significant increase of probing activity may be from a growing number of wireless clients using Windows XP, which has a default setting of periodically probing for an AP that has stronger signal strength. Alternatively, the probe requests may have been from wireless clients connected in an ad-hoc network, or they may be from wireless clients seeking a network to join by sending randomly timed requests. The probe responses may be from APs performing their periodic broadcast for wireless clients to join.

However, these results are not indicative of the number of ad-hoc networks that were detected, but suggest that this rise in overall network activity is largely due to the increase of probe requests and responses. This apparent ubiquity of wireless activity in the airwaves suggests that an attacker employing active methods of scanning, such as probing wireless networks for their information, could be well disguised amongst the sea of wireless traffic.

Figure 3 shows the total number of unique infrastructure networks from the total amount of unique networks that were detected. To determine which of the infrastructure networks were unique, the MAC address was identified in the BSSID of the captured wireless packets. Table 4 shows that the initial growth was nearly consistent at 41% and 42%, followed by a near doubled increase in round 4 August 2004.

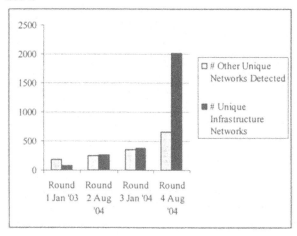

Fig. 3. Total number of unique infrastructure networks [13]

Table 4. Increase in number of unique infrastructure networks detected [13]

	Increase in number of unique infrastructure networks	% Growth
Round 1 Jan '03	n/a	n/a
Round 2 Aug '03	74	41%
Round 3 Jan '04	106	42%
Round 4 Aug '04	295	82%

The implications of these results are the growing number of infrastructure networks that exist in the Perth city area that are broadcasting their presence outside of the corporate walls. This was deduced because the packet sniffing was conducted from the inside of a vehicle that travelled over major public roads, around parks and through residential areas. Given the widespread exposure that many of these networks were transmitting over, it may be assumed that these organisations have not taken measures to restrict the broadcasting ability of their antennas and APs. Consequently, they have neglected to mitigate this basic security weakness by restricting access of their confidential information to outsiders.

An attacker could assemble similar artefacts to those used in the study and gather the same information without the knowledge of these organisations. From the rich selection of wireless networks available in the results given earlier, an attacker could seek the most visibly insecure networks to target. Kismet identifies wireless networks that use WEP and mask the network name as part of the network settings. An attacker could target networks that do not use these security settings because they may seem like easy targets compared to networks that appear secured and would require additional effort to compromise.

The use/non-use of WEP and masking of the network name does not indicate the level of security applied to the wireless network, nor is it the aim of this study to suggest this. The use of third party security is not detectable using passive methods of packet sniffing. Identifying any alternate use of security in a wireless network would require an active method of probing which is prohibited by law, and likely to be detected by a network Wireless Intrusion Detection System (WIDS). Hence, they were not examined in this study.

4. Results of Hiding the Network Presence in the Airwaves

The reporting of the following results focuses on the basic security weakness of failure to hide the network's presence in the airwaves by broadcasting the settings in use on the wireless network. The use of WEP and masking of the network names are two settings that may denote to an attacker that a network is potentially a weakly configured and easy target.

Table 5 shows the relationship between the growth of WEP enabled infrastructure networks and the growth of infrastructure networks that were detected. These results indicate that initially, WEP uptake increased by 10% while detected infrastructure networks increased by 1% from round 2 August 2003 to round 3 January 2004. Subsequently increases in WEP were 20% and increases in infrastructure networks were 40% from round 3 January 2004 to round 4 August 2004. These results suggest that the proportion of detected infrastructure networks that are using WEP is declining, although this is not an indication of security.

Table 5. Total number of infrastructure networks with WEP enabled [13]

	% Growth in infrastructure networks	With WEP enabled
Round 1 Jan '03	n/a	107
Round 2 Aug '03	41%	143
Round 3 Jan '04	42%	206
Round 4 Aug '04	82%	337

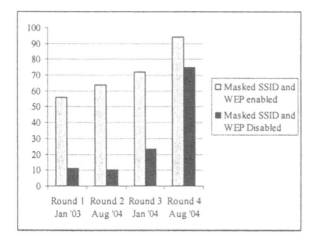

Fig. 4. Number of infrastructure networks detected with a masked SSID with WEP and without WEP enabled [13]

Figure 4 shows the number of networks that masked their SSID-network name, with and without WEP enabled; taken from the total number of infrastructure networks detected. The results in Table 6 show a substantial rise in the number of infrastructure networks that are masking their network name, particularly in round 4 August 2004 with a surge of 78%. This suggests that these organisations are limiting what an attacker or outsider may detect from packet sniffing, given that the SSID setting must be identified to connect to the wireless network. The additional use of WEP shows a 1% decline, followed by an 18% increase from round 3 January 2004 to round 4 August 2004. Networks without WEP enabled increased by over 100% on each round of scans, albeit the first.

Table 6. Total number of infrastructure networks detected with a masked SSID with WEP and without WEP enabled [13]

	% Growth of infrastructure networks with masked SSID	Infrastructure networks with masked SSID & WEP	% Growth of WEP users	Infrastructure networks with masked SSID & WEP disabled	% Growth of non WEP users
Round 1 Jan '03	n/a	56	n/a	11	n/a
Round 2 Aug '03	10%	64	14%	10	-1%
Round 3 Jan '04	28%	72	13%	23	103%
Round 4 Aug '04	78%	94	31%	75	226%

These trends may indicate that organisations deploying the detected infrastructure networks are aware that masking an SSID is a security option that can minimise foreign probing wireless clients that are not part of the organisation's WLAN. The decline in WEP adoption may suggest that other security solutions are in use or that no encryption is used at all. This may not be determined from the collected results.

Figure 5 shows the number of infrastructure networks that did not adopt a masked SSID, with and without WEP enabled. Table 7 shows the growth trends for these networks. An initial drop was shown in the number of detected infrastructure networks without a masked SSID, followed by a 30% rise. While the growth of WEP networks appeared to increase, the growth of non-WEP networks declined and then surged by 44%. Networks that did not mask their SSID and did not employ WEP may appear as the most attractive targets to an attacker seeking a network with the least amount of visibly detected security. These networks may be deploying third party security; however, broadcasting of the network name provides an attacker with a potential opportunity to attempt to connect to the wireless network.

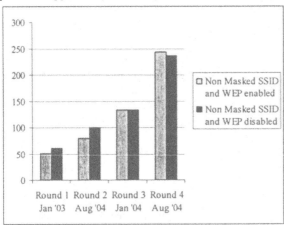

Fig. 5. Number of infrastructure networks detected without a masked SSID with WEP and without WEP enabled [13]

No explanation can be given for the rise and falls in growth of the detected wireless networks, nor can there be deductions on the fluctuations in numbers masking the SSID and using WEP. However, the results do indicate the number of networks that are broadcasting their network settings, which are detectable by passive packet sniffing. Moreover, an attacker may use this information to determine which networks are likely to be easier targets based on a lack of masking the network name and not using WEP. Alternatively, networks that do employ WEP may be cracked due to its inherent weaknesses.

Table 7. Total number of infrastructure networks detected without a masked SSID with WEP and without WEP enabled [13]

	% Growth in infrastructure networks without a masked SSID	Infrastructure networks without a masked SSID & with WEP	% Growth of WEP users	Infrastructure networks without a masked SSID & without WEP	% Growth of non WEP users
Round 1 Jan '03	n/a	51	n/a	61	n/a
Round 2 Aug '03	60%	79	55%	100	64%
Round 3 Jan '04	49%	134	70%	133	33%
Round 4 Aug '04	79%	243	81%	236	77%

5. Conclusion

The transparency of wireless networks has presented organisations with new challenges in securing the transmission of confidential information. While it is unlawful and difficult to ascertain the amount of security an organisation implements in their wireless network, it is possible to distinguish the number of corporate networks that are broadcasting outside of their physical environment, and networks that do not hide or mask their presence in the airwaves.

The results of this study show that although there is a declining growth in the number of detected networks, there is a significant surge of probing packets sent between wireless clients and APs. This indicates that the number of individual wireless users may be increasing and the likelihood of an outsider connecting to an organisation's corporate network, whether accidentally or intentionally could rise significantly. Additionally, the growth of detectable infrastructure networks, most likely belonging to organisations, suggests a growing problem of corporate networks broadcasting outside of their required area of usage or perimeter walls.

There are basic measures to take in securing a wireless network. Firstly, to reduce the power outage of the antennas that is used to transmit information. The default setting of an AP connected with an antenna may be to broadcast at full power, or at an unnecessarily high power, which is not required for the organisation's use. Reducing the power of the antenna's transmission can aid this leakage problem of broadcasting to outsiders of the organisation.

The study also reported on the growth of networks that implemented settings that masked the network name and enabled WEP. These results did not indicate the security of the networks. With similar growth trends of networks not masking their SSID and not implementing WEP, these networks could be the most attractive targets for an attack. Taking measures to mask the network name from broadcasts and minimising or disabling many of the settings that an AP periodically transmits would control this problem. Corporate clients of the wireless network should be pre-configured with the required settings and not have to probe for these rudimentary network settings.

Overall, the proliferation of detectable wireless networks that are broadcasting into the open areas of the Perth CBD provides attackers with an abundance of targets to intercept and potentially access the confidential information and services on the corporate network. It is intended to expand the study by conducting interviews or surveys into wireless usage and security to observe the trends of these basic security weaknesses within the corporate environment. Wireless networks that do not implement the basic security measures of restricting the distance of antenna transmission and masking details about the network's settings are placing themselves at risk.

6. References

[1] Fluher, S., Mantin, I., & Shamir, A. (2001). *Penetration testing: weaknesses in the key scheduling algorithm of RC4*. Retrieved 31 March, 2004, from http://lists.insecure.org/lists/pen-test/2001/Aug/0012.html

[2] Hegerle, B., & Bruestle, J. (2004). AirSnort (Version 0.2.3a).

[3] Pfleeger, C., & Pfleeger, S. (2003). *Security in computing* (3rd ed.). New Jersey: Pearson Education Inc.

[4] Valli, C., & Wolski, P. (2004). *802.11b wireless networks insecure at any speed.* Paper presented at the SAM2004, Las Vegas.

[5] Australian Communications Authority. (1997). *Telecommunications ACT 1997*. Retrieved November 4, 2004, from http://www.austlii.edu.au/au/legis/cth/consol_act/ta1997214/

[6] The Certified Wireless Network Professional Training & Certification Program. (2003). Certified wireless network administrator: Official study guide. Georgia: Planet3 Wireless Inc.

[7] Kershaw, M. (2004). Kismet (Version 2004-04-R1).

[8] Welch, D. J., & Lathrop, S. (2003). *A survey of 802.11a wireless security threats and security mechanisms*. New York: Information Technology and Operations Center.

[9] Webb, S. (2003). *Identifying trends in 802.11b networks in Perth*. Paper presented at the Australian Computer Network, Information & Forensics Conference, Perth.

[10] Yek, S., & Bolan, C. (2004, 26 November). *An analysis of security in 802.11b and 802.11g wireless networks in Perth, W.A.* Paper presented at the

2nd Australian Computer Network, Information & Forensics Conference, Perth, W.A.

[11]   Milner, M. (2004). Netstumbler (Version 0.4).

[12]   SourceForge. (2004). Wellenreiter (Version 1.9).

[13]   Yek, S., & Bolan, C. (2003). *A comparative study of wireless scans conducted in Perth, Western Australia and their network security implications* (report). Perth: Edith Cowan University.

SECTION III: Network Protocol Analysis & Cryptographic Applications

Attack on Undeniable Partially Blind Signatures

Song Han[1], Elizabeth Chang[1], and Jie Wang[2]

[1] School of Information Systems,
Curtin Business School,
Curtin University of Technology,
GPO Box U1987, WA 6845, Australia
[2] National Natural Science Foundation of China,
Shuangqing Road, Haidian District,
Beijing 100086, China

Abstract. Blind signatures allow a user to get a signature on any message without revealing the content of the message to the signer. Partially blind signatures allow the signer to explicitly include common information in the blind signature under some agreement with the user. Undeniable signatures can only be verified with the help of the signer. However, if a signature is only verifiable with the aid of the signer, a dishonest signer may disavow a genuine document. Undeniable signatures solve this problem by adding a new component called the disavowal protocol in addition to the normal components of signature and verification. Disavowal protocol can prevent a dishonest signer from disavowing a valid signature. The convertible undeniable signatures allow the signer to convert given signatures into universally verifiable signatures. To combine all the above characteristics, Huang et al. proposed a convertible undeniable partially blind signature scheme at IEEE AINA 2005. They extended the concept of partially blind signature to the convertible undeniable partially blind signature, in which only the signer can verify given signatures on messages, and confirm/disavow the validity/invalidity of given signatures, and convert them into universally verifiable signatures. However, their scheme is not secure. In this paper, we present an attack on the convertible undeniable partially blind signature scheme.

Keywords: Attack, Blind signature, Partially blind signature; Security protocol; Convertible undeniable signature.

1 Introduction

The concept of blind signatures was first introduced by Chaum [1] in 1982. A blind signature scheme allows a user to get a signature on any message m without revealing the content of the message to the signer. This blindness property plays a central role in real-world privacy-preserving protocols, such as electronic cash, electronic voting and selective disclosure protocols, where privacy is of great concern [2]. However, the signer has no control over the attributes except for those bound by the public key, and then the signatures may be used in an illegal way. Therefore, the concept of partially blind signatures [3] was proposed in 1996 to overcome the above weakness. Partially blind signatures allow the signer to explicitly include common information in the blind signature under some agreement with the user.

However, both the blind signatures [1, 6, 26, 27] and the partially blind signatures [3, 19] have the 'self-authenticating' property that anyone having a copy of any signature can check its validity using the corresponding public information, and signatures can be transferred in any way by anyone. From the signer's point of view, that will jeopardize the privacy of the signer. Therefore, it is necessary to merge the privacy-preserving or selective disclosure property into the blind signatures as well as the partially blind signatures.

Undeniable signatures were first introduced in 1989 [5]. One of the primary features of undeniable signature is that a signature can only be verified with the help of the signer. This protects the signer against the possibility that documents signed by herself are duplicated and distributed without her approval. However, if a signature is only verifiable with the aid of the signer, a dishonest signer may disavow a genuine document. Undeniable signatures solve this problem by adding a new component called the disavowal protocol in addition to the normal components of signature and verification. Disavowal protocol can prevent a dishonest signer from disavowing a valid signature. Therefore, undeniable signatures [7, 11, 13, 17, 23, 24] can be applied to this scenario: a software company is selling a useful software. To ensure that their software is virus-free, they embed an undeniable signature into each copy of the software. However, they hope that only legitimate buyers of the software are able to verify the signature. At the same time, if copies of the software are found to contain a virus, the software company should not be able to disavow a valid signature in the copies of the software.

The notion of designated verifier proofs was integrated into the design of undeniable signatures [21, 24, 25]. For example, a voting center can give a voter a proof that his vote was actually counted without giving him the opportunity to convince someone else of his vote. The use of designated verifier proof can provide non-interactive and non-transferable confirmation and disavowal protocols for undeniable signatures. This is because the verifier can use his private key to generate a valid proof, but he cannot convince other parties that a signer actually signed a message or not.

A variant of undeniable signature is the designated confirmer signatures [8, 9, 11, 12, 16, 22, 23]. It involves three parties: the signer, the confirmer and the recipient. If the signer is unavailable to confirm the signature , the confirmer can confirm for the recipient. The recipient of the signature cannot convince anyone else of the validity of the signature. The construction of designated confirmer signatures uses zero-knowledge proof [20] in the confirmation protocol. In order for the verifier to be convinced of the validity of the signatures, the confirmer and verifier interact in a zero-knowledge proof in which the confirmer proves to the verifier what he got is indeed a valid confirmer signature, while the verifier is unable to transfer the convince to other party.

In some situations, an undeniable signature needs to be transferred to a universally verifiable signature. In [5], Michels and Stadler extended the undeniable signature to the convertible undeniable signature supporting designated-verifier verification, in which the signer can convert given signatures into universally verifiable signatures. A number of convertible undeniable signatures were proposed [4, 10, 19].

Recently, Huang et at. proposed a convertible undeniable partially blind signature scheme [15]. They extended the concept of partially blind signature to the convertible undeniable partially blind signature, in which only the signer can verify given signatures, and confirm/disavow the validity/invalidity of given signatures to the verifier, and convert given signatures into universally verifiable signatures. They did not use the notion of designated verifier proofs in the confirmation protocol and disavowal protocol. They utilized the interactive zero-knowledge proof in the confirmation and disavowal protocols. That is, the signer and the verifier need to interact with each other for proving the validity or invalidity of the given signature. In this paper we present an attack on Huang at al.'s convertible undeniable partially blind signature scheme. We show that the signer can disavow any valid signature.

Why does the proposed attack on the undeniable partially blind signatures work? The principle behind this attack is that the signer of the signature scheme may be malicious or unreliable. For example, the signer may not comply with the procedures of the signature scheme; the signer may send an incorrect response to the receiver/verifier's challenge. However, the receiver/verifier is complying with the procedures of the signature scheme. This will lead to an acceptable round of communication to the receiver/verifier. That is, the receiver/verifier will accept the verification/disavowal process of the underlying signatures. Therefore, the signer would be successful in the attack on the undeniable partially blind signatures.

The organization of the rest of the paper is as follows: we review Huang et al.'s convertible undeniable partially blind signature scheme in section 2. We present an attack on the disavowal protocol of the signature scheme in section 3. In section 4, we conclude this paper.

2 Review on Undeniable partially blind signatures

We first review Huang et al.'s convertible undeniable partially blind signature scheme, and present the same settings in [15].

The system parameters are $\{p; q; g; \langle g \rangle; H(\cdot); F(\cdot)\}$, where p and q are large primes that satisfy $q|(p-1)$, and g is an element in Z_p^* with order q. Let $\langle g \rangle$ denote a subgroup in Z_p^* generated by g. We assume that there exists no algorithm running in expected polynomial time which decides with non-negligible probability better than guessing whether two discrete logarithms are equal. Let $H : \{0,1\}^* \mapsto Z_q$ and $F : \{0,1\}^* \mapsto \langle g \rangle$ be public secure hash functions. All arithmetic operations are done in Z_p in the following.

The signer's private and public key pair is $\{x, y = g^x\}$, where x is odd.

2.1 Convertible Undeniable Partially Blind Signature

Sign: To sign a message m, the user (requester) and the signer first agree on a common information $info$ in a predetermined way.

(1) The signer chooses $k, c, d \in_R Z_q^*$, computes $z = F(y\|info)$, $a = y^k$, $b = g^c z^d$, and then sends a, b to the user.

(2) The user chooses $t_1, t_2, t_3, t_4 \in_R Z_q^*$, computes $z = F(y\|info)$, $\alpha = a^{t_1} y^{t_2}$, $\beta = b^{t_1} g^{t_3} z^{t_4}$, $\epsilon = H(\alpha\|\beta\|z\|y\|info\|m)$, $e = (\epsilon - t_4) t_1^{-1} (\text{mod } q)$, and sends e to the signer.

(3) The signer computes $s = e - d(\text{mod } q)$, $r = k - sx(\text{mod } q)$, and then sends (r, s, c, d) and proves $\log_g(g^r y^s) = \log_y a$ to the user using **ZKP** (See [15] for the details of ZKP).

(4) If the sender accepts, computes $\rho = rt_1 + t_2(\text{mod } q)$, $\omega = st_1(\text{mod } q)$, $\sigma = ct_1 + t_3(\text{mod } q)$, $\delta = dt_1 + t_4(\text{mod } q)$, and publishes the signature $\{\rho, \omega, \sigma, \delta\}$ on message m with common information $info$. Otherwise, outputs **False**.

Verification: The signer can verify a given signature $\{\rho, \omega, \sigma, \delta\}$ by checking whether

$$z = F(y\|info),$$

$$\omega + \delta = H((g^\rho y^\omega)^x \| g^\sigma z^\delta \| z \| y \| info \| m).$$

Confirmation or Disavowal: Given an alleged signature $\{\rho, \omega, \sigma, \delta\}$ on a message m,

Step 1. The signer (the prover) computes $A = g^\rho y^\omega$ and $B = A^x$.

Step 2. The signer then sends (A, B) and proves $\log_A B = \log_g y$ to the verifier using **ZKP**.

Step 3. The verifier checks whether

$$A = g^\rho y^\omega, \tag{1}$$

$$z = F(y\|info), \tag{2}$$

$$\omega + \delta = H(B \| g^\sigma z^\delta \| z \| y \| info \| m). \tag{3}$$

If they all hold, the verifier accepts the signature as valid; otherwise, invalid.

Selective conversion: When the signer wants to convert a given signature $\sigma_{m,info} = \{\rho, \omega, \sigma, \delta\}$ into a universally verifiable one, he computes

$$A = g^\rho y^\omega,$$

$$B = A^x,$$

$$(c', s') = SEQDL(g, A, y, B, \sigma_{m,info}),$$

and publishes the receipt (c', s', B).

Universally verification: Anyone can verify the signature $\sigma_{m,info}$ with the receipt (c', s', B) by checking

$$c' = H(g\|g^\rho y^\omega\|y\|B\|g^{s'} y^{c'}\|(g^\rho y^\omega)^{s'} B^{c'}\|\sigma_{m,info}),$$

$$\omega + \delta = H(B\|g^\sigma z^\delta\|z\|y\|info\|m).$$

2.2 Security of Huang et al.'s Scheme

Huang et al. proved and claimed that their scheme has the following security properties. See [15] for the details.
(1) Completeness;
(2) Unforgeability;
(3) Untransferability;
(4) Blindness;
(5) Zero-knowledge and uncheatable.

3 Attack on Undeniable Partially Blind Signatures

In this section, we provide an attack on Huang et al.'s convertible undeniable partially blind signatures. We show that the signer can disavow any valid signature to the verifier. In other words, we show that the disavowal of their scheme is not uncheatable.

Assume $\sigma_{m,info} = \{\rho, \omega, \sigma, \delta\}$ is a valid undeniable partially blind signature on a message m with a predetermined agreeable common information $info$. Then, the signer can make the verifier accept the signature as invalid through the following interaction:

Step 1. The signer selects $s \in_R Z_q^*$, computes $A = y^{s\rho}$ and $B = A^x$, and sends (A, B) to the verifier.

Step 2. The verifier chooses $a, b \in_R Z_q^*$, computes $\alpha = A^a g^b$, and sends α to the signer.

Step 3. The signer chooses $t \in_R Z_q^*$, computes $\beta_1 = \alpha g^t$ and $\beta_2 = \beta_1^x$, and sends (β_1, β_2) to the verifier.

Step 4. The verifier sends (a, b) to the signer.

Step 5. If $\alpha = A^a g^b$, the signer sends t to the verifier.

Step 6. The verifier checks whether:

$$\beta_1 = A^a g^{b+t},$$

$$\beta_2 = B^a y^{b+t}.$$

If both of them hold, then the verifier accepts that $\log_A B = \log_g y$. Therefore, she believes that the signer does not cheat her. Otherwise, the signer is cheating her.

Step 7. The verifier checks whether:

$$A = g^\rho y^\omega,$$

$$z = F(y\|info),$$

$$\omega + \delta = H(B\|g^\sigma z^\delta\|z\|y\|info\|m).$$

These equations are the checking conditions of the **Confirmation or Disavowal** in Equation (1), (2) and (3) in section 2.

It is easy to see that

$$A \neq g^\rho y^\omega,$$

and

$$\omega + \delta \neq H(B\|g^\sigma z^\delta\|z\|y\|info\|m).$$

Therefore, the conditions in Equation (1), (2) and (3) do not hold. This results in that the verifier will accept that the signature is invalid.

From the above interaction, we have shown that the signer can disavow any valid signature to the verifier. That is, we have shown that Huang et al.'s convertible undeniable partially blind signature scheme has no soundness with respect to the disavowal protocol of the scheme [15]. Soundness means that the signer can not cheat the verifier with non-negligible probability. Therefore, Huang et al.'s scheme is not secure.

4   Conclusion

In this paper, we have shown that Huang et al.'s convertible undeniable partially blind signature scheme is not secure. To show it, we present an attack on Huang at al.'s convertible undeniable partially blind signature scheme. In this attack, the signer can disavow any valid signature. Thus, the signer can cheat the verifier. Therefore, their signature scheme has no soundness from the undeniable signature point of view.

Acknowledgment

The authors would present theirs thanks to the anonymous reviewers.

This work is supported by the Curtin Research Fellowship and ARC Funding within the Centre for Extended Enterprises and Business Intelligence and School of Information Systems at Curtin Business School, Curtin University of Technology.

References

1. D. Chaum, Blind signatures for untraceable payments, In: Advances in Cryptology Proceedings of CRYPTO'82, Prenum Publishing Corporation, 1982, pp.199-204.

2. T. Balopoulos, S. Gritzalis, S. K. Katsikas, Specifying privacy-preserving protocols in typed msr, Computer Standards & Interfaces, v 27 (5), June 2005, pp. 501-512.
3. M. Abe, E. Fujisaki, How to date blind signatures, In: Advances in Cryptology ASIACRYPT'96, Lecture Notes in Computer Science, Vol.1163, Springer- Verlag, Berlin, 1996, pp.244-251.
4. J. Boyar, D. Chaum, I. Damgard, T. Pedersen, Convertible undeniable signatures, Advances in Cryptology - Crypto'90, Lecture Notes in Computer Science vol. 537, Springer, pp. 189-208, 1990.
5. D. Chaum, H. van Antwerpen, Undeniable signatures, Advances in Cryptology - Crypto'89, Lecture Notes in Computer Science vol. 435, Springer-Verlag, pp. 212-216, 1989.
6. A. Boldyreva: Threshold signatures, multisignatures and blind signatures based on the Gap-Diffie-Hellman-Group signature scheme. Public Key Cryptography 2003: 31-46.
7. D. Chaum, Zero-knowledge undeniable signatures, Advances in Cryptology - Crypto'90, Lecture Notes in Com- puter Science vol. 473, Springer-Verlag, pp. 458-464, 1990.
8. J. Camenisch, M. Michels, Confirmer Signature Schemes Secure against Adaptive Adversaries. In: Preneel B, ed. Proceedings of the Advances in Cryptology- EUROCRYPT 2000. LNCS 1807, Springer- Verlag, Berlin, 2000. 243-258.
9. D. Chaum, Designated Confirmer Signatures, In: De Santis A, ed. Proceedings of the Advances in Cryptology- EUROCRYPT '94. LNCS 950, Springer-Verlag, Berlin, 1994. 86-89. 11
10. I. Damgard, T. Pedersen, New convertible undeniable signature schemes, Advances in Cryptology - Eurocrypt'96, Lecture Notes in Computer Science vol. 1070, pp. 372-386, Springer-Verlag, 1996.
11. S. D. Galbraith, W. Mao, Invisibility and anonymity of undeniable and confirmer signatures, In: M. Joye, ed. Topics in Cryptology CT-RSA 2003, Springer, LNCS 2612, 2003, 80-97.
12. S. Goldwasser, E. Waisbard, Transformation of Digital Signature Schemes into Designated Confirmer Signature Schemes, First Theory of Cryptography Conference, TCC 2004, LNCS 2951, Springer-Verlag, Heidelberg, 2004, 77-100.
13. R. Gennaro,H. Krawczyk, T. Rabin. RSA-based Undeniable Signatures. In: Burt Kaliski ed. Proceedings of the Advances in Cryptology-Crypto '97, LNCS 1294, Springer-Verlag, Berlin, 1997, 132-149.
14. F. Yang, J. Jan. A provable secure scheme for partially blind signatures. IACR eprint 2004/230.
15. Z. Huang, Z. Chen, Y. Wang, Convertible undeniable partially blind signatures, in: Proceedings of the IEEE 19th International Conference on Advanced Information Networking and Applications (AINA'05), Volum 1, Tamkang University, Taiwan, March 28-30, 2005, pp. 609-614.
16. Y. Li, D.Y. Pei, A New Designated Confirmer Signature Variant with Intended Recipient. IACR eprint 2004/288.
17. B. Libert and J.Quisquater, ID-based undeniable signatures, Advances in CT-RSA 2004, LNCS 2964, Springer-Verlag, Heidelberg, 2004. 112- 125.
18. M. Michels, M. Stadler, Generic constructions for secure and efficient confirmer signature schemes. In: Nyberg K, ed. Proceedings of the Advances in Cryptology-EUROCRYPT '98, LNCS 1403, Springer- Verlag, Berlin, 1998, 406-412.
19. M. Michels, M. Stadler, Efficient convertible undeniable signature schemes, in: Proceedings of Workshop on Selected Areas in Cryptography, (SAC'97), Ottawa, Canada, 1997, pp.231-244.

20. K. Nguyen, F. Bao, Y. Mu, V. Varadharajan: Zero-Knowledge Proofs of Possession of Digital Signatures and Its Applications. International Conference on Information and Communications Security, ICICS 1999: 103-118.

21. M. Jakobsson, K. Sako, R. Impagliazzo, Designated Verifier Proofs and Their Applications, Advances in Cryp- tology - Eurocrypt'96, Lecture Notes in Computer Science vol. 1070, Springer-Verlag, pp. 143-154, 1996.

22. T. Okamoto, Designated confirmer signatures and public-key encryption are equivalent. In: Desmendt YG, ed. Proceedings of the Advances in Cryptology- Crypto '94. LNCS 839, Springer-Verlag, Berlin, 1994. 61-74.

23. T. Pedersen: Distributed Provers with Applications to Undeniable Signatures (Extended abstract), In: Donald W. Davies ed. Proceedings of the Advances in Cryptology- EUROCRYPT '91, LNCS 547, Springer-Verlag, Berlin, 1991. 221-242.

24. A. Fujioka, T. Okamoto, K. Ohta, Interactive Bi-Proof Systems and undeniable signature schemes, Advances in Cryptology - Eurocrypt'91, Lecture Notes in Computer Science vol. 547, pp. 243-256, Springer-Verlag, 1991.

25. D. Pointcheval, Self-Scrambling Anonymizers, Proceedings of Financial Cryptography 2002, Lecture Notes in Computer Science vol. 1962, Springer-Verlag, pp. 259-275, 2001.

26. D. Pointcheval, J. Stern, Security arguments for digital signatures and blind signatures, Journal of Cryptology, vol. 13-Number 3, pp. 361-396, 2000.

27. J. Camenisch, M. Koprowski, B. Warinschi, Efficient blind signatures without random oracles. Security in Communication Networks (SCN 2004), LNCS 3352, pp. 134-148.

EVOLUTIONARY APPROACH IN THE SECURITY PROTOCOLS DESIGN

Pavel Ocenasek

Faculty of Information Technology, Brno University of Technology,
Czech Republic

ocenaspa@fit.vutbr.cz

Abstract. This paper proposes an evolutionary method that serves for designing security protocols. The principles of security protocols are outlined, followed by the specification of modal logic that is used to encode the belief and knowledge of communicating parties. The second part introduces the evolutionary optimization framework and proposes the techniques that can be used to automatically evolve basic security protocols.

Keywords. Security protocol, design, verification, modal logic, genetic algorithm, evolution, chromosome, crossover, state space exploring

1 Introduction

The increasing popularity of distributed computing and applications like internet banking and electronic commerce has created both tremendous risks and opportunities. Many of risks stem from security breaches, which can be ruinously expensive. One of the cornerstones of security is the use of security (cryptographic) protocols in which information is exchanged in a way intended to provide security guarantees.
Security protocols are becoming widely used and many new protocols are being proposed. Since security protocols are notoriously difficult to design, computer assistance in the design process is desirable.
In this paper we describe an evolutionary technique that may be useful in designing new security protocols. This approach supports the formalization in a BAN logic [4]. In the first part we outline the principles of security protocols and introduce a BAN logic. Then we explain a principle of genetic algorithms and show how they can be applied to the protocols design.

2 Security protocol

Security protocols are intended for secure communication of subjects over an insecure
network. A crucial goal is to prevent a spy from reading the contents of messages
addressed to others (secrecy). Most security protocols also guarantee an authenticity.
This means that if a message appears to be from subject A, then A sent precisely this
message and it contains the indication of its integrity.

Because security protocols may contain certain flaws, finding such attacks is the
purpose of formal validation using various approaches [5] [1] [2].

2.1 Introduction

A protocol is a recipe that describes how subjects should act to achieve some goal.
Protocols are often described using informal notation, for example as a sequence of
instructions explaining the actions taken by the subjects.

Each step describes an event A → B: X, which states that A exchanges the message X
with B. Messages consists of atoms, like subject names and nonces (randomly
generated strings), and are composed by tupling. Moreover, messages may be
encrypted using keys of subjects.

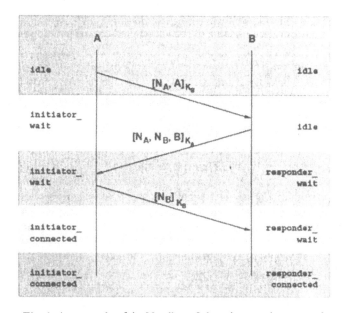

Fig. 1. An example of the Needham-Schroeder security protocol

However, describing the protocol components, cryptographic properties and
requirements in details is beyond the scope of this paper. For more information please
refer e.g. to [6].

2.2 BAN logic

For protocol description we decided to use the BAN logic. BAN logic (researched by Burrow, Abadi, Needham) [4] [2] [3] is a modal logic with primitives that describes the beliefs of subjects involved in a cryptographic protocol. Using the inference rules of BAN logic the evolution of the beliefs of subjects during a cryptographic communication can be studied. Here we present some typical rules.

The BAN-formalism is built on three sorts of objects: the subjects involved in a security protocol, the encryption/decryption and signing/verification keys that the subjects possess, and the messages exchanged between subjects. The notation $\{M\}_K$ denotes a message encrypted using a key K. For a symmetric key K we have $\{\{M\}_K\}_K = M$ for any message M i.e., decrypting with key K a message M that is encrypted with K reveals the contents M. For a key pair <EK, DK> of a public encryption key EK and a private decryption key DK it holds that $\{\{M\}_{EK}\}_{DK} = M$ for any message M. Likewise, for a key pair <SK, VK> of a private signing key SK and a public verification key VK it holds $\{\{H\}_{SK}\}_{VK} = H$ for any hash value H. Hash values are obtained by application of a one-way collision-free hash-function. Proving the hash value H(m) of a message m is a mean to demonstrate that m is known, without revealing it.

In BAN we have a number of operators describing the beliefs of subjects, for which the usual modal properties apply, like P believes (A → B) → (P believes A → P believes B). On the top of that we have the operators sees and possesses. The following rules are illustration of some of the authentication and encryption rules:

(1)   *P believes secret (K, P, Q) ∧ P sees {X}$_K$*
         → P believes Q said X
(2)   *P believes belongs.to (VK, Q) ∧ P sees {X}$_{SK}$*
         → P believes Q said X
(3)   *P believes fresh (X) ∧ P believes Q said X*
         → P believes Q believes X
(4)   *P possesses DK → P sees {X}$_{EK}$ ∧ P sees X*

Intuitively, (1) says that if an subject P believes that it shares the symmetric key K with an subject Q, and subject P receives a message encrypted under K, then subject P believes that Q once said message X. This rule addresses the symmetric encryption.

In a similar way, (2) models digital signatures. If a subject P believes that the verification key VK belongs to a subject Q, then P concludes, confronted with a message or hash encrypted with the corresponding secret key SK, that a message or hash originates from the subject Q.

Regarding rule (3), if an subject P believes that certain information is new, i.e. constructed during the current protocol run, and P furthermore believes that Q conveyed this information, then P concludes that the subject Q believes himself this information.

According to (4), if a subject P sees an encrypted message and P possesses a decryption key then P can read the message itself.

2.3 State exploration

Model checking [10] is a powerful technique and received a lot of attention recently. It models certain protocol as a finite state system. Finally it verifies by exhaustive search that all reachable states satisfy some property. Because exploration is performed on a finite model, the process can be automatic.

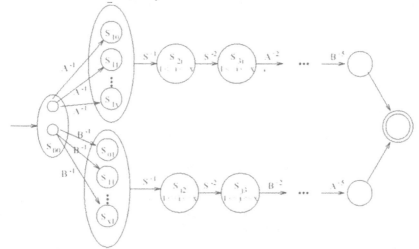

Fig. 2. State exploration while the protocol runs

3 Protocol example

The proposed technique for analyzing protocols using BAN could be explained on the well known Needham-Schroeder symmetric protocol.

The formal description of this protocol is as follows:

1. $A \to S$: A, B, Na
2. $S \to A$: $\{ Na, B, Kab, \{ Kab, A \}_{Kbs} \}_{Kas}$
3. $A \to B$: $\{ Kab, A \}_{Kbs}$
4. $B \to A$: $\{ Nb \}_{Kab}$
5. $A \to B$: $\{ Nb - 1 \}_{Kab}$.

The graphical representation could also be used for describing the protocol behavior and communication sequence:

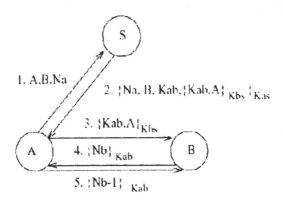

Fig. 3. Graphical description of Needham-Schroeder protocol

For analyzing the protocol behavior we can use the weakest-precondition calculus. The benefits of this approach to protocol verification include the automatic generation of protocol preconditions, the focus on recipient beliefs, and the detailed specification of the protocol sequence.

The process of protocol description differs for each involved subject. In our example we focus on subject B, which may be easier for understanding the principle:

	NS-B Step	Postcondition	Preconditions
NS-B1 ⟶ B: (K ab ,A) K_{bs}	8	B believes (B received N_b-1)	(?) B believes (B received $\{N_b\text{-}1\}_{K_{ab}}$) (?) B believes (B sees $\{N_b\text{-}1\}_{K_{ab}}$)
NS-B2 B: decrypt(K ab ,A) K_{bs}	7	B believes (B received $\{N_b\text{-}1\}_{K_{ab}}$) B believes (B sees $\{N_b\text{-}1\}_{K_{ab}}$)	(2) B believes (B sees K_{ab})
NS-B3 B proves (A $\overset{K_{ab}}{\longleftrightarrow}$ B)	6	B sent $\{N_b\}_{K_{ab}}$	(5) B sees $\{N_b\}_{K_{ab}}$
NS-B4 B proves fresh (K ab)	5	B sees $\{N_b\}_{K_{ab}}$	(p) B sees N_b (2) B sees K_{ab}
NS-B5 B: F(N b ,K ab) = (N b) K_{ab}	4	B believes fresh (K_{ab})	(p) B believes (S controls fresh (K_{ab})) (2) B believes (S says fresh (K_{ab}))
NS-B6 B ⟶ (N b) K_{ab}	3	B believes A $\overset{K_{ab}}{\longleftrightarrow}$ B	(p) B believes (S controls (A $\overset{K_{ab}}{\longleftrightarrow}$ B)) (2) B believes (S says A $\overset{K_{ab}}{\longleftrightarrow}$ B)
NS-B7 ⟶ B: (N b -1) K_{ab}	2	B believes (S said A $\overset{K_{ab}}{\longleftrightarrow}$ B) B believes (B sees K_{ab})	(p) B believes (B sees K_{bs}) (p) B believes (B $\overset{K_{bs}}{\longleftrightarrow}$ B) (?) ¬ B sent $\{K_{ab},A\}_{K_{bs}}$ (:) B believes (B received $\{K_{ab},A\}_{K_{bs}}$)
NS-B8 B: decrypt (N b -1) K_{ab}	1	B believes (B received $\{K_{ab},A\}_{K_{bs}}$)	(:0) ∃ C:C sent $\{K_{ab},A\}_{K_{bs}}$

Table 1: Calculated postconditions and predondicitions

During the specification of the protocol behavior we identify states that satisfy the security presumptions and those that don't. Finally the fitness is constructed according to the results obtained from the state space exploration.

4 Evolutionary approach

Genetic algorithms (GA) are a family of computational models inspired by natural evolution. These algorithms encode a potential solution to a specific problem as a chromosome and perform recombination operators on this data structure to propose new solutions.

The reproduction process is performed in such a way that the chromosomes representing better solutions are given more chances to reproduce than those representing worse solutions. The goodness/fitness is defined according to the desired property of the final solution.

The genetic algorithm manipulates the most promising chromosomes in the search space to obtain an improved solution. It operates through a simple cycle:

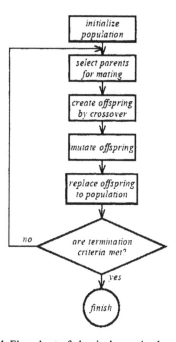

Fig. 4. Flowchart of classical genetic algorithm

Each cycle produces a new generation of possible solutions (individuals) for a given problem.

At the beginning, a population of possible solutions is created. Each individual in this population is represented as a string (the chromosome) to be manipulated by the genetic operators.

In the next stage, the individuals are decoded and evaluated according to their performance in relation to the target response. This determines how fit this individual is in relation to the others in population. Based on each individual's fitness, a selection mechanism chooses the best pairs for the genetic manipulation process. The selection policy is responsible to assure the survival of the fittest individuals.

Crossover is one of the genetic operators used to recombine the population genetic material. It takes two chromosomes and swaps parts of their genetic information to produce new chromosomes.

The recombination process alone cannot explore search space sections not represented in the population's genetic structures. This could make the search get stuck around local minima. Here mutation goes into action. The mutation operator introduces new genetic structures in the population by randomly changing some of its genes, helping the algorithm escape local minima traps.

After applying crossover and mutation to the set of promising solutions, the population of new candidate solutions replaces the original one and the next iteration is executed, unless the termination criteria are met. For example, the run can be terminated when the population converges to a single solution, or the population contains a good enough solution, or a maximum number of iterations has been reached.

5 Automatic protocol design

As we mentioned above, the protocol is a set of rules and conventions that define the communication framework between two or more subjects. These rules may be elementary instructions that consist of operations such as sending a message, encrypting/decrypting a message with a secret key; additionally for our approach we should mention a new basic operation: adding a nonce (random number) to the set of knowledge. This allows subjects to send in the rest of protocol these nonces as often needed in cryptographic protocols.

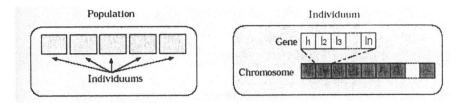

Fig. 5. Structure of a Population: Protocol (individual) is encoded as a sequence of instructions $(I_1, ..., I_n)$.

While the protocol runs, each instruction affects the corresponding sets of knowledge and belief, as explained in chapter 3.

From the evolutionary-optimization point of view, the sequence of protocol instructions is represented by a chromosome of variable length. There could be generated as many random chromosomes as required for initial population. Each chromosome represents a different protocol and its fitness is computed by simulating its run, according to the changed sets of knowledge and belief.

The following algorithm describes the whole flow we use to design security protocols:

1. Specifying security goals – in this first step we describe what should or shouldn't contain sets of knowledge and belief for each involved subject, which message is secret and cannot be sent unencrypted, which message can never be sent, number of recursive encryptions etc.

2. Generation of initial population – randomly generated protocols (instruction sequences) are encoded into the chromosomes. In this step the fitness of all individuals is calculated. This value depends highly on the security presumptions and satisfaction in each state of the protocol run. The use of additional verification tools for finding certain flaws might be helpful.

3. Choosing parents – like in standard genetic algorithms, the individuals with the best fitness are chosen to be parents for mating.

4. Performing crossover – the choice of the right locations in chromosomes for crossover is very important. It may highly affect the chances for a generation of chromosome with better fitness. The basic idea for mating is that two chromosomes may be mated at selected states (instructions) if both have corresponding sets of knowledge and belief. This means we have to prove that after crossing the instruction strings, the rest of protocols make sense for both individuals.

5. Performing mutation – avoiding jamming in local minima, the mutation is very useful step. By performing atomic changes in the instructions, mutation may affect both sets of knowledge and belief.

6. Replacing offspring to population - the produced individuals are replaced to the new population and the evolution process starts over again from step 3.

The whole design is finished when some individuals (with best fitness) satisfy the initial presumptions. The result is the chromosome with the best fitness which can be interpreted as a sequence of basic operations in the cryptographic protocol.

6 Automated tool

The practical output of our research should be a tool for designing security protocols. This tool would be highly automated. The most important step in the design is to specify the initial security presumptions and requirements. The designer decides which components of the messages are allowed to be sent through the communication and which are forbidden to transfer. There is also important task to correctly initialize the sets of knowledge and beliefs of the participants. Also the final sub-sets that should appear in the participants' knowledge and beliefs sets at the end of the protocols run are correspond with the security of protocols in the evolution process.

This means the more precise we specify the final sub-sets, the more secure protocol we obtain.

The whole design is automated and evolves according the algorithm specified above. The result of the design is the instruction sequence that mostly satisfies security requirements.

7 Conclusions and future work

This paper proposes the genetic algorithm for generating security protocols. With this approach the whole protocol design can be highly automated and adapted to various desired properties of the protocols. The basic crossover and mutation operators seem to be useful for generating simple security protocols. The usability for more complex protocols requires addition of heuristic strategies. Although the security requirements are specified at the beginning of the automatic generation, the use of additional verification techniques might be useful to check other security properties and the protocols correctness.

Our future work will focus on the combination of proposed approach with heuristic techniques to make the exploration of the space of possible protocols more effective.

ACKNOWLEDGEMENTS

This paper was created as a part of the research which has been supported by the Grant Agency of the Czech Republic through the following grants: GACR 102/05/0723: A Framework for Formal Specifications and Prototyping of Information System's Network Applications, GACR 102/05/0467: Architectures of Embedded Systems Networks, GACR 102/05/H050: Integrated approach to education of PhD students in the area of parallel and distributed systems, and by the Czech Ministry of Education in frame of MSM 0021630503 Research Intention MIKROSYN: New Trends in Microelectronic Systems and Nanotechnologies.

REFERENCES

1. Abadi M., Needham R.: Prudent Engineering Practice for Cryptographic Protocols. In: Proceedings of the 1994 IEEE Symposium on Security and Privacy, IEEE Computer Security Press (1994) p. 122-136
2. Abadi, M., Tuttle, N.: A Semantic for a Logic of Authentication. In: Proceedings of the ACM Symposium on Principles of Distributed Computing (1991) p. 201-216
3. Agray, N., van der Hoek, W., de Vink, E.: On BAN Logics for Industrial Security protocols. CCEMAS (2001) p. 8
4. Burrows M., Abadi M., Needham R.: A Logic of Authentication. ACM Transactions on Computer Systems, 8 (1) (1990) p. 18-36
5. Gritzalis S.: Security protocols over open networks and distributed systems: Formal methods for their Analysis, Design and Verification. University of Aegean, Greece, Computer Communications, 22 (8) (1999) p. 695-707
6. Ma, L., Tsai, J.: Formal Verification Techniques for Computer Communication Security Protocols. Handbook of Software Engineering and Knowledge Engineering, World Scientific Publishing Company (2000) p. 23
7. Očenášek, P.: On Inductive Approach in Security Protocol Verification. In: Proceedings of the 10th Conference and Competition STUDENT EEICT (2004) Brno, CZ, p. 272-276
8. Očenášek, P.: The Security Protocol Design Using Genetic Algorithms Paradigms. In: Proceedings of the 11th Conference and Competition STUDENT EEICT (2005) Brno, CZ, p. 576-580
9. Očenášek, P.: Towards Selected Problems in the Security Protocol Design and Verification. 1st Doctoral Workshop on Mathematical and Engineering Methods in Computer Science MEMICS (2005) Znojmo, CZ, p. 9
10. Shmatikov, V., Stern, U.: Efficient Finite-State Analysis for Large Security Protocols. In: Proceedings of the 11th IEEE Computer Security Foundation Workshop, IEEE Computer Society Press (1998) p. 10

Improvement of Adaptive Threshold RSA *

Feiyu Lei, Wen Chen and Kefei Chen

Department of Computer Science and Engineering,
Shanghai Jiao Tong University,
1954 Hua Shan Road, Shanghai, 200030
aflylei@gmail.com

Abstract. We put forward a solution to secure threshold RSA cryptosystems in the *adaptive adversary model*. Most protocols in the current literature for threshold cryptosystems were secure only against *static adversary*, especially for threshold RSA which is harder to be distributed than discrete logarithm schemes due to the unknown order of RSA exponents. In this paper, we point out that Canetti's solution to RSA is not secure. Then we propose a simple efficient adaptive secure RSA signature. And the proofs of adaptive secure simulation is given.

Keywords: cryptography, threshold, RSA, adaptive, simulation

1 Introduction

When networks becoming more practical for real life, threshold cryptography provides for increased security of the distributed platform by distributing protocols among a number of participants. The researches in the field always focus on the threshold signature [1, 2]. A t out of n threshold signature scheme is a protocol that we can combine partial signatures to a original signature after we collective at least t valid partial signatures (Note that each player should compute his partial signature.). An adversary who corrupts at most $t - 1$ players (the adversary knows all the secrets of corrupted players) cannot obtain any available information about the secret key of the system or forge a valid signature.

1.1 Static Adversaries and Adaptive Adversaries

Before Canneti proposed the adaptively security in [7], all previously known efficient protocols for threshold cryptosystems were proven secure only against static adversary such as [9–12]. Here, we also take into account the powerful adaptive adversary.

If the set of corrupted parties is fixed before the protocol begins, we call the adversary non-adaptive or static. Alternatively, adaptive adversary is allowed to choose whom to corrupt at any time. The non-adaptive or adaptive

---

* This work was partially supported under NFSC 60273049,60303026,90104005

adversaries both take full control corrupted parties. We must point out that the adaptive adversary is more powerful and realistic than the static adversary [3, 7]. Consider the following secret sharing protocol, the static adversary may corrupt t out of n players. A dealer D distributed a secret by a m out of m secret sharing scheme where $m \ll t$, then the secret is shared in a small set S which the dealer chooses. Obviously, any static adversary cannot learn D's secret only if they can choose the pre-defined set of corrupted players that is identical to S. But any adaptive adversary can compute the D's secret, that chooses about corrupted players in a unpredicted manner so that they can find the S.

1.2 The simulation

The common idea to prove threshold security [3] [4] [5] is that the adversary $\mathcal{A}$'s view in the threshold setting can be simulated by a simulator θ that runs in the original scheme. θ only accesses to public information of the threshold protocol and a signing oracle of the original scheme. Then θ has to show a simulated view of threshold scheme that is indistinguishable from a view of a real interaction with players running the threshold scheme. For instance, by a successful simulation, the security of threshold DSS can be made a reduction to the security of the original DSS. If we assume that the original scheme is secure, the threshold scheme must also be secure.

Difficulties of Adaptive Secure Simulation. An adaptive adversary can corrupt players at any time. The simulator should be able to provide the current internal states of any corrupted player which must be consistent with the previous information seen by the adversary [3]. A simple classic example can demonstrate the difficulties. Assume that the $A = g^x$, and x distributed as the $t - 1$ degree polynomial shares in a n players group , where g is a known group generator. Then the adversary sees all g^{x_i}. Since the simulator cannot predict which servers will be corrupted, the simulator has to create "fake" x_i of all the players. However, the simulation fails because the simulator cannot publish $A_i = g^{x_i}$ for any $t - sized$ set of players, and then open the x_i which can be interpolate secret x. We refer the readers to [3] [4] for more details.

1.3 Related Works and Our Contributions

After the idea of threshold cryptography was proposed in [6], threshold cryptography received a lot of attention. For a long time, the threshold cryptosystems only secure in the static adversary model where the adversary fixes the corrupted players before the protocol starts. Recently, Canetti et al. [7] and Frankel et al. [8] put forward the first schemes against the adaptive adversary.

Our Contributions are as follows:

Canetti Scheme's Drawback: Firstly, we point out that Canetti's RSA scheme cannot provide adaptive security. Canetti et al. [7] proposed a adaptive secure threshold cryptosystem based on discrete logarithm, and he said that his solution can build the adaptive secure threshold RSA of [10]. But he ignored that $\phi(N)$ cannot be as input of players in the the phase of Distribution Key Generation where $\phi(N)$ is the Euler Totient Function of RSA module N. Once any player is corrupted, the adversary $\mathcal{A}$ can know $\phi(N)$. That is to say, $\mathcal{A}$ can compute the divisor p and q of N. So Canetti's RSA scheme fails in the phase of Distribution Key Generation.

Our Improvement: Our work builds on [7, 9, 10, 12]. We firstly propose Pedersen-Z_N-VSS which doesn't compromise $\phi(N)$, and use Pedersen-Z_N-VSS as a subroutine to construct an adaptive threshold RSA. In this paper, we combine and simplify these protocols [7, 9, 10, 12] to achieve adaptive secure RSA signature. Our scheme is more efficient than [7] [8] both in communication and computation. Comparing with [7] [8], our scheme has fewer communication rounds and computations costs.

The remainder of the paper is organized as follows. We first describe models of threshold schemes and their security in section 2. In section 3, we present an implementation of our scheme. In section 4, efficiency analysis is given in a table. In section 5, we make detailed security proof. In section 6, we draw a conclusion.

2 System Model and Security Requirements

2.1 System Model

Communication Model. We have a set of n players $\{P_1, ..., P_n\}$, indexed $1, ..., n$, and an adversary $\mathcal{A}$. We consider a network that provides authenticated, service undeniable, point-to-point connections [10]. In addition, the players have access to a dedicated broadcast channel.

The Adaptive Adversary. We assume that the adaptive adversary can corrupt up to $t - 1$ of the n players.

System Parameters. We choose the same system parameters as [10], the public key is denoted by N, e where $N = pq$ and p, q are primes of the form $p = 2p' + 1, q = 2q' + 1$, and p', q' are primes. The private key is d where $ed \equiv 1 mod \phi(N)$, the number of players is n and the threshold is t, where $n \geq 2t + 1$. An element g of the high order is chosen, and $g \triangleq g_0^{L^2} mod N$ where g_0 is an element of high order and $L \triangleq n!$.

2.2 Security Requirements

The threshold signature should satisfied the following properties [13]:

Unforgeability. We say that the threshold RSA signature should be as unforgeable as the standard RSA signature, even the adversary controls the $t - 1$ of the n players.

Robustness. The robustness of threshold signature scheme means that an adversary who corrupts less than $t - 1$ players should not be able to prevent uncorrupted players from generating valid signatures.

3 Adaptive Threshold RSA Signature

In this section, firstly, based on the schemes [9,10,12], we propose Pedersen-Z_N-VSS and Joint Pedersen-Z_N-VSS. Then we put forward the adaptive threshold RSA signature scheme.

3.1 Pedersen-Z_N-VSS and Joint Pedersen-Z_N-VSS

Verified Secret Sharing is a main component of threshold signature. Our Pedersen-Z_N-VSS is based on Pedersen-VSS [9], we refer to it as Pedersen-Z_N-VSS.

Algorithm: Pedersen-Z_N-VSS
Sharing Phase:
Input: secret value $s \in [-nN^2, ..., nN^2]$ and composite N, element g of high order in Z_N^*, n number of players, t threshold value.

1. The dealer chooses $a_1, ..., a_t \in [-nL^2N^3, ..., nL^2N^3]$, $b_0, ..., b_t \in [-nL^2N^3, ..., nL^2N^3]$ where $L = n!$, and defines $f(x) = a_0 + a_1x + ... + a_tx^t, a_0 = sL, f'(x) = b_0 + b_1x + ... + b_tx^t$

2. The dealer computes $s_i = f(i), s_i' = f'(i)$ for $1 \le i \le n$, and hands P_i the value s_i, s_i'

3. The dealer broadcasts $C_k = g^{a_k}h^{b_k} \bmod N$ for $0 \le k \le t$

Verifications steps: The parties do as follows.

1. The parties check that the value s_i, s_i' really define a secret by checking that $g^{s_i}h^{s_i'} = \prod_{k=0}^{t}(C_k)^{j^k}$

2. if the party P_i holds a share that does not satisfy the equation above, then he request that the dealer make $s_i = f(i), s_i' = f'(i)$ public. If any of the revealed shares still fails the verification, the dealer is disqualified.

We have pointed out in section 1.3 that the Canetti's solution [7] fails in the phase of Distribution Key Generation. So we avoid the Distribution Key Generation in threshold RSA. A non-fault Trusted Third Party chooses and hands P_i value $d_i \in [-nN^2, ..., nN^2]$ for $1 \le i \le n$, set $d_{public} = d - \sum_{i=1}^{n} d_i$, and broadcasts d_{public}. Then Joint Pedersen-Z_N-VSS makes each player's additive share d_i be the interpolate polynomial share x_i, where $d = d_{public} + \sum_{i=1}^{t} x_i \prod_{i=1}^{t}(0 - j)/(i - j)$. The adaptive simulation will fail if we only use additive shares or interpolate polynomial shares to realize threshold RSA. The combination of additive shares and interpolate polynomial shares can avoid the barrier of the simulation, then we can provide the internal states of players at any time except a single consistent player [7] [8].

Algorithm: Joint Pedersen-Z_N-VSS
Threshold Parameters: t, n, t'
Input: the same (g, h, N) as Pedersen-Z_N-VSS.

Public Output: C_{ik} for $i = 1..n, k = 0..t'$. Set $QUAL$ of non-disqualified players.

Secret Output of P_i: x_i and x_i', $f_i(z)$ and $f_i'(z)$, s_{ij}, s_{ij}' for $j = 1..n$

1. Each player P_i performs a Pedersen-Z_N-VSS of a random value d_i as a dealer:

   (a) P_i chooses $a_1, ..., a_t \in [-nL^2N^3, ..., nL^2N^3]$, $b_1, ..., b_t \in [-nL^2N^3, ..., nL^2N^3]$ where $L = n!$, and defines $f_i(z) = a_0 + a_1 z + ... + a_t z^t, a_0 = d_i L$, $f_i'(z) = b_0 + b_1 z + ... + b_t z^t$, P_i sends shares $s_{ij} = f_i(j), s_{ij}' = f_i'(j)$ to each P_j for $1 \le i \le n$, P_i broadcasts $C_{ik} = g^{a_{ik}} h^{b_{ik}} mod N$ for $0 \le k \le t'$.

   (b) Each P_j verifies the shares he receives from the other players by checking for $i = 1, ..., n$, $g^{s_{ij}} h^{s_{ij}'} = \prod_{k=0}^{t'} (C_{ik})^{j^k} mod N$, If the check fails for an index i, P_j broadcasts a complaint to P_j.

   (c) Player p_i (as a dealer) reveals the share s_{ij} matching the equation in Step 1b for each complaining player P_j.

   (d) Each player builds the set of $QUAL$ which excludes any player: who received more than t complaints in Step 1b, or answered to a complaint in Step 1c with values that violate the equation in Step 1b.

2. Each P_i sets his share of the secret to $x_i = \sum_{j \in QUAL} s_{ji}$ and the associated random value $x_i = \sum_{j \in QUAL} s_{ji}'$, then broadcasts the witness $w_i \triangleq g^{x_i} mod N$.

3.2 Adaptive Threshold RSA

We presented the adaptive threshold RSA as follows.

Input: the same (g, h, N) as Pedersen-Z_N-VSS, the secret key d
Public Output: y the standard RSA signature
Output of P_i: s_i the partial signature
Generating x_i and s_i: We first generate shares x_i of d and partial signature s_i.

1. A non-fault Trusted Third Party chooses and hands P_i value $d_i \in [-nN^2, ..., nN^2]$ for $1 \le i \le n$, set $d_{public} = d - \sum_{i=1}^{n} d_i$, and broadcasts d_{public}.

2. Players execute Joint-RVSS(t, n, t). Player P_i gets the following outputs of Joint-RVSS:
   − x_i his share of the secret
   − all witnesses $w_j \triangleq g^{x_i} mod N$ about x_j.
   Players also get public outputs C_{ik} for $i = 1..n, k = 0..t$ and the set $QUAL$. Each player broadcasts $m^{d_i} mod N$ as partial signature.

Computing $y = m^d mod N$: Next we combine the partial signature to the standard RSA signature.

1. P_i proves his partial signature using the protocol of [12] that $Dlog_{m^{x_i}} = Dlog_{g^{w_i}}$.

2. Any at least t qualified players can combine original RSA signature as following: $y = m^d mod N = m^{d_{public}} \prod_{i=1}^{t} m^{x_i} \prod_{i=1}^{t} (0-j)/(i-j) mod N$.

4 Efficiency Analysis

Comparing with two previous adaptive secure threshold schemes [7,8], we show the communication and computation costs of these schemes as following table. Clearly, our scheme is more efficient than [7,8].

Table 1. comparison with previous solutions

The Scheme	Numbers of Broadcasts	Numbers of Exponentiation
[7]	$5n \leq Numbers \leq 5n + 5t$	$Numbers \geq 16t$
[8]	$4n + 2t \leq Numbers \leq 5n + 4t$	$Numbers \geq 20t$
Our Scheme	$4n \leq Numbers \leq 4n + 2t$	$Numbers \geq 15t$

5 Security Proofs

We consider the following properties as described in Section 2.

5.1 Unforgeability

The successful adaptive secure simulation gives us a proof of unforgeability. Next we present a simulator for Joint Pedersen-Z_N-VSS and the adaptive threshold RSA signature as following:

Input: message m, the same (g, h, N) as Pedersen-Z_N-VSS, $y = m^d mod N$ the standard RSA signature.
  1. we denote set $\{1 \leq i \leq n\}$ as $SETOFALL$. A non-fault Trusted Third Party chooses at random one uncorrupted player P, and chooses and hands P_i value $d_i \in [-nN^2, ..., nN^2]$ for $i \in SETOFALL$. Then compute s_p such as
  $y = m^d mod N = s_p \cdot m^{d_{public}} \prod_{i \in SETOFALL \setminus \{P\}} m^{d_i} mod N$. s_p is the partial signature of the player P, where we don't know the secret key d_p such as $s_p = m^{d_p} mod N$.
  2. Players execute Joint-RVSS(t, n, t).Player P_i gets the following outputs of Joint-RVSS:
     - x_i his share of the secret
     - all witnesses $w_j \triangleq g^{x_i} mod N$ about x_j.
     Each player except P broadcasts $m^{x_i} mod N$ as partial signature. P broadcasts s_p as his partial signature.
Computing $y = m^d mod N$: Next we combine the partial signature to the standard RSA signature.

1. P_i proves his partial signature using the protocol of [12] that $Dlog_{m^{x_i}} = Dlog_{g^{w_i}}$. The special player P's zero knowledge proof can be simulated as the protocol of [7]

2. Any at least t qualified players can combine original RSA signature as follows: $y = m^d mod N = m^{d_{public}} \prod_{i=1}^{t} m^{x_i \prod_{i=1}^{t} (0-j)/(i-j)} mod N$.

Clearly, we show that the simulator above outputs a probability distribution which is identical to the distribution that the real adversary sees in an real execution of our adaptive threshold RSA signature. The technique of single inconsistent player is the same as the protocol of [7] [8]. If a player is corrupted in Step1 or Step2, the simulator can provide consistent view. After Step2 the simulator can reveal a consistent internal state d_i for all but the special player P of the players it controls. If the special player P is corrupted, which happens with at most 1/2 probability, the simulator rewinds the adversary to the beginning of Step2 and select a different special player.

5.2 Robustness

In this paper, we adopt the protocol of [12] to guarantee the Robustness. We refer readers to [12] for details. Any adversary who corrupts less than $t - 1$ players should not be able to prevent uncorrupted players from generating valid signatures.

6 Conclusion

Threshold cryptosystem is a useful tool to protect system security, and adaptive adversaries are more realistic and powerful than static adversaries. In this paper, we firstly discuss the adaptive security of threshold scheme. Then we propose an efficient adaptive threshold RSA scheme which is provable secure. Comparing with two previous adaptive secure protocol [7] [8], the proposed simplified scheme is more efficient than them both in the communication and computation overheads, and still inherits the adaptive security.

References

1. Y.Desmedt and Y.Frankel. Shared generation of authenticators and signatures.In J. Feigenbaum, editor, Advances in Cryptology CRYPTO' 91,LNCS VOL.576,pp.457-469, Springer Verlat, 1992
2. Y.G.Desmedt. Threshold cryptography. European Transactions on Telecommunications, 54; 449-457, July 1994
3. Ran Canetti, Uri Feige, Oded Goldreich, and Moni Naor. Adaptively secure multiparty computation. In Proceedings of the Twenty-Eighth Annual ACM Symposium on the Theory of Computing, pages 639-648, Philadelphia, Pennsylvania, 22-24 May 1996.

4. S.Micali and P.Rogaway, Secure computaion. In Joan Feigenbaum, editor, Advances in Cryptology - Crypto'91, pages 392-404, Berlin, 1991. Springer-Verlag. Lecture Notes in Computer Science Volume 576.

5. D.Beaver, Foundations of secure interactive computing. In Joan Feigenbaum, editor, Advances in Cryptology - Crypto'91, pages 377-391, Berlin, 1991. Springer-Verlag. Lecture Notes in Computer Science Volume 576.

6. Y.Desmedt. Society and group oriented cryptopraphy: A new concept. In Advances in Cryptology-proceedings of CRYPTO'87, LNCS, pp.120-127,1988

7. R.Canetti,R.Gennaro, S.jarecki,H.Krawczyk, and T.Rabin. Adaptively security for threshold cryptosystems. In Advances in Cyptology-CRYPTO 99. Springer-Verlag, 1999.

8. Y.Frankel, Phlip MacKenzie, and Moti Yung. Adaptively secure optimal-resilience proactive RSA. IN advances in cryptology ASIACRYPT 99.Springer-Verlag, 1999.

9. T.Pedersen. A threshold cryptosystem without a trusted party. In Eurocrypt'91, pp 522-526, 1991. LNCSNo.547

10. T.Rabin. A simplifed approach to threshold and proactive RSA. In crypto'98, PP 89-104, 1998, LNCS No.1462

11. R. Gennaro, S. Jarecki, H. Krawczyk, and T. Rabin. The (in)security of distributed key generation in dlog-based cryptosystems. In Eurocrypt '99, pages 295310, 1999. LNCS No.

12. R.Gennaro, S.jarecki,H.Krawzyk, and T.Rabin. Robust and efficient sharing of RSA functions. In Crypto'96, pp157-172, 1996. Springer-Verlag. LNCS No.1109

13. V.Shoup. Practical threshold signatures. IBM Reseearch Report RZ3121(April 19 1999).

SECTION IV: Intrusion Detection & Prevention

A LOG-BASED MINING SYSTEM FOR NETWORK NODE CORRELATION

Yongzheng Zhang, Binxing Fang, Yue Chi and Xiaochun Yun

Research Center of Computer Network and Information Security Technology,
Harbin Institute of Technology, Harbin 150001, China

zyz@pact518.hit.edu.cn

Abstract. In the field of network security, people become aware of the importance of study on the connectivity between network nodes. Based on analyzing the connectivity, this paper introduces a conception of network node correlation (NNC) and designs a novel log-based NNC mining system which adopts a typical distributed architecture based on agent. By means of bayesian network, this system can accurately and effectively mine high-level NNCs on application layer. The mined results can provide useful information for some security fields such as network risk assessment, vulnerability and intrusion detection, and virus propagation.

Keywords   Network Risk Assessment, Network Node Correlation, Bayesian Network, System Log

1. Introduction

1.1 Motivation

To protect information resources from network viruses, malicious codes and attempted intrusions, people have been conducting research in many fields of network security in recent years, such as modeling and automated generation of network attack graph [1~3], network vulnerability detection and risk assessment [4,5]. In their work, to effectively detect network attacks or vulnerabilities, they correlate the individual attacks or vulnerabilities on different nodes by means of network node connectivity. Ritchey et al indicates that one of the requirements of a successful attack is to ensure the interconnection between network nodes and connectivity is defined as a host's ability to communicate with other hosts [4]. Afterward, he proposes a model for representing TCP/IP connectivity for topological analysis of network security in the literature [6]. Moreover, Mayer et al implements a firewall analysis engine for finding the connectivity between network nodes [7]. So it can be seen that deeply understanding and studying the

167

connectivity is an important step of detecting network attacks and vulnerabilities, and is also the basis of accurately evaluating network security risk.

However, the previous work only considers TCP/IP connectivity. We argue that the connectivity is not enough to reflect some special logical relation over physical connection, such as one party's control on resources of the other party. To illustrate the shortage of the previous work, we try to give an example that an attacker lies on node A and is not a user, node B without any vulnerability is an attack object, a user on node A can logon node B as root. In the example, the previous work can not identify the risk of node B due to no vulnerabilities on B. But in fact, because the user on node A can control the resources of node B, sometimes the attacker probably gains the root password of B by sniffer or social engineering.

As stated above, it is necessary to mine and analyze this logical relation. Therefore, a conception of network node correlation (NNC) is introduced in this paper. According to the ascending-order hierarchy of access privilege to resources, NNC can reflect the correlations of different degree between network nodes. Based on TCP/IP connectivity, NNC emphasizes the privilege relations between services or users on application layer.

1.2 Related Work

Currently, there are four main NNC detection methods: active scanning [5], passive sniffing, analyzing configuration files of network or safety devices [7], and reporting from users. The description and comparison of these approaches are as follows:

- **Active scanning** Use known scanning tools like Nmap [8], Nessus [9] and Traceroute [10] to respectively detect a network from different spots in and out of managing domain. Thus a part of NNCs on TCP/IP layer can be found. The quantity of identifying NNCs depends on that of distribution of scanning tools. But NNCs on high level like application layer can't be obtained by this method.
- **Passive sniffing** Collect communication data to find a part of NNCs on TCP/IP or application layer. The precision and quantity of identifying NNCs lie on the quality and quantity of captured network data. To some extent, this method is supplement and improvement of active approach.
- **Analyzing configuration files** Analyze configuration files of network or safety devices like switch, router and firewall to gain NNCs on TCP/IP layer. This method can be used to update promptly to avoid time delay. But it also can't gain NNCs on high level and needs the ability to control the devices.
- **Reporting from users** Users on hosts can accurately report high level NNCs by manually analyzing network configurations and operation characteristics.

1.3 Contributions

Through analyzing the above methods, we can see that each method has its own particular effect. However, these methods are unfit to automatically identify high level NNCs. Therefore, this paper designs a novel log-based NNC mining system which adopts a classical distributed architecture based on agent. This system can accurately and effectively mine NNCs on high level like application layer. The mined results provide useful information for some security fields such as network risk assessment, vulnerability and intrusion detection, and virus propagation.

In the next Section 2, we simply introduce the definition and classification of NNC. In Section 3 we give some details of main modules in the mining system. We then give an applied example to illustrate a good effect of this system in Section 4. We conclude with Section 5.

2. Definition and Classification of NNC

2.1 Definition of NNC
Firstly we give the notion of a component.

Def.1. Component A computer in a network information system is stated to be a network node. A user, operating system, application or service on network node is said to be a subject. Thus, a pair (n,s) constructed by network node n and its owning subject s is said to be a component on node n.

Reference to [11], this paper aims at the problems in security risk to introduce a concept of "Network Node Correlation" as follows:

Def.2. Network Node Correlation After an attacker has successfully intruded a network node A, as long as he possibly exploits an access relation from a certain component C_i on node A to a certain component C_j on node B, so as to attack node B, then we can say this access relation to be a NNC from node A to node B. It can be written to NNC_{AB}. Furthermore, from the viewpoint of a component, it is also written to NNC_{ij}. A NNC is expressed to an ordered 6-tuples: $<A,S_a,B,S_b,P_{SaSb},V_{SaSb}>$, where, S_a and S_b is respectively a subject on node A and B. An ordered component pair of (A,S_a) and (B,S_b) is a unique identification of the NNC, while P_{SaSb} and V_{SaSb} are two descriptive attributes. Different attributes are chosen in terms of different requirements. In this paper, P_{SaSb} means the correlative probability of component (A,S_a) and (B,S_b). V_{SaSb} is a value which quantifies component (A,S_a)'s ability to control the resources of component (B,S_b) and belongs to real number set. The product of P_{SaSb} and V_{SaSb} denotes the correlative impact between components.

2.2 Classification of NNC
Because NNC emphasizes a privilege correlation, we classify NNCs by different control privileges. Table1 shows ranks and quantification of NNCs. In this paper, we expect measuring the control degrees between two components in terms of numeral. The quantification standard mainly derives from our subjective expectation and design idea. But the quantification must comply with a partial order relation according to the importance and quantity of control privileges, namely $V_7 > V_6 > V_5 > V_4 > V_3 > V_2$. This classification reflects a multi-hierarchy characteristic of NNC.

170

Ranks	Value	Description
V_7	10	Visitors can execute commands as system administrator of servers and completely control all system resources.
V_6	7	Visitors can execute commands as regular user of servers and control this user resources and parts of system resources.
V_5	5	Visitors can receive or publish information as registered user of service components, but can't execute system commands
V_4	3	Visitors can receive or publish common information as anonymous user of service components. This relation only implies the connectivity on transport layer, such as access to inside services through firewall.
V_3	2	Visitors can only access to servers on network layer. This relation indicates the connectivity on network layer.
V_2	1	Visitors can only access to servers on data link layer. This relation indicates the connectivity on data link layer. It is designed for solving the problem about ARP attacks.
V_1	8	This relation is a special NNC. It reflects the relation of sniffing and sniffed between access nodes and service nodes.

Table 1: Ranks and quantification of NNCs

3. Mining System

The log-based mining system proposed in this paper has a distributed architecture as shown in Fig.1., where, a broken line means a control flow and a real line is a data flow. This system mainly contains mining agents, a processing center and a NNCB (NNC database). Mining agents has to be installed in the nodes which need to be analyzed. Its task is to collect and analyze target system logs and then generate NNCs by means of a mining algorithm to be transported to the processing center. The processing center is a central managing module of this system. It periodically sends commands and configurations to every agent and receives NNCs to be stored in NNCB which provides information for further security researches.

The main design characters of this system are as follows:
- **High level** Adapted to automatically mine high level NNCs.
- **Expandability** Adopt a distributed architecture based on agent to conveniently add or remove mining units.
- **Flexibility** Users can modify mining policies and means according to different environments or applications.
- **Security** Communications between the processing center and the mining agents are encrypted to ensure transportation safety.

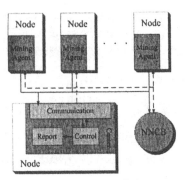

Fig. 1: Architecture of our mining system

3.1 Processing Center

Processing center which takes charge of contacting and controlling all mining agents consists of three submodules: 'Communication', 'Control' and 'Report'. Because the mined NNCs have great influences on network security, it is demanded that an encrypted channel should be established between the processing center and an agent in module 'Communication'. Module 'Control' provides a managing interface for users which can configure mining parameters, send control commands and receive resulting data. Module 'Report' can show mined results to users in a friendly form.

3.2 Mining Agent

Mining agent which is the technical core of this system completes the processes of mining NNCs as shown in Fig.2.

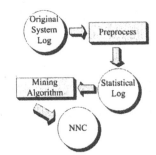

Fig. 2: Processes of mining NNCs

3.2.1 System Log

To record various actions and events occurring on operating systems and help administrators to find the problems when systems are at fault, almost all operating systems write system logs. Because we are concerned with remote accesses of legal users, for the example of current popular operating systems Windows and Linux, we only gather the security log of Windows (normally stored under the directory of %systemroot%\system32\config) and the wtmp log of Linux (normally stored under the directory of /var/log, and the case of Unix is similar). These two files record the login information of users generally including name, login IP, login time, exit time etc. Although they are binary files, they can be exported to text files by system commands and we store each original log record in the following form.

```
typedef struct _t_log_ {
  char user[USER_MAX]; //User
  char ip[IP_MAX];      //IP
  char term[USER_MAX]; //Term, login terminal
  unsigned int lt;      //LT, login time
  unsigned int et;      //ET, exit time
} s_log;
```

3.2.2 Log Preprocessing

In this subsection we preprocess the original log to generate "statistical log" whose format is as follows, where, User and IP are stated in the original log format.

```
typedef struct _t_S_ {
  unsigned int ot;    //OT, the sum of online time of User from IP in this time
                        zone.
  unsigned char lot; //LOT, the sum of online time of User from IP in the previous
                        time zone.
  unsigned char lli;  //LLI, the interval between the previous login time of User
                        from IP and the start time of this time zone.
  unsigned char login; //Login, the value is yes or no.
} s_S;
typedef struct _t_rcd_ {
  char user[USER_MAX];    //User
  char ip[IP_MAX];        //IP
  s_S S[TIME_ZONE_MAX]; //Statistical items
} s_rcd;
```

The main idea of preprocessing is as follows:

1) Specify the time interval T in unit of hour, $T=24n$ $(n=1,2,...)$.

2) From beginning of the first log record, a time zone is plotted out each T hours. These time zones are supposed as A_1, A_2, K, A_{t+1}, where, $t = \left\lfloor \dfrac{H_{last} - H_{first}}{T} \right\rfloor$, H_i=Hour(i.LT),

denotes the login time of record i in the form of hour.

3) According to all pairs of User and IP which appear in the original log, respectively make statistical analysis of records in time zone A_1, K, A_t to fill the statistical log. Because it is possible that the records in the last zone A_{t+1} are not full, we never consider them.

To make computing simple and effective, we transform continuous variables into discrete variables of LOT and LLI, as shown in Formula (1) and (2). LOT' and LLI' denote respectively continuous variables of LOT and LLI. AverOT and MaxOT mean respectively the average and maximum of all OTs in the statistical log.

$$LOT = \begin{cases} short & LOT' \in [0, AverOT/2) \\ medium & LOT' \in [AverOT/2, AverOT) \\ long & LOT' \in [AverOT, (MaxOT + AverOT)/2) \\ verylong & LOT' \in [(MaxOT + AverOT)/2, MaxOT] \end{cases} \tag{1}$$

$$LLI = \begin{cases} short & LLI' \in [0, T/2) \\ medium & LLI' \in [T/2, T) \\ long & LLI' \in [T, 2T) \\ verylong & LLI' \in [2T, +\infty) \end{cases} \tag{2}$$

3.2.3 Mining Algorithm

The key of generating a NNC is how to calculate the correlative probability P. In this subsection we apply bayesian network to learn the data in the statistical log, and then evaluate the probability of a certain user's access to a target host in the next time zone.

Firstly, define random variables. We respectively regard User, IP, LOT, LLI and Login in the statistical log format as five random variables X_i (i=1,…,5). According to practical knowledge, the structure of bayesian network is defined as S, as shown in Fig.3.

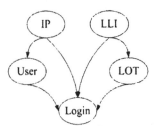

Fig. 3: Bayesian network structure

Secondly, learn the probability distribution of bayesian network. The papers [12,13] expatiate the theories of bayesian network. This paper applies those theories and methods to our work. By reason of the length, the related conceptions and deductions are ignored. We can draw a conclusion as shown in Formula (3).

$$p(X_5 = Yes \mid Pa_5^j, D, S^h) = \frac{\alpha_{5j1} + N_{5j1}}{\alpha_{5j1} + \alpha_{5j2} + N_{5j1} + N_{5j2}} \tag{3}$$

S^h is the hypothesis of bayesian network structure S. Pa_5^j denotes that the state of parent node set Pa_5 of X_5 is j. $D = \{D_i \mid i = 1,2,K\}$, is the statistical log, where D_i expresses a log record. $\alpha_{ijk}(k = 1, K, r_i)$ is the parameter of Dirichlet distribution. $N_{ijk}(k = 1, K, r_i)$ equals the number of records in D when $X_i = x_i^k, pa_i = pa_i^j$.

Finally, the mining algorithm is as follows:

Suppose:

Q is a set of all pairs of User and IP which appear in the original log, $|Q| = n$; $\left\lfloor \dfrac{H_{last} - H_{first}}{T} \right\rfloor = t$; $D_{(u,ip)}^j = \{D_i \mid D_i.User == u \wedge D_i.IP == ip \wedge D_i \text{ belongs to time zone } j\} \in D$;

Algorithm:

For each $(u_i, ip_i) \in Q$

{

  $N_{5j1} = N_{5j2} = 0$;

  For each $j \in \{2, K, t\}$

  {

    If $D_{(u_i,ip_i)}^j.LOT == D_{(u_i,ip_i)}^{t+1}.LOT \wedge D_{(u_i,ip_i)}^j.LLI == D_{(u_i,ip_i)}^{t+1}.LLI \wedge D_{(u_i,ip_i)}^j.Login == Yes)$

      $N_{5j1} ++$;

    ElseIf $D_{(u_i,ip_i)}^j.LOT == D_{(u_i,ip_i)}^{t+1}.LOT \wedge D_{(u_i,ip_i)}^j.LLI == D_{(u_i,ip_i)}^{t+1}.LLI \wedge D_{(u_i,ip_i)}^j.Login == No)$

      $N_{5j2} ++$;

  }

  According to Formula (3), we can figure out the correlative probability $P_{(u_i,ip_i)}$;

  According to u_i and the taxonomy in Table 1, we can gain $V_{(u_i,ip_i)}$;

  Generate a NNC $< ip_i, 'User', IP_{system}, u_i, P_{(u_i,ip_i)}, V_{(u,ip_i)} > \rightarrow NNCB$;

}

4. An Example

In this section we give a real-world example of local network to illustrate the usefulness of this system. The real local network structure is shown in Fig.4. Mining agents are installed on each server. 'Processing center' and 'NNCB' are installed on a host. For simplicity and without loss of generality, we only focus on a RedHat Linux 8.0 server (192.168.1.160). We collect 320 system log records of this server and configure the following parameters:

1) Let $n=7$, namely $T=24*7$(hours);

2) Assuming the login user is u and the login IP is ip, the parameters of Dirichlet prior probability distribution are α_{5j1} and α_{5j2}. α_{5j1} means the number of records in D

when $Login = Yes, User = u, IP = ip$. α_{5j2} equals the number of records in D when $Login = No, User = u, IP = ip$.

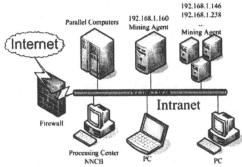

Fig. 4: Real network structure in this example

Node_A	Subject_A	Node_B	Subject_B	Prob	Value	Impact	Is Login?
192.168.1.204	User	192.168.1.160	root	60.00%	10	8	
192.168.1.232	User	192.168.1.160	root	75.00%	10	7.5	
192.168.1.200	User	192.168.1.160	xyp	78.57%	7	5.5	
192.168.1.233	User	192.168.1.160	sl	61.54%	7	4.31	
192.168.1.191	User	192.168.1.160	root	37.50%	10	3.75	
192.168.1.243	User	192.168.1.160	root	35.29%	10	3.53	
192.168.1.197	User	192.168.1.160	root	30.77%	10	3.08	
192.168.1.235	User	192.168.1.160	root	14.29%	10	1.43	
192.168.1.233	User	192.168.1.160	root	14.29%	10	1.43	
10.10.10.187	User	192.168.1.160	ww	15.00%	7	1.05	
192.168.1.235	User	192.168.1.160	pact	20.00%	5	1	
pact04	User	192.168.1.160	vw	14.29%	7	1	
192.168.1.146	User	192.168.1.160	root	9.09%	10	.91	
192.168.1.153	User	192.168.1.160	pact	15.00%	5	.75	
192.168.1.183	User	192.168.1.160	sl	9.09%	7	.84	
192.168.1.235	User	192.168.1.160	sl	9.09%	7	.84	
192.168.1.199	User	192.168.1.160	rt	9.09%	7	.84	
192.168.1.197	User	192.168.1.160	rt	9.09%	7	.84	
192.168.1.204	User	192.168.1.160	xyz	9.09%	7	.84	
wwserver20	User	192.168.1.160	ww	7.14%	7	.5	
server25	User	192.168.1.160	vw	7.14%	7	.5	
server24	User	192.168.1.160	vw	7.14%	7	.5	
server20	User	192.168.1.160	vw	7.14%	7	.5	
wwserver25	User	192.168.1.160	ww	7.14%	7	.5	
pact05	User	192.168.1.160	vw	7.14%	7	.5	
192.168.1.200	User	192.168.1.160	pact	10.00%	5	.5	
wwserver45	User	192.168.1.160	vw	7.14%	7	.5	
pact06	User	192.168.1.160	vw	7.14%	7	.5	
192.168.1.232	User	192.168.1.160	pact	9.09%	5	.45	
192.168.1.191	User	192.168.1.160	pact	9.09%	5	.45	
192.168.1.233	User	192.168.1.160	pact	9.09%	5	.45	
192.168.1.191	User	192.168.1.160	xm	4.55%	7	.32	
192.168.1.191	User	192.168.1.160	oxf	4.55%	7	.32	
192.168.1.243	User	192.168.1.160	pact	4.55%	5	.23	

Fig. 5: Mined results from server 160

The mining agent on this server generates 34 NNCs which are sorted in descending order of attribute 'Impact' as shown in Fig.5. Where, 'Impact' ='Prob'×'Value', denotes the correlative impact of a NNC. Red colored in the field 'Is Login?' of a record means the access related to this record assuredly occurs during the last week. We can see that most of red-colored records concentrate on the top of the figure. This indicates that the higher the correlative impact of a mined NNC is, the greater the probability of this NNC's real occurrence during the future time zone is. Thus it can be seen that our mining system has a good effect.

5. Conclusions

This paper designs a novel log-based NNC mining system which adopts a classical distributed architecture based on agent. This system has good expansibility, flexibility and security. By means of bayesian network, it can accurately and effectively mine NNCs on high level like application layer. The mined results of this system provide useful information for some security fields such as network risk assessment, vulnerability and intrusion detection, and virus propagation.

6. Acknowledgement

This research is supported by the National Natural Science Foundation of China under Grant No. 60403033 and the "Tenth Five-Year Plan" of Chinese National Defense Pre-research Program under Grant No. 4131571.

7. References

[1] Swiler, L., Phillips, C., Ellis, D. and Chakerian, S.: Computer-Attack Graph Generation Tool, in Proceedings of the DARPA Information Survivability Conference & Exposition II, Anaheim, California (2001) 307–321

[2] Daley, K., Larson, R., Dawkins, J.: A Structural Framework for Modeling Multi-Stage Network Attacks, in Proceedings of the International Conference on Parallel Processing Workshops (ICPPW'02). Tulsa Univ., OK, USA (2002) 5–10

[3] Sheyner, O., Haines, J., Jha, S. (eds.): Automated Generation and Analysis of Attack Graphs, in Proceedings of IEEE Symposium on Security and Privacy, Oakland, California (2002) 273–284

[4] Ritchey, R., Ammann, P.: Using Model Checking to Analyze Network Vulnerabilities, in Proceedings of IEEE Symposium on Security and Privacy, Oakland, California (2000) 156 –165

[5] Jajodia, S., Noel, S., O'Berry, B.: Topological Analysis of Network Attack Vulnerability, in Managing Cyber Threats: Issues, Approaches and Challenges, Kumar, V., Srivastava, J., Lazarevic, A., eds., Kluwer Academic Publishers, Boston (2004)

[6] Ritchey, R., O'Berry, B., Noel, S.: Representing TCP/IP Connectivity for Topological Analysis of Network Security, in Proceedings of 18th Annual Computer Security Applications Conference, Las Vegas, Nevada (2002) 25–31

[7] Mayer, A., Wool, A., Ziskind, E.: Fang: A Firewall Analysis Engine, In Proceedings of the IEEE Symposium on Security and Privacy, Oakland, CA (2000) 177–187

[8] Nmap, Security Scanner, information on the web at http://www.insecure.org

[9] Nessus, Remote Security Scanner, information on the web at http://www.nessus.org

[10] Traceroute, information on the web at ftp://ftp.ee.lbl.gov/traceroute.tar.gz

[11] Yau, S.S., Zhang, X.Y.: Computer Network Intrusion Detection, Assessment and Prevention Based on Security Dependency Relation, in Proceedings of COMPSAC '99, Phoenix, USA (1999) 86–91

[12] Shi, Z.Z.: Knowledge Discovery (In Chinese). Tsinghua University Press, Beijing (2002)

[13] Mu, C.D., Dai, J.B., Ye, J.: Bayesian Network for Data Mining (In Chinese), Journal of Software, Vol.11, No.5 (2002) 660–666

EXPLORING VULNERABILITIES OF AGENT-BASED IDS: THE NEED FOR AGENT SELF-DEFENCE

Eni E Oyegoke, Theodore Tryfonas and Andrew J Blyth

Information Security Research Group, School of Computing, University of Glamorgan
Pontypridd CF37 1DL, Wales, United Kingdom

{Eoyegoke, Ttryfona, Ajcblyth}@glam.ac.uk

Abstract. Distributed intrusion detection is considered as a robust technique for the detection of complicated attacks in high traffic flow and heterogeneous network environment. It has become one of the main research subjects in information security. The use of agents fits in a distributed computational environment and it provides an effective method for detecting distributed attacks. However, when agents are used, as software entities they are exposed to external attacks when they run. It is therefore important to ensure the security of agent entities and the confidentiality and integrity of their exchanged messages. In this paper we analyse the different vulnerabilities of agent-based IDS, review security threats that can be imposed on agents by malicious hosts and provide a classification of these threats before looking further into the need for agent self-defence.

Keywords   Intrusion Detection, Mobile Agents, Self-defence

1. Introduction

1.1 Mobile Agents

As an independent and autonomous program, a mobile agent migrates between nodes in a heterogeneous network, acting as a personal assistant by performing tasks on behalf of its owner. It carries along with it its complete implementation, and interacts with host systems, other network entities, as well as other mobile and stationary agents [1]. An agent is comprised of the code and state information needed to carry out some computation. Mobility allows an agent to move, or hop, among agent platforms [3].

Therefore we define a Mobile agent as an autonomous software entity that can halt itself, transport itself to another agent-enabled host on the network, and continue execution, deciding where to go and what to do along the way. These agents are autonomous because they are independently-running entities. Because agents are independently-running entities, they can be added, removed and reconfigured without altering other components and without having to restart the intrusion detection system. [2]

Mobile agents are goal-oriented, can communicate with other agents, and can continue to operate even after the machine that launched them has been removed from the network. In the following subsection we will refer to the mobile agent-based intrusion detection systems (IDS) computing paradigm. One of the main obstacles to the widespread use and adaptation of this new technology are the several security concerns stemming from the use of mobile agents. A broad categorisation of security risks that can be encountered in mobile agent environments includes malicious hosts, malicious agents and malicious network entities.

Threats to the security of mobile agents generally fall into four comprehensive classes: disclosure of information, denial of service, corruption of information, and interference or nuisance. These classes of threats are usually the major inner security issues faced by agent-to-agent, agent-to-platform, platform-to-agent, and other-to-platform security issues.

1.2 Agent-based IDS
Autonomous agent-based IDS is a software IDS implementation utilising mobile agents that perform certain security monitoring functions at a host. There has been various types of Agent-based IDSs developed in recent years such as AAFID [6], DIDS [7], EMERALD [8], GRIDS [9], etc. which have all implemented the concept of distributed intrusion detection either by capturing misuse or anomaly or both. All these agent-based IDS have various components to which they use in order to perform their security functions.

These systems mostly have a hierarchical architecture; hierarchical systems scale better than the first generation intrusion detection systems, but they can be also more vulnerable. If an attacker is able to disable any part of the internal nodes or the root node, the functioning of that branch of the IDS is compromised. As agent-based IDSs make use of the mobile agent concept, they are prone to the security issues affecting agents, as well as code size and performance issues.

There are several types of security threads against agent-based IDS such as execution of exploits of different agents, malicious activities against running platform, etc. The major countermeasures presently available for some of these security problems involve signed agents, encryption and authorization methods.

1.3 Current Implementations
AAFID (Autonomous Agents For Intrusion detection) [6] is a distributed anomaly detection system that employs autonomous agents at the lowest level for data collection and analysis. At the higher levels of the hierarchy, transceivers and monitors are used to obtain a global view of activities. A single monitor may control several transceivers located at different hosts and may itself report to other monitors above it. Monitors this way get a global view of the network that facilitates in the decision process.

DIDS (Distributed Intrusion Detection system) [7] is another intrusion detection system that aggregates audit reports from a collection of hosts on a single network. The architecture consists of a host manager, a monitoring process or collection of processes running in background.

EMERALD (Event Monitoring Enabling Responses to Anomalous Live Disturbances) [8] is an analysis and response system that is able to address unanticipated misuse in large network-based enterprises, within an interoperable and scalable modular system framework. It has a hierarchical framework for distributed intrusion detection. It has service monitors at the lowest level that monitor the network traffic. Information gathered by service monitors is then communicated to client monitors that then pass it on to domain monitors, which then pass it on to enterprise monitors. Communication between the monitors is subscription based. The data at each monitor is collected, analyzed, reduced and then passed on to the top layers.

GRIDS [9] construct graphs to analyze and represent host and network activity. It lays out the organization as a hierarchy of departments and each department creates its own graph during analysis. Any material relating to other departments is passed up the hierarchy.

The remaining sections of this paper are organized as follows; section 2 discusses in detail security issues of agent-based IDS, providing examples of compromise. Section 3 describes the mobile agent self defence and control approach and discusses the current proposals. Finally, section 4 identifies open issues and further research areas.

2. Security Issues of Agent-based IDS

While mobile agents can help improve IDS in many areas, there is still the issue of security when it comes to applying the mobile agent technology into intrusion detection systems. That is, the use of mobile agents may introduce vulnerabilities that can be exploited by an attacker to propagate an attack or subvert detection by the IDS.

Security threats for the mobile agent computing paradigm can be classified into four broad categories:
- agent-to-agent,
- agent-to-platform,
- platform-to-agent, and
- other-to-platform.

The agent-to-agent category represents the set of threats in which agents exploit security weaknesses of or launch attacks against other agents residing on the same agent platform. The agent-to-platform category represents the set of threats in which agents exploit security weaknesses of or launch attacks against an agent platform where they reside. The platform-to-agent category represents the set of threats in which agent platforms compromise the security of agents that reside there. The other-to-platform category represents the set of threats in which external entities, including agents and agent platforms situated elsewhere on the network, threaten the security of an agent platform, including its underlying operating system and network communications service.

Agent against Agent Platform

This category represents the set of threats in which agents exploit security weaknesses of an agent platform or launch attacks against an agent platform. These threats include, masquerading, denial of service and unauthorized access [4].

The theory behind the mobile agent paradigm requires it to have an agent platform in order to be able to accept and execute codes. An incoming malicious agent can usually attack in two different ways. The first is to gain unauthorized access to information residing at the agent platform; the second is to use its authorized access in an unexpected and disruptive fashion.

Unauthorized access may occur simply through a lack of adequate access control mechanisms at the platform or weak identification and authentication, which allows an agent to masquerade as one trusted by the platform. Once access is gained, information residing at the platform can be disclosed or altered. Besides confidential data, this information could include the instruction codes of the platform. Depending on the level of access, the agent may be able to completely shut down or terminate the agent platform so has to make intrusion easy.

Even without gaining unauthorized access to resources, an agent can deny platform services to other agents by exhausting computational resources, if resource constraints are not established or not set tightly. Otherwise, the agent can merely interfere with the platform by issuing meaningless service requests wherever possible.

Agent Platform against Agent

The set of threats that could take place under this category include masquerading, denial of service, eavesdropping, and alteration [4].

A receiving agent platform can easily isolate and capture an agent and may attack it by extracting information, corrupting or modifying its code or state, denying requested services, or simply reinitializing or terminating it completely. An agent is very susceptible to the agent platform and may be corrupted merely by the platform responding falsely to requests for information or service, altering external communications, or delaying the agent until its task is no longer relevant.

Modification of the agent by the platform is a particularly insidious form of attack, since it can radically change the agent's behaviour (e.g., turning a trusted agent into malicious one) or the accuracy of the computation (e.g., changing collected information to yield misleading results).

Agent against Other Agents

The agent-to-agent issue is actually the kind of attack in which agents exploit the security weakness of other agents in order to launch an attack against those. These threats also include masquerading, denial of service, unauthorized access and repudiation [4].

An agent can target another agent using several general approaches which include actions to eavesdrop upon conversations, or interfere with an agent's activity. An agent can gain information by serving as an intermediary to the target agent (e.g., through masquerade) or by using platform services to eavesdrop on intra-platform messages. If the agent platform has weak or no control mechanisms in place, an agent can access and modify another agent's data or code. Even with reasonable control mechanisms in place, it is possible for an agent to attempt to send messages repeatedly to other agents in order to make it impossible for the agents to communicate in a planned timely fashion.

Other Entities against Agent System
There is always a possibility that there will be problems in protecting mobile agents from malicious sites, even assuming that locally active agents and the agent platform are well behaved. For example these sites could tamper with agents' state making it possible for them to disclose control information [4]. Also other entities both outside and inside the agent environment may be able to initiate actions to disrupt, harm, or subvert the agent system.

The major attack method used is to attack the inter-agent and inter-platform communications through either masquerading, or interception. Its is possible for an attacking entity to intercept agents or messages in transit and modify their contents, substitute other contents, or simply replay the transmission dialogue at a later time in an attempt to disrupt the synchronization or integrity of the agent framework. Denial of service attacks through available network interfaces is another possibility. Also at a protocol level below the agent-to-agent or platform-to-platform protocol, an entity may eavesdrop on messages in transit to and from a target agent or agent platform to gain information [5].

3. Mobile Agent Control and Defence

For mobile agents to be applied to intrusion detection, participating nodes must have an agent platform installed in order to execute agent codes. With mobile agent technology, the collection nodes, internal aggregation nodes, and command and control nodes which all comprise of an agent do not have to be continuously resident on the same physical machine. For example, a mobile agent may function as an aggregation node and move to whatever physical location in the network is best for its purposes. The mobile agent paradigm also offers specialization in which the agents may be different for different functions, each looking for distinct attacks and processing data accordingly.

Even though the intrusion detection systems mentioned in section 1.3 are considered to be of a higher standard than that of the conventional IDSs, there still exist vulnerabilities which need to be addressed. As they are usually implemented through a hierarchical approach, the failure of nodes at higher levels in the hierarchy can be proved to be very costly. The fact that data needs to be transferred to the highest level for it to be analyzed gives an opportunity for the intruder to intercept the data.

It is known that within classical hierarchical IDS, trust relationships are strong in the downward directions (i.e., subordinates trust superiors), but weaker in the reverse (i.e., superiors do not trust subordinates) [11]. By successfully subverting a node high in the hierarchy, an attacker can isolate a control branch of an IDS, or completely disable it by taking out the root.

To resist direct attacks, conventional IDSs rely on hardened systems for their critical components. Similarly, mobile agents can also take advantage of hardened systems by restricting the movement of the critical components they embody to such systems. That is, the trustworthiness of an agent platform **can be a factor in the itinerary of an agent;** mobile components have an advantage in being able to move away from danger, within well specified safe areas.

Mobile agents migrate in potentially hostile environments, so they must be protected from potential threats in-transit and on-site. For agents on migration, the confidentiality, authentication and integrity of their components during network transmission must be ensured. Communication content between mobile agent platforms must be secured from eavesdropping in order to protect data transmission. The sender and receiver should be able to identify whether the other party is legal. Any tampering of agents in the process of network transmission must be detected as quickly as possible.

In terms of agent execution security, because agents as processes execute locally in plaintext form, they may be vulnerable to eavesdroppers on the host while executing. No effective solution has been found so far to protect executing agent code [12]. The platform-to-agent category is one aspect which is difficult to defend against, because it concerns applications that require unrestricted movement of agents across the inter-networked systems [13].

A protection mechanism against tampering with the agent can be the application of digital signatures. The code of at least all management agents **must be signed and successfully pass validation** before the agent platform allows execution. This countermeasure prevents an attacker from modifying an agent's code or forging a bogus management agent. In combination with the ability of most agent platforms to mutually authenticate one another before allowing an agent to move, this measure makes it difficult to attack the mobile agent paradigm directly.

To circumvent the agent system, an attacker would need to penetrate successfully the host system supporting the agent platform, using the same techniques as with any conventional IDS. An attacker may delay or terminate incoming management agents, falsify information to them, or modify their state information. The latter is a particularly insidious form of attack, since it can radically change the agent's behaviour or the accuracy of the computation. The problem an attacker faces with delaying or terminating agents is that the IDS may note their absence, raise the level of suspicion of an intrusion, and launch a replacement agent or response agents to deal with the situation.

To counter the impact of a highly skilled intruder successfully taking control of a host and tampering with an agent's state information, many agent systems [3, 16, 17] provide a means to limit an agent's capabilities through privilege management. Authorizations, conveyed either internally within some data structure or externally along with the agent, are encoded into a protected object and bound to an agent, serving in effect as a kind of agent passport or visa. For example, a signed digital certificate, issued by the domain authority (e.g., system security officer) and containing the needed authorizations, can be cryptographically bound to the agent's code and serve this purpose. Any attempts to violate those authorizations are raised to the agent platform to take appropriate action.

Whilst not all agents performing management tasks need a high level of authorization, some agents may need to run with administrative or root privileges. For additional protection, a management agent can encapsulate collected results to prevent tampering, such that each result entry obtained at a platform is cryptographically bound to all previous entries and to the identity of the subsequent platform to be visited [14]. Each platform digitally signs its entry using its private key, and uses a secure hash function to link results and identities within an entry.

Known Threats	Countermeasures
An attacker gains access to a host and attempts to corrupt an agent's state information	The Cryptographic encapsulation of the partial results should be collected in order to allow detection of any modification.
An attacker has been able to gain access to a host and terminates or tries to indefinitely retain an agent	There must be in process Hardening of the platforms commensurate with their use by network management agents.
An attacker attempts to introduce a malicious agent in order to infiltrate the other agents	Agent platforms must be designed to mutually authenticate each other successfully before communicating. A process must be in place to make sure a security officer signs all management agents all agents must pass validation before being executed.
An attacker gains access to a host and terminates or indefinitely retains an agent	There must be a quick detection of the lost or tardy agent by the IDS and a possible initiation of a response.

Table 1: Threats against IDS and countermeasures [4].

Besides forward integrity, the encapsulation technique also provides confidentiality by encrypting each piece of accumulated information with the public key of the originator of the agent. The technique also ensures that a platform is unable to modify its entry in the chain, should the agent revisit it, or to collude with another platform to modify entries, without invalidating the chain. Other techniques also exist for encapsulating partial results having somewhat different properties [15, 18].

Solutions and applicable countermeasures to some of the common threats faced by agents and agents platforms as discussed here, are summarized in table 1 [4].

4. Conclusions

At the moment, the majority of the implementations of the agent-based IDS paradigm try to resolve security issues by the use of signed agents, encryption and authorization methods. However, even when those countermeasures are in place, they can only protect from specific scenarios, e.g. known agent-to-platform attacks etc. Most of the current proposals address the issue in a system-wise fashion, in a sense that they require configurations of the entire IDS to be in place and the protection mechanisms address the entire IDS.

However, as most of the vulnerabilities of agent-based IDSs stem from the agents per se, providing rigorous mechanisms for developing agent self-defences would be a step forward. The objectives of such further research would be to allow agents to move amongst comparable trustworthy hosts within their security domain whilst been able to defend themselves from outside attacks, without further centralised IDS configuration; also to be able to ensure that each platform will allocate each agent under the appropriate security policy, granting or denying the same privileges it had on its previous platforms. The authors are presently researching in ways of making agents capable of protecting themselves, as well as to be able to detect malicious hosts and platforms with minimal overhead.

5. References

[1] TRIPATHI, A.R., KARNIK, N.M., AHMED, T., SINGH, R.D., PRAKASH, A., KAKANI, V., VORA, AND M.K., PATHAK, M. 2001. Design of the Ajanta system for mobile agent programming. *The Journal of Systems and Software.*
[2] M. Crosbie, G. Spaford, Active defense of a computer system using autonomous agents, Technical Report 95-008, COAST Group, Department of Computer Sciences, Purdue University, West Lafayette, IN 47907-1398, February 1995.
[3] Wayne A. Jansen "INTRUSION DETECTION WITH MOBILE AGENTS" National Institute of Standards and Technology.
[4] JANSEN, W.A. 2000. Countermeasures for Mobile Agent Security. Computer Communications. Special issue on advanced security techniques for network protection. Elsevier Science.
[5] E. H. Spafford and D. Zamboni. Intrusion detection using autonomous agents. *Computer Networks*, 34(4):547{570, October 2000.

[6] Balasubramaniyan, J., Garcia-Fernandez, J. O., Isacoff, D., Spafford, E. H., and Zamboni, D. An Architecture for Intrusion Detection using Autonomous Agents, Department of Computer Science, Purdue University: Coast TR, 98-05, 1998.

[7] J. B. S. Snapp and G. D. et al. Dids (distributed intrusion detection system) motivation, archi-tecture, and an early prototype. In *Fourteenth National Computer Security Conference*, Washington, DC, October 1991.

[8] Porras, P.A. and Neumann, P.G. EMERALD: Event Monitoring Enabling Responses to Anomalous Live Disturbances, National Information Systems Security Conference, October 1997.

[9] Staniford-Chen, S., Cheung, S., et. al., GrIDS – A Graph Based Intrusion Detection System for Large Networks, In the Proceedings of the 19th National Information Computer Security Conference (Baltimore, MD), October 1996.

[10] G. White, E. Fisch, and U. Pooch. Cooperating security managers: A peer-based intrusion detection system, IEEE Net-work, vol. 10, no. 1, pp. 20–23, 1994.

[11] Deborah Frincke, Don Tobin, Jesse McConnell, Jamie Marconi, and Dean Polla, "A Framework for Cooperative Intrusion Detection," Twenty-first National Information Systems Security Conference, pp.361- 373, October 1998.

[12] Chunsheng Li, Qingfeng Song, and Chengqi Zhang, *Senior Member, IEEE* MA-IDS Architecture for Distributed Intrusion Detection using Mobile Agents. Proceedings of the 2nd International Conference on Information Technology for Application (ICITA 2004).

[13] Wayne Jansen and Tom Karygiannis, "Mobile Agents and Security," NIST Special Publication 800-   19, September 1999.

[14] Günter Karjoth, N. Asokan, and Ceki Gülcü, "Protecting the Computation Results of Free-Roaming Agents," Second International Workshop on Mobile Agents, Stuttgart, Germany, September 1998.

[15] Sergio Loureiro, Refik Molova and Alain Pannetrat, "Secure Data Collection with Updates, "Workshop on Agents on Electronic Commerce, First Asia Pacific Conference on Intelligent Agent Technology December 1999, pp. 121-130.

[16] Srilekha Mudumbai, Abdeliah Essiari, and William Johnston, "Anchor Toolkit - A Secure Mobile Agent System," Mobile Agents '99 Conference, October 1999.

[17] Joseph Tardo and Luis Valente, "Mobile Agent Security and Telescript," IEEE COMPCON '96, pp.58-63, February 1996.

[18] Bennet S. Yee, "A Sanctuary for Mobile Agents," Technical Report CS97-537, University of California in San Diego, April 28, 1997.

Detecting and Classifying Attacks in Computer Networks Using Feed-Forward and Elman Neural Networks

V. Alarcon-Aquino[1], J. A. Mejia-Sanchez[1], R. Rosas-Romero[1]
J. F. Ramirez-Cruz[2]

[1] Department of Electrical and Electronic Engineering
Communication and Signal Processing Group, CENTIA
Universidad de las Américas-Puebla
72820 Cholula, Puebla MEXICO
vicente.alarcon@udlap.mx

[2] Department of Computer Science
Instituto Tecnologico de Apizaco
Tlaxcala, MEXICO

Abstract. In this paper, we present an approach for detecting and classifying attacks in computer networks by using neural networks. Specifically, a design of an intruder detection system is presented to protect the hypertext transfer protocol (HTTP). We propose the use of an application-based model using neural networks to model properly non-linear data. The benefit of this perspective is to work directly on the causes of an attack, which are determined directly by the commands used in the protected application. The intruder detection system is designed by defining three different neural networks, which include two multi-layer feed-forward networks and the Elman recurrent network. The results reported in this paper show that the Elman recurrent network achieved a performance around ninety percent of good detection, which demonstrates the reliability of the designed system to detect and classify attacks in high-level network protocols.

Keywords: Intrusion Detection, Neural networks, HTTP protocol.

1 Introduction

With the explosive growth of computer networking and electronic commerce environments, security of networking systems has become very important [3], [5]. Currently, network anomaly and intrusion detection in wide area networks and e-commerce infrastructures is gaining practical importance (see e.g., [5], [8]). Detecting computer attacks thus poses significant problems of the global Internet so that the network intrusion detection (NID) area is devoted to detecting this activity [3], [5].

Several approaches have been proposed to solve the problem of network intrusion detection (see e.g., [3], [5], [8]-[11], [13]-[14]). The problem of NID may be solved from the statistical perspective as discussed in [5] or as discussed in [3] a security issue as the one we are facing may find a correct solution depending on whether we use a host-based model or a network-based model. For a host-based model, intrusion detection systems (IDS) find their decisions on information obtained from a single or multiple host systems, while for a network-based model, IDS find their decisions by monitoring the traffic in the network to which the hosts are connected [15].

It has been shown that neural networks have special advantages in IDS such as the self-adaptive ability and the internal parallel computation (see e.g., [3], [9]-[11], [13]-[14]). Elman recurrent neural networks have been recently considered for network intrusion detection (see e.g., [9], [11], [14]). In the work reported in this paper we propose an intruder detection system to detect and classify correctly attacks in high-level network protocols by using two feed-forward neural networks and the Elman recurrent neural network. The aim is to compare and prove the underlying fundamentals of our approach using these networks in network intrusion detection. Furthermore, a competitive transfer function to classify attacks is reported. We present the use of an application-based model using neural networks to model properly non-linear data. The benefit of this perspective is to work directly on the causes of an attack, which are determined directly by the commands used in the protected application. The remainder of this paper is organised as follows. In Section 2, we present a description of intrusion detection techniques. Section 3 discusses the HTTP protocol. In Section 4, we present a brief overview of neural networks. In Section 5, we propose the IDS to detect and classify attacks in high-level network protocols by using neural networks. Performance evaluation of the intruder detection system is presented in Section 6. In Section 7, conclusions of this paper are reported.

2 Intrusion Detection Techniques

In this section we present a brief description of intrusion detection techniques. There are two primary models for analyzing events to detect attacks [9], [15]: the misuse detection model and the anomaly detection model. The misuse detection model uses patterns of known systems attacks to match and identify attacks. In other words, the misuse detection approach bases its performance on comparing an Internet command with a database of signatures (or known attacks) in order to recognize whether the Internet requirement has an intrusive nature or normal behaviour. However, this solution is a static approach in the sense that an intrusive requirement that is not in the database is not recognized as an attack. This is due to the fact that the database is built based on past experience but not on future attacks [8]. Note that new variations of an attack may find a way inside the network system because there is no record of this type of attack in the database, making this type of system very vulnerable and dependent of database constant actualizations [9].

The anomaly detection model detects intrusions by searching abnormal network traffic (see e.g., [5]). That is, this model tries to determine if a deviation from the established normal usage patterns can be flagged as intrusion [15]. The anomaly detection approach, which is based on finding patterns on Internet data, determines whether the data have an intrusive nature or normal behaviour. With this type of characterization we may be able to decide if unknown data is an attack without having to know previous information about it [10].

3 Description of HTTP protocol

According to the Spanish company S21SEC [12] the hypertext transfer protocol (HTTP) is the main and most used protocol for computer communications, and it is therefore the main source of attacks in the Internet. To design an intruder detection system to detect attacks on this protocol, it is thus necessary to assemble an amount of data corresponding to normal and intrusive behaviour. These data serve as training data and have to be characterized by the proposed system; afterwards the system may be able to classify the nature of new data. There are at least five categories in a HTTP requirement [7], [11]:

NORMAL: This classification includes the normal behaviour of a system command meaning that no attack is involved.

COMMAND INJECTION: This category includes all commands executed directly on the system due to vulnerabilities on data validation, basically executing shell codes written in machine language.

SQL DATABASE ATTACK: This is another type of command injection attack, but this is executed on SQL databases.

XSS (CROSS-SITE SCRIPTING): This includes all commands executed via HTML, JAVA, or JAVASCRIPT.

PATH MODIFICATION: This is the path manipulation of a file or directory that provides privileges to the attacker.

The intruder detection system reported in this paper should be able to detect and classify adequately the HTTP requirement in one of these five categories.

4 Feed-forward and Elman neural networks

Neural networks may be used to work as a pattern extractor of an intruder detection system, which may characterize adequately the nature of any HTTP requirement. Figure 1 shows a single artificial neuron model [4]. The input vector $\{X_1, X_2, K, X_p\}$ is multiplied by a weight vector $\omega_{kj}, j = 0, 1, K, p$ and then summed to get a single scalar number υ_k, which is then passed through a transfer function $\varphi(\cdot)$ that delivers the neuron's output y_k. Letting the input vector and the desired neuron's output fixed, we only have to determine the weight vector that allows this neuron to deliver the desired output for the corresponding input vector. The artificial neuron can deliver any output value for any input vector as long as we can find the corresponding weight vector. This process is known as the learning process of a neuron [4]. An output value between one and zero can be obtained with the sigmoid transfer function. These values are then used to decide whether an input vector is an attack or normal behaviour. The input vector to the neural network system represents the HTTP requirement made by any user in the communication network.

190

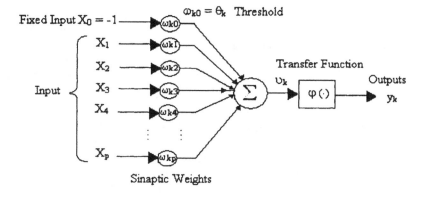

Fig. 1. Neuron Model

4.1 Feed-forward neural networks

It is necessary the use of more than one neuron to be able to correctly model a non-linear data flow. A multi-layer feed-forward neural network consists of a number of neurons structured on several layers, that is, an input layer, hidden layers, and an output layer (see Fig. 2). The output layer may be a layer of one or more neurons, allowing the network to deliver one or more outputs for one or more inputs. As for a single neuron, the training process for a neural network consists in correctly finding the value of each weight vector corresponding to each neuron so that we can obtain the desired output for each combination of inputs. This process is accomplished by an algorithm known as Back-propagation [4].

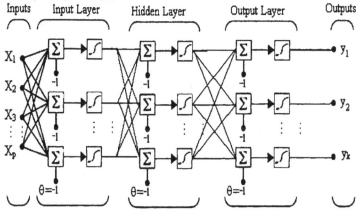

Fig. 2. Multi-layer feed-forward neural network

4.1.1 Back-propagation

The back-propagation algorithm changes weight vectors value in recursive propagation over the network from the output layer to the input layer and the main objective of this algorithm is to minimize the error from network's output by modifying weight vectors. The back-propagation algorithm is based on a gradient descent algorithm where the main goal is to search over the error surface, corresponding to a neural network, for the combination of weights that allow the network to perform with minimum error. This search is accomplished by calculating the gradient of the error surface in which the negative of gradient's direction indicates the direction where the surface decreases more rapidly, and the gradient's magnitude indicates the amount of distance over which this direction is valid. With this algorithm we may be able to train the neural network to design the intruder detection system. However, there are important considerations we must know before using this algorithm. First, for a pattern classification problem, as the one we are facing, neurons work near to the limits of zero and one because we train them to deliver this kind of output to indicate whether a requirement is an attack or normal behaviour. The problem with the back-propagation algorithm is that it computes the gradient of the error surface based on partial derivation of the transfer function at each neuron. This partial derivative represents the change of slope for this transfer function; a sigmoidal transfer function has its minimum slope change at the output limits of one and zero [6]. Minimum slope change will decreases the magnitude of the gradient making the algorithm very slow for this kind of problem. The problem of working with a slow algorithm to train a neural network is that it can get stuck in a local minimum of the surface. If a local minimum is far to the global minimum the network performs poorly.

4.1.2 Faster training

RESILIENT BACK PROPAGATION: The purpose of the resilient back-propagation training algorithm is to eliminate the harmful effects of the small magnitudes of the partial derivatives as discussed above. Only the sign of the derivative is used to determine the direction of the weight update. The magnitude of the derivative has no effect on the weight update. The size of the weight change is determined by a separate update value. The update value for each weight and bias is increased by a factor Δinc if the derivative of the performance function with respect to that weight has the same sign for two successive iterations. The update value is decreased by a factor Δdec if the derivative with respect that weight changes sign from the previous iteration. Whenever the weights are oscillating the weight change is reduced. If the weight continues to change in the same direction for several iterations, then the magnitude of the weight change is increased allowing faster training [1].
CONJUGATE GRADIENT: The basic back-propagation algorithm adjusts the weights in the gradient descent direction (negative of the gradient). This is the direction in which the performance function is decreasing more rapidly. It turns out that, although the function decreases more rapidly along the negative of the gradient, this does not necessarily produces the fastest convergence. In the conjugate gradient algorithms a search is performed along conjugate directions, which produces generally faster convergence than gradient descent directions. In the basic back-propagation algorithm the learning rate is used to determine the length of the weight update (step

size). In the conjugate gradient algorithm, the step size is adjusted at each iteration. A search is made along the conjugate gradient direction to determine the step size, which minimizes the performance function along that line [1].

4.2. Elman recurrent neural network

Another option to design the intruder detection system based on neural networks is the Elman recurrent neural network which consists of the same structure of a multi-layer feed-forward network with the addition of a feedback loop which enables the network to find temporal training patterns. The Elman neural network is a recurrent network that connects the feedback loop from the output of the hidden layer to its input [2], [4]. This recurrent connection allows the Elman network to both detect and generate time-varying patterns. This neural network structure is used to obtain a different performance allowing us to take a design decision.

5 Detection of Attacks based on Neural Networks

As mentioned previously, any HTTP requirement may fall in one of five categories which include normal and abnormal behaviours. The intruder detection system is designed to take an HTTP requirement and determine the correspondent category, which is accomplished by a MATLAB® script. For this purpose, the dataset is divided into two parts. The first part is seventy percent of the dataset corresponding to training data, and the second part is the remaining thirty percent corresponding to test data. To this point we count with 488 requirements corresponding to abnormal behaviour and 285 corresponding to normal behaviour [7].

5.1. Data Pre-processing

An example of a typical HTTP requirement is given by //nombre.exe?param1=..\..\archivo. Most of this string consists of filenames, parameters, and alphanumeric strings which normally changes from system to system. The most significant part of this string is the file extensions, and special characters. As a result, every alphanumeric string is replaced with the special character '@' [7]. Thus, the example requirement shown before takes the following shape //@.exe?@=..\..\@. Now we have only the significant part of every requirement. The next step is to convert these characters to their corresponding ASCII decimal value. Once data is formatted to decimal, we need to consider that HTTP requirements do not have a fixed length; however, a neural network needs a fixed input length because the number of neurons in the input layer depends on this fixed length. The next step in data preprocessing is to fix the requirement's length. This is accomplished by a sliding window approach; its main function is to convert a variable length vector in several fixed length vectors. The length is determined by a constant defined by the problem's nature. The sliding window approach can be described as follows. Consider a decimal vector with six elements. Now suppose that a neural network requires a fixed input length M equal to three. The sliding window approach delivers (N-M+1) vectors of fixed length M, where N is the length of the original vector. As a result, we have static length vectors which are able to work as input vectors for a neural network. In order to have a better network performance, these vectors are then converted to their binary form [7]. After the binary conversion, a binary matrix is obtained, which has to be converted to a single vector of length Mx8, where M is the fixed length defined by the sliding window.

5.2. Neural Network Architecture

As explained previously, the length of the input vector is Mx8. In this case we have chosen M equal to eight; thus, for this problem an input length equal to 64 is obtained. The value of M was chosen to generate an adequate size for the dataset after using the sliding window approach. Therefore, the neural network has 64 neurons in the input layer, while the output layer is conformed by five output neurons corresponding to each of the five categories where a HTTP requirement may fall. The network is trained to output a 1 in the correct position of the output vector corresponding to the desired HTTP requirement and to fill the rest of the output vector with 0's. Three neural networks are defined with 64 input neurons and five output neurons but with different number of hidden neurons and structure. The first network is a multi-layer feed-forward network (FF1) with two hidden layers with 15 neurons each (see Fig. 3a). The number of hidden layers and hidden neurons is selected by guesswork and experience. This network is trained with a resilient back-propagation algorithm and all neurons are sigmoid to enable the network to output a one or a zero as this is a pattern classification problem. This neural network is trained with 70% of the dataset achieving an error goal of .015 (see Fig. 3b).

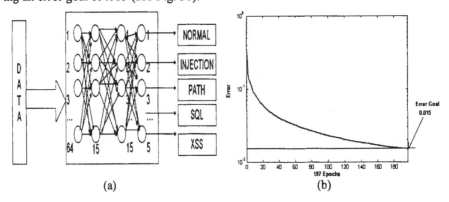

(a)   (b)

Fig. 3. (a) Multilayer feed-forward neural network. (b) First feed-forward network training

The second network is a multi-layer feed-forward network (FF2) with two hidden layers with 20 neurons each. This network differs from the first one in the training algorithm, which in this case is a conjugate gradient algorithm. This neural network is also trained with 70% of the dataset achieving an error goal of .015 (see Fig. 4a). The third network is the Elman recurrent network with two hidden layers with 30 neurons each. According to [2] the number of neurons used by an Elman network to face a problem is larger than what a multi-layer feed-forward network would use for the same problem. This is the reason why we choose 30 neurons for each hidden layer. A resilient back-propagation algorithm is used to train this network. Training results are shown in Fig. 4b.

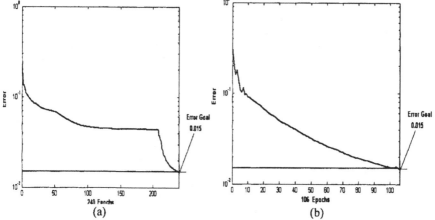

(a)   (b)

Fig. 4. (a) Second feed-forward network training (b) Elman network training

6   Performance Evaluation

The three neural networks are assessed with 30% of the dataset, delivering, for each training vector, an output which is passed through competitive MATLAB® transfer function. This ensures that the output corresponding to the most activated neuron is a value of one and the rest of the neurons are a value of zero [7] (see Fig. 5). Then we compared outputs with targets and counted errors. For this particular problem we have chosen two performance criteria for each network. The first criterion is identification percentage corresponding to the amount of outputs that exactly correspond to a desired target identifying correctly the category of any HTTP requirement. The second criterion is detection percentage corresponding to the amount of outputs that exactly detects a normal or an abnormal requirement, without taking care of the category in which an abnormal requirement may fall. The detection percentage should be larger than identification percentage because of the level of accuracy that each percentage uses. Table 1 shows the percentage obtained for each neural network as well as false positives and negatives. A false positive occurs when the system classifies an action as intrusion when it is a valid action, whereas a false negative occurs when an intrusion actually happens but the system allows is to pass as non-intrusive behaviour. It can be seen that the best performance is accomplished by the Elman network with 90% of good detection and 87% of correct identification. However, the other networks performed almost as well as the Elman. Once the network is correctly trained weight vectors are defined and we are able to work with this trained network as an intruder detection system for the HTTP protocol.

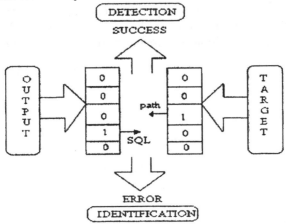

Fig. 5. Identification and detection.

Table 1. Performance of each neural network

	FF1	FF2	ELMAN
Identification	84.85	84.42	87.01
Detection	88.74	89.18	90.91
False Positives	4.97%	5%	4.86%
False Negatives	0.97%	0.96%	0.94%

7 Conclusions

This paper has presented an approach for detecting and classifying intrusions in high-level network protocols by using neural networks. The results reported in this paper show that the best performance is accomplished by the Elman network with 90% of good detection and 87% of correct identification. Note that a better performance may be achieved if the network is trained with more training data keeping the neural network's knowledge updated. The approach of anomaly detection has proven to be a good solution for this kind of problem, performing a 90% of good detection which is by far a better performance than what misuse detection can accomplish with new and unknown data. Future work will focus on investigating further enhancements using recurrent neural networks trained by real-time recurrent learning algorithms. Furthermore, a hardware implementation on an FPGA, which may work with a firewall for detecting intruders and protecting the system, is also considered.

References

[1] M. Beale, and H. Demuth, *Neural Network Toolbox*, Math Works, Inc. Massachusetts, USA, (2003).

[2] C. Bishop, *Neural Networks for Pattern Recognition*. Oxford University Press, Nueva York, USA, (1995).

[3] A. Bivens, C. Palagiri, R. Smith, B. Szymanski, and M. Embrechts, Network-Based Intrusion Detection Using Neural Networks, *Intelligent Engineering Systems through Artificial Neural Networks*, Proc. of ANNIE-2002, vol. 12, ASME Press, New York, (2002) pp. 579-584.

[4] S. Haykin S., *Neural Networks: A Comprehensive Foundation*, McMMillan, New York, (1994).

[5] C. Manikopoulos, C. and S. Papavassiliou, Network Intrusion and Fault Detection: A Statistical Anomaly Approach, *IEEE Communications Magazine*, October (2002) pp. 76-82.

[6] T. Masters, *Practical Neural Network Recipes in C++*, Academic Press, Inc. California, USA, (1993).

[7] J. A. Mejia-Sanchez, *Detección de Intrusos en Redes de Comunicaciones Utilizando Redes Neuronales*, Department of Electrical and Electronic Engineering, Universidad de las Américas Puebla, Mexico, May (2004).

[8] B. Mukherjee, L. T. Heberlein, and K. N. Levitt. Network Intrusion Detection, *IEEE Network*, May/June (1994).

[9] J. P. Planquart, Application of Neural Networks to Intrusion Detection, *SANS Institute*, July (2001).

[10] N. Pongratz, Application of Neural Networks to Recognize Computer Identity Hijacking, *University of Wisconsin*, (2001).

[11] E. Torres, *Immunologic System for intrusion detection at http protocol level*, Department of Systems Engineering, Pontificia Universidad Javeriana, Colombia, May (2003).

[12] S21SEC, http://www.s21sec.com

[13] L. de Sa Silva, A. C. Ferrari dos Santos, J. D. S. Da Silva, A. Montes., A Neural Network Application for Attack Detection in Computer Networks, *IEEE International Joint Conference on Neural Networks*, Vol. 2, July (2004) pp. 1569-1574.

[14] X. Jing-Sheng, S. Ji-Zhou, Z. Xu., Recurrent Network in Network Intrusion Detection System, *IEEE International Conference on Machine Learning and Cybernetics*, Vol. 5 August (2004) pp. 2676-2679.

[15] Y. Bai, and H. Kobayashi, Intrusion Detection Systems: Technology and Development, *IEEE International Conference on Advanced Information Networking and Application (AINA '03)*, (2003)

DATA AUTHENTICATION AND TRUST WITHIN DISTRIBUTED INTRUSION DETECTION SYSTEM INTER-COMPONENT COMMUNICATIONS

John Haggerty, Qi Shi, Paul Fergus & Madjid Merabti

School of Computing and Mathematical Sciences, Liverpool John Moores University, James Parsons Building, Byrom Street, Liverpool, L3 3 AF, Tel: 0151 231 2279 {J. Haggerty, Q. Shi, P. Fergus, M. Merabti}@livjm.ac.uk

Abstract. Networks are a fundamental technology for users and businesses alike. In order to achieve security in ever-increasing distributed environments, recent advances in intrusion detection have led to the development of distributed intrusion detection systems (DIDS). A key concern in these systems is that inter-component communication of data regarding potential network intrusions must be authenticated. Thus, a level of trust is maintained within the distributed system that data has not been altered by a malicious intruder. This paper presents a novel scheme that provides security in the transmission of data between DIDS components. A key consideration in the provision of this security is that of the computational and network overhead that this data transfer incurs. Therefore, this paper presents a scheme that ensures the high level of trust required within DIDS, and as demonstrated by a case study, with minimal computational or network impact.

Keywords   Distributed Intrusion Detection Systems, Authentication

1. Introduction

Networks are a fundamental technology for both users and businesses alike. These networks allow disparate and heterogeneous hosts or systems to interact and communicate over large distances irrespective of geo-political borders. Underlying the use of these networks is the need for the provision of a secure environment through a variety of deployed countermeasures such as firewalls, intrusion detection systems (IDS), and access control. Just as networks are increasingly distributed, so the countermeasures that are employed must be so too. Therefore, recent advances in intrusion detection have seen the development of IDS for deployment in large networks [1] or distributed intrusion detection systems (DIDS). These systems consist of a number of system components; network monitors, that report and act on potential intrusions within the network, and analysis engines that provide the command and control required by those monitors.

197

Within DIDS, a wide range of devices may potentially connect and share data regarding potential intrusions over networks. A fundamental design goal within IDS is the security of the security system itself [2]. Therefore, a key consideration in DIDS is the securing of inter-component communications to prevent shared data from being exploited by a malicious attacker. There are three foundations of trust that are required during data transactions between a monitor and the analysis engine. First, the reporting monitor is who they say they are. Second, the analysis engine is in fact who they say they are and that it is the service advertised. Finally, that the the transfer of the intrusion information is not intercepted and modified in any way *en route* to either host. For example, a monitor A forwards an intrusion report to its analysis engine B. B supplies the response to the intrusion via a network connection. Listening in on the connection is C, a malicious user. C intercepts the data *en route* from B to A, modifies the data in some way, and forwards the modified data to A. In the traditional network model, A has no way of knowing that the data has been modified for malicious purposes and trusts the data as if it comes from B.

Therefore, in order to achieve the trust required within a DIDS, the monitor, the analysis engine and in particular the data must in some way be authenticated. Authentication ensures that the data has not been modified in any way, or if it is modified, that modification is discovered by either party. The security of this data is paramount as undermining any such information passed between IDS and DIDS entities will undermine the security of the network under protection. IDS are prime targets for attack due to the protection that they provide [3]. In order to provide the authentication and trust that these systems require, it is assumed that traditional authentication schemes are to be used. However, these schemes are not designed for deployment in high-speed, large-volume networks that DIDS operate within and therefore add unacceptable computational and network load.

The novel contribution of this paper is that it presents a cryptographic scheme to provide the authentication and trust required within DIDS inter-component data communications. This scheme, presented in section 3, relies on one-way hash functions and public-key encryption to ensure security of DIDS information. The case study presented in this paper demonstrates that the hashing algorithm will have an impact on network and computational load but this effect may be significantly reduced by careful choice of algorithm.

This paper is organised as follows. In section 2, related work in authentication and intrusion detection is discussed. Section 3 posits our approach for authentication and trust within DIDS. Section 4 presents the implementation and results from our case study. Finally, section 5 presents further work and concludes.

2. Related Work

Authentication ensures that a principal's identity or data origin is genuine [4] and is widely used in network security. In addition, authentication techniques are used to maintain the integrity and non-repudiation of the data itself. Early work in authentication focused on public-key encryption in order to meet the requirements of authentication. However, many of these schemes, such as [5, 6] do not scale to the requirements of high-speed, large volume networks due to their complexity and associated overhead that they incur.

Recent work, such as [7, 8, 9] has demonstrated the requirement for authentication schemes within multicast systems to reflect the needs of today's networks. These schemes focus on high multimedia data throughput within networks and therefore operate in similar high-level, large-volume network environments to DIDS. These approaches suggest schemes for source authentication for applications such as broadcasting stock quotes, film distribution and video-conferencing. However, these schemes are not without their problems for adoption in intrusion detection. Primarily, due to their complexity they are not flexible enough, nor computationally light, for deployment in DIDS.

Intrusion detection is the "art" of detecting and responding to computer misuse [10]; or more accurately, it is the identification of evidence of intrusions [1]. IDS are the system manifestations of this effort that alert legitimate system users to the possibility of an attack either whilst the attack is ongoing or after the fact.

Intrusion detection is viewed as an "art" in that there is no one accepted methodology or set of methodologies as to how this effort is to be performed. There are two main approaches to IDS; misuse detection and anomaly detection. *Misuse detection* is the identification of anomalous network traffic by applying known attack signatures to the traffic under inspection. *Anomaly detection* uses models of user behaviour and inspects systems under their control for deviations of these expected operations. Irrespective of the approach, the IDS is often placed within the network under protection. As such, various network entities are required to communicate any results that they find regarding evidence of intrusions. This can occur within a centralised architecture (client-server) or decentralised architecture (host-to-host with a higher-level entity acting as a reference point if required).

Recent work within intrusion detection recognises some of the failings in perimeter model devices such as IDS in dealing with distributed attacks such as denial of service or Internet worms. Therefore, DIDS are often deployed beyond the network perimeter to provide *distributed detection* of *distributed attacks*. For example, [11] propose a system for detecting distributed attacks through network traffic analysis. *Groups Of Strongly SImilar Birthdays* (GOSSIB) [12] detects attacks to provide traceback to attack sources across distributed networks. The *DIstributed Denial-of-Service DEtection Mechansim* (DiDDeM) [13] provides a distributed detection system for deployment against denial-of-service attacks, and through this detection effort, provides traceback to attack sources and response through throttling the source of the attack. These approaches have in common that they are deployed within the network infrastructure, and therefore system components must communicate to provide a co-ordinated defence posture.

However, a key issue remains; that of how to secure the data of DIDS inter-component communications within a distributed network environment to ensure the authentication and trust required by the system. In the next section, such a scheme is presented.

3. Authentication and Trust in DIDS

Source authentication approaches and the defence against modification required by DIDS share a common problem; that of the trade-off between computational overhead and network overhead. *Computational overhead* refers to the additional processing power placed on the host by implementing a security service. For example, the use of complex cryptographic schemes require more overhead than lighter approaches although they provide more security. A complex cryptographic scheme will be too computationally exhaustive to be used within a high-speed detection environment where devices have limited resources available to them due to the large volume of network traffic inspected. *Network overhead* refers to the load placed on the network connections by placing additional traffic on the connections between devices or increasing packet size when reporting intrusions.

Therefore, this paper proposes a lightweight, cryptographic authentication scheme for protection of data from modification within a DIDS. This approach differs in those discussed above in that it does not focus on the authentication of particular hosts within data transactions, but focuses on the data transaction as an entity requiring authentication in its own right. Therefore, the approach has two requirements. First, that the encryption algorithm is simple to reflect the types of hosts served by a DIDS, so the algorithm must be computationally light whilst complex enough to ensure security. Second, that the approach requires that only a small amount of data be added to the packet to ensure that the additional information does not have a negative impact on network performance.

Data authentication in DIDS is required to ensure that data comes from who it purports to come from. Thus, message authenticity, non-repudiation, and integrity are maintained. In the case where a secret key $K_{x,y}$ is shared between two communicating hosts X and Y, a cryptographic one-way hash function $H(z)$ (e.g. [5]) can be applied to ensure this aim. The one-way hash function serves as a check for the authenticity and integrity of a message from one host, e.g. X, to the other in the following way. A hash result of the message denoted as M_x is computed using shared key $K_{x,y}$ by message sender X, which is expressed as $H(K_{x,y}, M_x)$ where '$K_{x,y}, M_x$' means the concatenation of $K_{x,y}$ and M_x. X sends both the message and hash result to message recipient Y. The same way is used by Y to compute another hash result from the shared key and message received to compare the two hash results. If they are different, then a change has occurred. One-way hash functions must be made easy to compute from input to output, but not in the opposite direction. An advantage of using hash functions for authentication is that they are computationally faster than public-key-based signature schemes [14].

In the case of a key not being shared between the two communicating hosts, X and Y, a one-way hash function in conjunction with a public-key cryptographic scheme such as RSA [5] can be applied to generate digital signatures for message authentication. Figure 1 defines such a communication protocol. Suppose that RSA is applied for signature generation, X has a pair of private/secret and public keys, SK_x and PK_x, and public key PK_x has been certified by a CA and known by Y. The message in figure 1 consists of X's identity, ID_x, its message, M_x, a timestamp, t_x, and X's signature. The signature is the encryption of the hash result with X's private key.

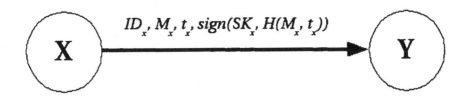

Figure 1. Authentication with no shared secret key.

Y receives the message, and using X's public key, PK_x, decrypts the signature to recover the hash result. Y then computes its own hash result from the message and timestamp received. If the recovered and computed hash results match, the authenticity and integrity of the message are assured as no other host could forge X's signature without knowing its private key. To ensure that the message is not part of a replay attack, a timestamp is included. In any dispute, the message signature will be used to resolve the dispute.

The use of public-key cryptographic schemes adds computational overhead. Therefore, symmetric encryption schemes may be used to reduce this overhead. Figure 2 illustrates a communication protocol using symmetric encryption such as the Data Encryption Standard (DES) [14]. Suppose that the confidentiality of host X's message content needs to be protected, and a key, $K_{x,y}$, is shared between hosts X and Y. X sends its identity, ID_x, and encrypts its identity, message, M_x, and timestamp, t_x using this shared key, which is denoted as $SE(K_{x,y}, ID_x, M_x, t_x)$.

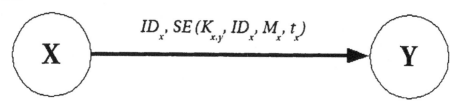

Figure 2. Authentication with shared secret key.

Y decrypts the encrypted part of the message it has received from X using the shared key. If the decryption is successful, the message has been sent by X as only X and Y know the key. This is verified by comparison of the two ID_x to ensure that they are the same. To ensure that the message is not part of a replay attack, a timestamp is included.

4. Case Study and Results

This section demonstrates that the computational overhead placed on the DIDS can be reduced through the choice of hashing algorithm. In addition, the choice of hashing scheme will also affect packet size, and therefore the choice of algorithm may be used to reduce network overhead.

The encryption algorithm is developed using Java, which uses the java.security namespace. Our authentication scheme has the provision to encrypt the MessageDigest using either MD5 or SHA1. The scheme also allows every packet to be encrypted before it is streamed to the client or it can encrypt every nth packet where n is a value bigger than zero and less than the pre-defined packet size. The MessageDigest generated for a packet is appended onto the front of the streamed data byte array. MD5 uses the first 16 bytes of the array containing the hash for the packet and in SHA1 the first 20 bytes. When the client receives the data it either extracts the first 16 or 20 bytes depending on the hashing algorithm used by the two devices. The case study uses two PCs connected using a RJ45 cross-over cable. Data packets containing 192 bytes of data and either 16 or 20 bytes containing the hash value for the data, depending on the hashing algorithm, are transmitted between the two PCs.

Figure 3 illustrates the time to stream 10,000 packets of data, where every 100th packet is hashed. Streaming data with no hashing takes 30.717 seconds and using the MD5 and SHA1 algorithms takes 31.739 and 32.747 seconds respectively. The results suggest that the MD5 hashing algorithm is 3.3275% slower and the SHA1 hashing algorithm is 6.608% slower than when no hashing is used.

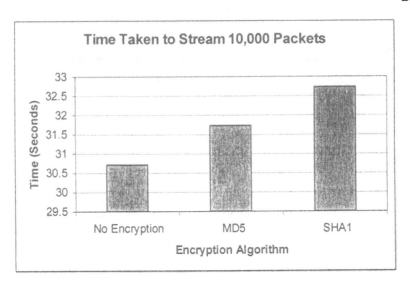

Figure 3. Time taken to stream 10,000 packets.

Figure 4 demonstrates the average processing time for each packet. When no hashing is used the computational overhead is 3.012776 milliseconds per packet with a standard deviation of 6.72351.

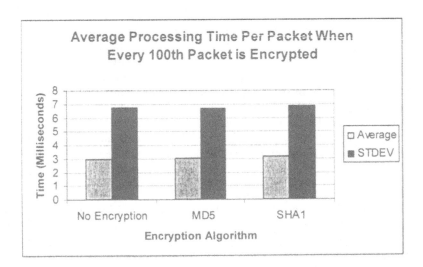

Figure 4. Every 100th packet encrypted using the MD5 hashing algorithm.

The computational overhead for MD5 is 3.069518 milliseconds per packet with a standard deviation of 6.63902 when every 100th packet is hashed. Using SHA1, the computational overhead was calculated as 3.17036 milliseconds per packet with a standard deviation of 6.870593.

The results of this case study suggest that hashing every 100th packet using either MD5 or SHA1 incurs a minimal computational overhead. For example, MD5 incurs on average an additional 0.056742 milliseconds computational overhead per packet with the standard deviation being 0.08449 less than when no hashing is used. The SHA1 algorithm incurs an additional 0.157584 milliseconds computational overhead per packet with a standard deviation of 0.147083.

Figure 5 illustrates the percentage of additional computation needed to implement the lightweight hashing scheme. The results suggest that the SHA1 hashing algorithm performs worse than MD5, however this does not necessarily mean that the SHA1 hashing algorithm should not be used. The decision is a trade-off between performance and strong encryption. For example computational costs may be kept minimal at the expense of security. Conversely security costs may be increased at the expense of computation. Consequently, which hashing algorithm is used is dependent on the trade-off. However, our results suggest that either mechanism could be used without impeding the overall performance of the system.

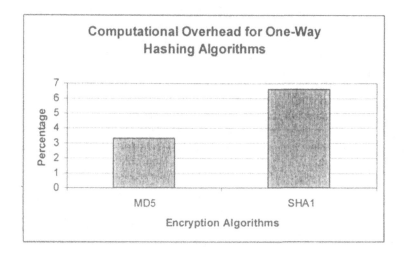

Figure 5. Computational overhead for one-way hashing algorithms.

The network overhead incurred when streaming all 20833 packets is minimal. When the MD5 hashing algorithm is used, an additional 17.36 packets of data are required to send the 16-byte message digest for every 100th packet that is hashed. When the

SHA1 hashing algorithm is used an additional 20.70 packets of data are required to send the 20 byte message digest for every 100th packet that is hashed.

The case study demonstrates that encrypting packets using either MD5 or SHA1 incurs minimal computational overhead compared to not encrypting the data. In addition, the choice of hashing algorithm can further reduce these overheads. However, a small computational overhead is justified in that data communications within a DIDS can be authenticated. This provides the level of trust required within such systems at a very low cost between disparate network entities.

5. Conclusions and Further Work

Networks have become increasingly distributed, and recent advances in intrusion detection has seen the development of DIDS to meet the requirements for security in these disparate environments. DIDS monitor traffic in high-speed, large volume networks and alert legitimate users to potential intrusions or attacks against their systems. These systems consist of a number of interacting components, from network monitors to analysis engines, that holistically provide the security of the network(s) as a whole. To achieve this, system inter-components must communicate, and the data that is passed between hosts must be trusted and authenticated.

This paper has presented a novel scheme for authentication between DIDS inter-component communications to ensure the trust that is required by these systems. This scheme provides a lightweight, cryptographic mechanism to provide authentication between DIDS components. A key consideration in the authentication scheme is the computational or network load that is placed on the DIDS. Through the use of a case study presented in section 4, this paper has demonstrated that the choice of hashing algorithm can severely impact the computational and network load. Therefore, the choice of an efficient hashing algorithm reduces the impact on this load. Further work will extend the authentication scheme to provide further reductions in computational and network load as required in DIDS. In addition, the scheme will be evaluated for its applicability to other high-speed, large-volume network uses such as mutlimedia distribution.

References

1.   Kemmerer, R.A. & Vigna, G., "Intrusion Detection: A Brief History," *Computer*, vol. 35, no. 4, pp. 27-30, 2002.
2.   Zhang, Y. & Paxson, V., "Detecting Backdoors," in *Proceedings of USENIX Security Symposium*, Denver, CO, USA, 2000.
3.   Ptacek, T.H. & Newsham, T.N., "Insertion, Evation, and Denial of Service: Eluding Network Intrusion Detection," *Secure Networks Inc. Technical Report*, available from http:///www.clark.net/~roesch/idspaper.html, January 1998.
4.   Hassler, V., *Security Fundamentals for E-Commerce*, Artech House, USA, 2001.
5.   Rivest, R.L., Shamir, A. & Adelman, L.M., "A Method for Obtaining Digital Signatures and Public-Key Cryptosystems," *Communications of the ACM*, vol. 21, pp.

120-126, 1978.

6. Rabin, M.O., *Digital Signatures Foundations of Secure Communications*, New York Acemic Press, NY, USA, 1978.

7. Aslan, H.K., "A Hybrid Scheme for Multicast Authentication Over Lossy Networks," *Computers and Security*, vol. 23, no.8, pp. 705-713, 2004.

8. Dittman, J., Katzenbeisser, S., Schallart, C. & Veith, H. "Ensuring Media Integrity on Third Party Infrastructures," in Sasaki, R., Qing, S., Okamoto, E. & Yoshiura, H. (eds.) *Security and Privacy in the Age of Ubiquitous Computing*, Springer/IFIP, NY, USA, 2005.

9. Challal, Y., Bettahar, H. & Bouabdallah, A., "SAKM: A Scalable and Adaptive Key Management Approach for Multicast Communications," *ACM SIGCOMM Computer Communications Review*, vol. 32, no. 8, 2004.

10. Proctor, P.E., *The Practical Intrusion Detection Handbook*, Prentice Hall, Saddle River, NJ, USA, 2001.

11. Ning, P., Jajodia, S. & Wang, X.S., "Design and Implementation of a Decentralized Prototype System for Detecting Distributed Attacks," *Computer Communications*, vol.25, pp. 1374-1391, 2002.

12. Waldvogel, M., "GOSSIB vs. IP traceback Rumors," in *Proceedings of the Annual Computer Security Applications Conference (ACSAC)*, Las Vegas, NV, USA, 2002.

13. Haggerty, J., Berry, T., Shi, Q. & Merabti, M., "DiDDeM: A System for Early Detection of TCP SYN Flood Attacks," in *Proceedings of Globecom 04*, Dallas, TX, USA, 2004.

14. Pfleeger, C.P. & Pfleeger, S.L., *Security in Computing 3rd ed.*, Prentice Hall, Upper Saddle River, NJ, USA, 2003.

Design and Implementation of a Fast String Matcher Utilizing Content Addressable Memory

Mohamed Azab[1], Mohamed Rizk[2], Mohamad Abou-El-Nasr[1]

Arab Academy for Science, Technology and Maritime Transport[1],
Alexandria University[2]
E-mail: Mohamed_Azab@aast.edu

Abstract

This work aims at designing a fast string matcher using the content addressable memory technology. It is appropriate for use in applications that require a variable width dynamic string matcher, where the content of the matching module has to be varied within a certain time period. This alteration includes the need to add, remove or even modify the content without the need to change the module. The content of the string matcher is padded with don't cares in order to solve the length difference problem between words. A software program was developed in order to extract, merge and reformat the data to be matched.

In this work, we provide an FPGA-based hardware implementation for the rule matching module that can be employed as a network intrusion detection system (NIDS). This module can be used in applications that require packet-level fire-wall based security systems. Moreover, we present a detailed comparison with different hardware implemented NIDS algorithms.

1. Introduction

The proliferation of the Internet and networking applications, coupled with the widespread availability of system hacks and virus threats, have increased the need for network security against intrusions. Such applications called network intrusion detection system (NIDS). The main task of such a security system is to process the network data searching for potential threats without decreasing the network throughput. One anticipates that a general purpose processor may not be capable for handling such tasks while keeping up the network throughput. One method to solve this problem is to share some of the CPU heavy tasks and convert some or part of the software-based applications into hardware modules. In this work, the string matcher part of an (IDS) is to be hardware-implemented to meet the required the performance constraints of today's high speed networks.

The IDS basic task is to compare the incoming network payload to a predetermined variable width suspicious pattern in order to detect an intrusion. As time goes by, one can expect that new patterns will be discovered then a reconfiguration of the hardware will be required. A reconfiguration of such system has to be simple and must not require a module replacement. The main contribution of this work is to implement a "variable word-width string matcher" using content addressable memory (CAM). This memory is implemented by utilizing field programmable gate arrays technology (FPGA). Section 2 provides an overview of IDS, whereas the string matcher design is detail described comprehensively in section 3. The simulation results and implementation reports are summarized in section 4 and the summary and our conclusions are given in section 5.

2. Intrusion Detection Systems (IDS)

Researchers found by simulating attacks that there are certain patterns that occur more often than others in the cases of intrusion [2]. The challenge, when using IDS, is to monitor a high speed network looking for these patterns. Snort [2] is a popular Network IDS (NIDS) because it is an "open source" software and runs under most popular operating systems. In addition, it offers full control over its "rule-set configuration" [5]. A rule is also known as a signature and may contain a string that must be compared with the contents of an incoming packet to detect intrusions. Although Snort has over 1400 rules it is not common or practical to activate all of them at the same time [3]. We can only load the needed rules at a certain time and change them whenever needed.

An IDS relies on string content matching [4] [5]. String matching based on software has not been able to keep up with high network speeds, and hardware solutions are needed [6]. A CAM by itself may be used for high performance systems, but it is known to offer little or no flexibility [7].

Available CAMs has a major defect all the cam word's has to be the same size and has to be static and unchangeable no modification or insertion of any new data can be done. Thus they are not suited for implementations with Snort rules. The string matching module based on CAM design presented here solves the different word width problem. Thus it is well suited for Snort rules and also solves many other limitations for the existing systems [8].

3. String matcher using CAM

Content addressable memory also called Associative Memory can be defined as a storage device capable of recalling a complete pattern or associated data based on matching an input pattern. One can compare CAM to the inverse of RAM. When read, RAM produces the data for a given address. Conversely, CAM produces an address for a given data word. When searching for data within a RAM block, the search is performed sequentially. Thus, finding a particular data word can take many cycles. On the other hand, CAM searches all addresses in parallel and produces the address storing a particular word. A traditional way of describing the size of a CAM is given by "width * words". The width conveys the size in bits of one storage location in the CAM, while words provide the number of storage locations.

A simple string matcher illustrated in Figure 1. A four-input AND-gate, with optional inverters on the inputs, is capable of matching any four-bit string and a shift register on the input. In this case we could say that we have a CAM of one word that is four-bit wide.

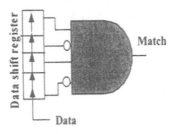

Fig. 1. Simple String Matcher for (1010 String)

Many applications have the following list of design constraints that the existing string matcher's dose not satisfy or only satisfies a subset of them.

1. The length of the strings to be matched to a certain input data stream should be independent from each other. That is, the String Matcher should be able to compare strings of different lengths at the same time. The smallest element of the string matcher is a single character (one byte) as it is the smallest element of any string.
2. The number of words should not be restricted.
3. The comparison between an incoming packet and the stored string patterns must be fast, preferably around 1 clock cycle.
4. It should be possible to change the content, the number and the length of words in the String Matcher without having to reconfigure the whole design.
5. The time spent for changing the content of the String Matcher should be insignificant compared to the decision making time because it is a very simple task and a software module will handle it.

3.1 Using SRL16E to design a CAM

The basic building block of this design is a 16-Bit Shift Register acting as a Look-Up-Table (LUT) SRL16E; Figure 2 illustrates how it can be utilized to design an 8 bit word cam. At the writing phase where the CAM contents is being stored into the look up tables , the Input pattern is compared to a 4-bit down counter, and the result is of the comparison is shifted into the (LUT), this process takes 16 clock cycles for the counter 16 states. If the counter value equals the input data value then a "1" is shifted into the SRL16E. Otherwise, a "0" is shifted in. At the reading phase the input data to be compared is used as an address of the Shift Register. Only one out of the 16 locations in the SRL16E has a "1" corresponding to the data stored previously. If the input data addresses this location, a match is found [17].

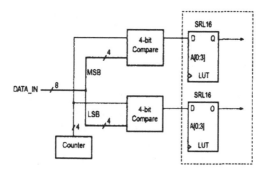

Fig. 2. 8-bit CAM Word [17]

Ternary Content Addressable Memory (TCAM) devices implemented with SRL16 primitives, has three supported ternary mode options using ternary bits 0, 1, X. The bit X matches either 1, 0, or X (1010 = 1X1X = 10XX) and is referred to as don't care bit. Snort rules have a variable content size. The chosen rule width for the presented implementations where in between of 4 to 32 character where the most appropriate rule size is in range of 12 characters [11] because most of snort rules within that range see Figure 3. Therefore a pipelined variable width module implementation is included, where each module is a fixed size CAM capable of storing contents up to its word width, where any entry having less width will be padded with X don't care bits the Chosen word width for that CAM modules has been made in a way that can utilize as much rules as it can with minimum space usage.

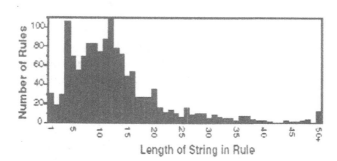

Fig. 3. Distribution of the lengths of the unique strings found in the Default Snort database [1].

The main advantage of this design implementing a CAM with the maximum rule size is the ability to load all rules at runtime from an off-chip ram. Rules will be padded with X bits in order to equate different rule width. The comparison occurs at run time. Simulation results shows that it will take only one clock cycle to produce an output. The input data to be compared will be sent to the cam inputs through a shift register which will shift the payload one byte "one character" at a time until a match occurs.

The CAM Design illustrated in Figure 4 is a (5, 9, 4, 6) byte CAM. Each location in the shift register is connected to all matching units in the corresponding row as indicated by horizontal lines in Figure4. The CAM has a latency of a single clock cycle until the output is updated. By giving new data to the shift register each clock cycle, we will get a new valid output. The Loading the cam contents latency is of less interest in this work, and details are therefore omitted here because.

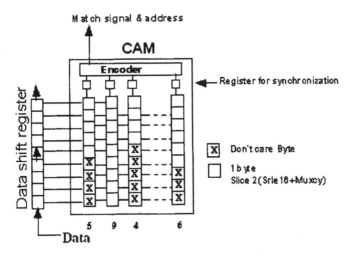

Fig. 4. String Matching Process

Solving the variable width of the snort rules by padding, in order to have the ability to change the cam contents without reconfiguration of the chip, has a space loss drawback, but using rule merging technique described in the next section will cover that loss.

3.2 Rule Merging and extraction

We have developed a software program in order to obtain a realistic dataset for testing the CAM. The requests that should be satisfied in that software are as follows:

1. Store a string if there is only one "content" part in the rule see Figure5 for an example of a Snort rule with one content part.
2. Store a string if it would not generate a multiple match.
3. Store strings that are at least 4 bytes and no more than 32 bytes.
4. Write these strings in appropriate format. There were 1083 Snort rule strings that matched the above criteria it is not common to activate all of them at the same time

212

[3] we can load only the needed rules at a certain time and change them whenever needed.
5. Convert the extracted contents into its binary form

```
    alert   tcp   $EXTERNAL_NET   any   ->
$HOME_NET 12345:12346 (msg:"BACKDOOR
netbus getinfo";
    flow:to_server,established;
content:"GetInfo|0d|"; reference:arachnids,403;
classtype:misc-activity; sid:110; rev:3;)
```

Fig. 5. pseudo code for a typical Snort Rule with one content part [2]

Based on the fact that determining which rule has been violated by a certain packet, is not as important as detecting that violation itself, we only interested in finding a match if any. While identifying which rule cause that match is not important, we can select the most similar pair of strings and swab dissimilarities with don't' care bits, then merge them into one string reducing the total number of strings into one half. See Figure 6 for an example of rule merging

```
    Rule A      010010101111
    Rule B      110110111111
    New Rule  x10x101x1111
```

Fig. 6. rule merging

A C# program was developed to extract the ASCII and Hex contents of the snort rules that satisfies the constraints illustrated before, and convert the content into its a binary string, then the software groups the converted strings into a similar size groups, where a similarity factor is set for each pair of rules, and the most similar pair of strings will be merged into one string. Using that technique we can store one pattern for each pair of rules, this will increase the system performance to a great extent and will reduce the chip usage to one half without decreasing the number of rules to be matched.

Figure 7 shows how string matching module can be used in IDS. The payload to be matched is sent to the system. Comparison takes place in parallel, payload is compared to all strings (words) stored in the CAMs. If a match is found, it is indicated by a *Match* Signal.

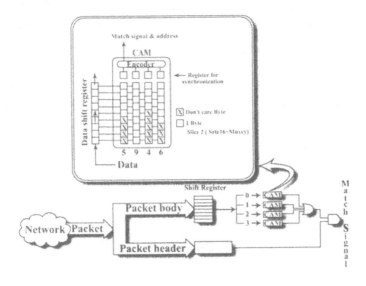

Fig. 7. String Matching Process

4. Results and comparisons

A variable word width string matcher module has been implemented, having the ability to change its content without any reconfiguration, just a simple memory rewrite task. Also a software module has been developed to compress the matching contents allowing it to store twice its capacity without any performance dropdown. In this section we compare the results of this research with the results of previous work on FPGA pattern matchers for network security applications. The chosen bodies of work represent the highest-performing implementations of each algorithmic approach bruteforce, DFA, distributed comparator NFA, and shared decoder NFA. The metrics used for comparison illustrated in Table 1are throughput (in Megabits per second) and capacity (LE /Char) where LE is a single logic element.

The throughput of a design is calculated by multiplying the amount of input data (in bits) processed per cycle by the maximum clock frequency (in Megahertz). The capacity of a design is the number of characters that can be stored into a given FPGA device. For comparison purposes, a device-neutral metric called logic element per character (LEs/char) is used. This figure
is determined by dividing the total number of logic elements used in a design (including the input and output circuitry) by the sum of the lengths of all patterns programmed into the design. A logic element is the fundamental unit of FPGA logic and consists of a four-input look-up table and a flip-flop. Since throughput and

capacity generally have an inverse relationship, any comparison of designs must consider both metrics.

Here, a value called Performance is defined as throughput time's density [4]. Density is the character density, or the reciprocal of LEs/char. The performance increases as throughput and density increase and decreases as throughput and density decrease. Therefore, a design with higher Performance provides a better tradeoff between throughput and area, or, in other words, a smaller increase in area as throughput is increased.

The proposed design has been synthesized using the Xilinx tools (ISE 7.1i) for several devices (the -N suffix indicates speed grade): VirtexE xcv2000E-8,Virtex2 6000-6. The structure of each device is similar how ever the area cost of our design turned out as expected to be almost identical for all devices, with the main difference in the performance. Figure 8 and Table 1 illustrates the performance metrics for the implemented designs, and previous work on FPGA pattern matchers for network security applications. Taking into consideration that number of patterns illustrated in the description part for our design is set to the actual number of patterns applied to the module while each of these patterns represents two merged snort rules.

The chosen rule width for the presented implementations where ranging from 4 to 32 characters, this is based on the fact that the most appropriate rule size is in range of 12 characters [11]. Therefore a pipelined variable width module implementation is included where we have distributed the available space on the different patterns in a way that covers the widest range of snort rules.

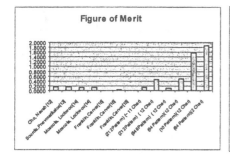 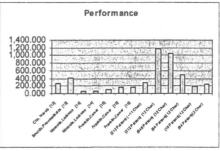

Fig 8. Performance and figure of merits for the proposed system and other systems

	Description	Logic Cells	Freq/MHz	Through put	Figure of Merit	Total # of Char	Cell / Char	Device	Input/bits	Performance
Brute Force	Cho, Navab,Mangione-Smith [12]	17,000	90	2880	0.1694	1,611	10.552	Altera EP20K	32	272.922
	Sourdis,Pnevm atikatos [13]	47,686	252	8064	0.1691	2,457	19.408	Virtex2-6000	32	415.494
DFA	Moscola, Lockwood,Et. al. [14]	2,318	37	296	0.1277	420	5.519	VirtexE-2000	8	53.632
		8,134	37	1184	0.1456	420	19.367	VirtexE-2000	32	61.136
NFA	Franklin, Carver,Hutchings [15]	20,618	30.9	247	0.0120	8,003	2.576	Virtex-1000	8	95.875
		20,618	52.5	420	0.0204	8,003	2.576	VirtexE-2000	8	163.026
		40,232	49.5	396	0.0098	16,028	2.510	VirtexE-2000	8	157.762
Our Design	(212 Pattern) Variable Width Modules (~11 Char)	7000	115	916.48	0.1309	2,272	3.081	VirtexE-2000	8	297.463
	(212 Pattern) Pipelined Modules (12 Char)	7398	107	3439.04	0.4649	2,544	2.908	Virtex2-6000	32	1,182.606
	(848 Pattern) Pipelined Modules (12 Char)	23927	76.9	2461	0.1029	10,176	2.351	Virtex2-6000	32	1,046.648
	(64 Pattern) Fixed Width Modules (12 Char)	2817	169	1352	0.4799	1,024	2.751	VirtexE-2000	8	491.462
	(10 Pattern) Fixed Width Modules (12 Char)	872	171	1366.8	1.5674	120	7.267	VirtexE-2000	8	188.092
	(64 Pattern) Fixed Width Modules (2 Char)	642	151	1208	1.8816	128	5.016	VirtexE-2000	8	240.847

Table 1 Performance metrics for the proposed system and other systems

216

The proposed design includes different rule sets implementations. A pipelined version combines a variable size sets has been implemented, including a set of 216 Patterns (432 rules) to show performance and cost for a medium size rule set, has the following sub sets.

A set of 100 Patterns (200 rules) in length of 4 characters, 30 Patterns (60 rules) in length of 8 characters, 70 Patterns (140 rules) in range of 16 character and 16 Patterns (32 rules) in 32 character. Also a large size rule set of 848 Patterns (1696 rules) 12 character length, has been implemented in a pipelined architecture to test the scalability of our approach for large rule sets.

The presented performance matrices shown in Figure 8 and Table 1 demonstrate that the over all performance of the proposed system, is much better than the performance of most of the previously implemented NIDS, even with both 8-bit and 32-bit input widths. While a 32 bit input gives better results but we have to read the input packet from different offsets that is why it is not suitable for many network protocols like TCP/IP with non fixed packet length.

5. Conclusion

A fast dynamic content string matcher with single clock cycle latency has been designed. A software program is used to compress and reformat the matcher content in a way makes it well suited for string matching with Snort rules. All cam contents are loaded from an off-chip ram, changing this contents change the cam contents as well. This makes the content changing phase is simply a memory rewrite task with no need for chip reconfiguration. Where the flexibility of such matcher, and the short time needed to change the contents, are vital constraints for NIDS. The rule merging phase saves half the chip space without reducing the number of stored rules. Future work involves designing and implementing interfaces to the string matcher module with the proper data communication elements. Also a parallel data fetch will reduce the total time to a great extent. The data shift register will be modified to be able to shift a whole word every clock cycle instead of a single character.

6. References

1 Peter Bellows et al. "GRIP: A Reconfigurable Architecture for Host-Based Gigabit-Rate Packet Processing," FCCM 2002.

2 Snort open source network intrusion prevention system http://www.snort.org

3 Y. H. Cho et al. "Specialized Hardware for Deep Network Packet Filtering," FPL 2002.

4 C. Jason Coit et al. Towards Faster String Matching for Intrusion Detection or Exceeding the Speed of Snort. In Proc. of DARPA Information Surviability Conference and Exposition, DISCEXII, 2001.

5 B. L. Hutchings et al. Assisting Network Intrusion Detection with Reconfigurable Hardware. In Proc. of the 10th Annual IEEE Symposium on Field-Programmable Custom Computing Machines FCCM 2002.

6 S. Dharmapurikar et al. Deep packet inspection using parallel Bloom filter. In Proc. of Hot Interconnections 11 (HotI-11), Stanford, CA, 2003.

7 D. E. Tylor et al. Scalable IP Lookup for Interne Routers. In IEEE journal on selected areas in communications, Vol. 21, No. 4, May 2003.

8 Shaomeng Li et al. Exploiting Reconfigurable Hardware for Network Security. FCCM 2003.

9 J-L Brelet and B. New. Designing Flexible, Fas CAMs with Virtex Family FPGAs. Xilinx Application Note 203, September23, 1999 (Version 1.1).

10 Xilinx Virtex-II Pro Platform FPGAs. Functional Description. Datasheet ds083

11 Nathan Tuck, Timothy Sherwood,Brad Calde, George Varghese, " Deterministic Memory-Efficient String Matching Algorithms for Intrusion Detection" Department of Computer Science and Engineering, University of California, San Diego

12 Young H. Cho, Shiva Navab, and William H. Mangione-Smith, "Specialized Hardware for Deep Network Packet Filtering," Proceedings of 12th International Conference on Field Programmable Logic and Applications, 2002.

13 Ioannis Sourdis and Dionisios Pnevmatikatos, "Fast, Large-Scale String Match for a 10 Gbps FPGA-based Network Intrusion Detection System," Proceedings of the 13th International Conference on Field Programmable Logic and Applications, Sept. 2003.

14 James Moscola, John Lockwood, Ronald P. Loui, Michael Pachos, "Implementation of a Content-Scanning Module for an Internet Firewall," Proceedings of IEEE Symposium on Field-Programmable Custom Computing Machines, pp. 31-38, Apr. 2003.

15 R. Franklin, D. Carver, and B.L. Hutchings, "Assisting Network Intrusion Detection with Reconfigurable Hardware," Proceedings of IEEE Symposium on Field- Programmable Custom Computing Machines, pp. 111-120, Apr. 2002.

16 Christopher R. Clark "Design of Efficient FPGA Circuits for Matching Complex Patterns in Network Intrusion Detection Systems" Electrical and Computer Engineering Georgia Institute of Technology December 2003

17 XILINX Content-Addressable Memory v5.1 Tutorial DS253 November 11, 2004

Zero hour outbreak prevention using distributed traffic anomaly detection

András Korn, Dr. Gábor Fehér

Budapest University of Technology and Economics,
Department of Telecommunication and Mediainformatics
{korn,feher@tmit.bme.hu}

Abstract. Network worms have been a constant threat to computers for the past few years. One remotely exploitable vulnerability after the other is found in widely used desktop software; and if that were not enough, worm authors can always rely on the curiosity and gullibility of users. No end seems in sight; even antivirus programs aren't much help against new and unknown worms. In this paper, we propose an algorithm that can detect network worms based on the traffic anomalies their infection attempts effect. Using simulations, we demonstrate that this algorithm can drastically reduce the ability of worms to infect remote computers.

Keywords: worm, anomaly detection, intrusion detection, portscan

1 Introduction

MyDoom ($5.25 billion). Sasser ($3.5 billion). Netsky ($2.75 billion). Bagle ($1.5 billion). These are some of the better known recent worms that relied on the Internet to infect other computers and the amount of financial damage they caused according to Computer Economics, Inc. of Carlsbad, CA. A quick web search for "virus damage" yields damage figures in the tens of billions of dollars, often attributed to a single piece of malware. Apparently, our current defence mechanisms are not up to the task of stopping network worms, because new ones manage to infect tens of thousands of computers (and to cause millions of dollars of damage) every month.

Dealing with worms using traditional methods is challenging primarily for two reasons. First, apparently many users cannot be assumed to act intelligently: they will run programs they receive from unknown people via email if the text of the message is sufficiently tempting (promising revealing photos of sports celebrities is known to have been enough). Thus, worms don't even need to rely on exploitable weaknesses in software in order to be run. Social engineering does the trick just fine[1].

Second, antivirus programs still primarily rely on signatures to detect malware. This means that a worm will typically be detected and identified by an antivirus suite only after it has been "in the wild" for several days (for example, 17 days in the case of Sasser) and done its share of infecting tens of thousands of computers. Some popular antivirus software is shipped with a default configuration of fetching updated signatures once a week; even if a worm is added to the signature database immediately after it appears, more than three days can be expected to pass before users will update their signatures. The situation is even worse if the signatures must be updated manually, or if the computer is turned off or offline at the time the update job would run.

All this leads us to believe that there is no way to win the worm war on the desktop front by any means except possibly a whitelist of programs that can be run, which would be next to impossible to maintain. Therefore, if something is to be done about worms, it must be done in the network, and without relying on signatures. Worm defence in the network also appears to be more viable because network devices are fewer in number and typically better managed than desktop computers.

In this paper, we propose an algorithm that can help severely limit the ability of even new and unknown worms to infect other computers. We call the algorithm "WANDA" – Worm ANomaly Detector Algorithm.

2 How Worms Reveal Themselves

We need to find some aspect of worms that distinguishes their network behaviour from benign applications. A trivial difference between worms and legitimate applications is that the latter don't spread from system to system.

Indeed it is the very act of spreading that can be spotted by looking at network traffic. There are, from a network perspective, two ways in which a worm can spread. One of them is mailing themselves to many different addresses via an SMTP smarthost (e.g. that of the infected computer). The other involves connecting to many different network addresses, either to exploit an exploitable weakness in software running on the remote computer, or to deliver an SMTP email message that contains the worm directly (instead of through the smarthost). From the network perspective, it doesn't make a difference: what we're going to see in the latter case is a lot of short-lived connections to lots of different addresses. If the worm is trying to exploit a weakness, many of these connection attempts may be unsuccessful.

Exploiting weaknesses only makes sense if the weakness is present in a widely deployed application that uses a well-known port number; otherwise, the worm couldn't spread very effectively because it would have to spend too much time looking for vulnerable systems, and the maximum total number of infected systems would also be very limited.

Another thing to consider is that a decisive majority of worms target Microsoft Windows computers; thus, whatever service they try to exploit a weakness in will be one that is often found on Windows. This practically rules out common Unix services such as syslog and NFS (Network File System) – however, we can monitor those as well, just to be on the safe side.

Thus, detecting a spreading worm boils down to the following:
- Detect a huge increase in the volume of mail originating from a host/subnet (if the worm uses a smarthost). This would be relatively easy to do on the smarthost itself; we will not deal with this scenario here. [2]

- Detect if a host/subnet tries to connect to one of at most a few dozen well-known ports on many different remote systems[3]. This is what the algorithm we describe in this paper can do.

3 Detecting the Traffic Anomaly

In order to detect the traffic anomaly we expect worms to create, we need an efficient way of coming up with the statistics we expect to change. That is, for each port we monitor, we need to keep track of how many different addresses are being contacted each time unit. This can be done using an approach similar to what is done in MULTOPS[4] and RESPIRE[5].

We allocate a tree structure for each port that we monitor. The root node contains 256 pointers (initially NULL) and a counter that counts the number of leaves in the tree. The leaves of the tree correspond to IP addresses. Leaf nodes are four levels away from the root; all intermediate nodes contain 256 pointers. A node for IP 22.33.44.55 is added by allocating root→22 if it doesn't exist yet; then allocating root→22→33, root→22→33→44 and finally root→22→33→44→55. A sorted linked list could be used instead of a tree for a reduction of memory consumption at the expense of processing (because lookups to find whether a given node already exists would be slower). The total size of the tree is bounded by the value of a "suspicion threshold", discussed below.

3.1 Detecting a Worm Inside our Network

The same algorithm can be used to detect worms that try to spread from a box within our network as to detect ones that try to infect our hosts from the outside. However, there are a few optimizations that are specific to each case. We will discuss detecting an internal worm first.

Each time a new connection to the given port is detected, we check whether the destination IP has a corresponding leaf in our tree. If yes, we do nothing. If not, we add the leaf and increase the counter in the root node. We reset the tree periodically (every few minutes). Memory consumption is bounded, because we can stop counting (and thus allocating new nodes) once a suspicion threshold is reached.

If the counter exceeds this threshold, we assume that a worm attack is taking place. The threshold would typically differ from port to port; while it is probably normal for a desktop system to contact up to several dozen different webservers per hour, it is unlikely that an ordinary user would need to access more than a handful of different MS SQL servers a day, for example. The threshold will also depend on the size of the subnet being monitored and even the behaviour patterns of the users. In our simulation (see section 5), the IDS (Intrusion Detection System) tries to guess the correct threshold by observing traffic declared to be normal for a few hours.

Once we are relatively certain that we are infected, we can do a number of things. We can block all further traffic on that port until administrator intervention. This would definitely stop the worm but probably inconvenience the users. A somewhat more lenient approach would still permit traffic to and from hosts on a whitelist; this runs the risk of infecting those hosts but ensures that users still have access to critical services.

We can also try to determine which specific boxes in our subnet are infected; we can do this by finding out which source IP is communicating with more than the normal number of different destinations on the now known infection port. This is done in much the same way as above, except that each source address now has its own tree of destinations, and the threshold can probably be substantially lower than for the entire subnet.

It would be impractical to monitor each source separately from the beginning because that would obviously require a lot more memory; whether it can be done for a single port (the single one of the several dozen well-known ports we monitor that we now know the worm uses to propagate) depends on the size of the subnet we have to keep track of. It is entirely realistic for a class C subnet, but probably out of the question for a class B (where it can only be done, in a distributed manner, if we partition the network into much smaller subnets, all of which have their own IDS).

Once we have the addresses of the boxes we suspect of being infected, we can block just their traffic on the propagation port (preferably at the switch level so they can't infect other systems in the same subnet either). At the cost of some time, memory and processing power, we can thus avoid disrupting the work of users with uninfected computers.

The algorithm could be refined by assigning a larger weight to failed connection attempts than to successful ones; this would speed up worm detection, because legitimate connection attempts mostly succeed, whereas a worm typically tries to connect to random addresses, many of which will not run the targeted service or be unreachable altogether. Our simulator does not yet take this into account.

Another possible heuristic is to enumerate some servers we know our users will attempt legitimate connections with and not count their IPs (by, for example, initializing the tree with their nodes already in place and the counter set to zero). This can help lower the suspicion threshold.

3.2 Detecting External Worm Attacks

The algorithm described above is primarily useful for detecting worms *within* our network that try to infect other internal or external hosts. A very similar approach can be used to detect worms that try to infect our network from the *outside*. All we need to do is use the algorithm discussed previously to count the number of different internal addresses that external hosts attempt to connect to on each of the monitored well-known ports. In a controlled (e.g. corporate) environment, we have a priori knowledge of the distribution of services, so it is sufficient to keep track of connections to the ports actually in use. In more liberal (for example, university) networks, no such assumptions can usually be made, and the full list of a few dozen well-known and possibly exploitable ports must be considered.

The threshold of suspicion can, in most cases, be much lower for external worms, because we may *know* how many different IPs in our network actually run a service on each port. If someone is trying to connect to more than twice as many, there is something fishy going on. Also, the additional weight for failed connection attempts to addresses that we know don't run the service could be much larger than in the case of the internal worm (where we don't know for sure that the remote service isn't supposed to be there anyway, and the connection failure could be intermittent).

The main difference between the case when the worm is on the inside and the case when it comes from the outside is how we can react. In the latter case, we don't need to find the specific source IP(s) the worm tries to infect our network from; in case of a major outbreak, the list entries would number in the hundreds of thousands, which would be challenging for firewalls to handle. Instead, it is probably sufficient to identify the class C networks the worm attacks originate in (so the tree can be one level less deep in this case). We can block incoming connections to the infection port from these networks without a second thought. The relevant firewall rules can be arranged hierarchically to speed up processing. Unfortunately, this policy can backfire if attackers simulate a worm infection attempt from spoofed addresses in order to have those addresses blocked by our firewall. If this is a concern (and the possibility should indeed not be dismissed out of hand), heuristics that help identify spoofing (e.g. [6]) may increase our confidence somewhat. Whitelists of hosts/networks that absolutely must retain access to our network even if they are infected by worms can also reduce the potential impact of spoofing.

3.3 Distributed Detection

There are two problems with the WANDA algorithm as presented above: the problem of the suspicion threshold, and the problem of resource consumption.
WANDA makes heavy use of an arbitrary suspicion threshold. Choosing the right threshold is difficult, but making the wrong choice can have severe consequences: blocking of legitimate traffic if it is set too low and the failure to detect a worm if set too high.

Another problem is that for large, busy internal networks with several thousand hosts, much memory may be needed to hold the data structures related to the algorithm.

Both of these problems can be extenuated by distributing the detection algorithm to several IDSes that each keep track of only a portion of all traffic. If the internal network is hierarchical, a natural choice would be to equip each smaller subnet with an IDS; if not, the scope of each IDS can be chosen arbitrarily.

Detection accuracy can be increased by making the suspicion threshold "fuzzy". Let us call the suspicion threshold "red alert threshold". If an IDS reaches some appreciable fraction of its red alert threshold (the "yellow alert threshold"), it can raise its "alert level" to "yellow". When going to yellow alert, the IDS initiates a vote on whether to go to red alert; if a pre-determined amount of IDSes are at yellow alert for the service (port) in question, the entire network can go to red alert even if the red alert threshold hasn't been reached yet. The assumption behind this approach is that worm outbreaks will in many cases not be isolated; thus, if several subnets exhibit the same slightly anomalous behaviour, it is safer to assume that a worm attack is in progress than if only one subnet is acting up, which could just be an overzealous user.

The memory footprint and CPU cost is naturally reduced if each IDS only has to track a fraction of all hosts on the internal network.

3.4 Possible False Positives

WANDA is a new algorithm that we first implemented in a simulator; thus, no experiments in real network were possible yet, so we can only try to predict how likely false positive detection would be.

Extreme usage burstiness of a particular service may cause false detection; for example, if a user suddenly decides to run an Internet survey to determine the distribution of name server software in use, we may wrongly decide to block their DNS traffic. This probably can't be helped; the user would need to make prior arrangements with network management to prevent being identified as a worm.

Another likely-looking case of false positive detection would be peer-to-peer filesharing activity, provided the application uses a well-known port (possibly in order to bypass firewall restrictions). While some international business alliances may strongly feel that blocking p2p would be good riddance, not all network operators may share this sentiment. Fortunately, the problem can be avoided at the cost of some processing overhead by using, for example, the Layer-7 Packet Classifier for Linux[7] to determine whether the connections bound for the port being monitored are actually related to the service that normally runs on that port.

4 Other uses

The traffic anomaly we are looking for is very similar to the one caused by port scanning. In fact, the worm carries out an extreme form of port scanning; instead of trying to connect to several different ports of the same IP, it tries to connect to the same port on several different IPs. The detection algorithm can be modified to detect portscans in addition to worms, at the cost of a larger memory footprint.

The usefulness of detecting portscans is questionable; ideally, an attacker shouldn't be any closer to breaking into a system after a successful portscan than before. Furthermore, portscans can be arbitrarily slow and arbitrarily distributed, so that it is a theoretical impossibility to detect all of them while avoiding false positives.

On the other hand, scripted attacks that sweep entire networks looking for a small set of vulnerable services are becoming increasingly common. For example, TCP port 22 (SSH) is often being probed on all hosts, and SSH servers that are discovered are subsequently attacked with primitive dictionary attacks. A server may experience one of these every few hours.

In a large, heterogeneous network (for example, a university campus network), it may be next to impossible to ensure that no computers offer public services using vulnerable software. Therefore, it may still make sense to try and detect portscans and block blatant portscanners; while this will not make the network more secure in the sense of preventing successful exploitation of a flaw, it could noticeably delay the inevitable and may thus be deemed worth the effort nevertheless.

When trying to detect portscans, we must be aware that the attacker will probably use spoofed source addresses (so-called decoys) in addition to their own address. If they can sniff our outgoing traffic, they may not even need to send packets with their real address at all, in which case there is no way we can block them. It's no longer enough to look at our small set of well-known ports; we need to track connection attempts to every port (carefully avoiding counting connections related to e.g. active FTP).

4.1 Detecting Incoming Portscans

In order to detect incoming portscans, we need to store the {IP, destination port} pair of each new incoming connection that our session tracking doesn't account for (i.e. we must ignore, for example, FTP data and IRC DCC connections). If the number of different internal {IP, port} pairs contacted in the last time unit exceeds a threshold (which need not be much larger than the total number of public services offered by the "internal" network behind the detector), we can assume that we are under attack. The size of the data structure used to track the {IP, port} pairs (a slightly modified version of the tree from before could be used, where each leaf has a bitfield to track individual ports) is bounded, because we can stop counting once the threshold is reached. Again, it is possible to speed up detection by increasing the weight of failed connections.

Finding the (possibly spoofed) addresses of the attackers works by building a list of contacted destination ports and a list of contacted destination addresses for each class C network that attempts a connection (the specific address within the subnet can probably be spoofed even if the subnet itself can't). Networks that try to reach few ports and few addresses are probably legitimate; networks that reference few ports but many addresses are sweeping for particular services; networks that reference many ports but few addresses are carrying out a classic portscan; finally, networks that access many addresses and many ports are probably trying to portscan several different computers at the same time. The memory requirements of this stage can be large even though we reduced it drastically by decoupling the {IP, port} pairs (counting different destination ports and destination addresses separately).

The memory footprint can be further reduced by first only tracking incoming traffic by class B (or even class A) networks and only "zooming in" on class C networks if their parent class B or class A exceeds our suspicion threshold. This increases detection time, which has the drawback that the portscan may be over by the time we could determine the presumed address of the perpetrator.

Once we discover what address the portscan seems to be coming from, there is little we can do. If the attack is a network sweep, it may seem safe to block further packets to the scanned ports from the attacking subnet(s) for a few minutes; the attack script would presumably just assume that our boxes are down and move on to the next victim network. However, the attack could be using a spoofed source address. Having traffic from that address blocked by our defence mechanism may be its very purpose. Automatic traffic blocking should always be employed with extreme caution and with a human administrator available on short notice.

4.2 Detecting outgoing portscans

Detecting outgoing portscans makes more sense, because we actually stand a realistic chance of finding the culprit. There are a number of measures that can be taken to prevent address spoofing in an IP network, both at the switch and at the router level; these are however, beyond the scope of this paper. If our network is spoofproof, the offending computer can be found; if the investigators are brave enough to be favoured by fortune, the attacker himself or herself can also be identified and subsequently subjected to appropriate attitude readjustment measures.

The detection algorithm is the same as the one we used for incoming portscans, but it is reasonable to expect a much smaller memory footprint.

5 Simulations

In order to demonstrate that the algorithm is useful (i.e. that the predicted traffic anomaly is there and can be detected), we ran a simulation. Before we describe the setup, let us introduce two shorthand notations: let $U[x;y]$ denote a uniformly distributed random variable between x and y and let $exp(x)$ denote an exponentially distributed random variable with an expected value of x.

We simulated 20 "internal" subnets: one with 50 and one with 200 computers; the others each had $U[100; 240]$ computers. The packet transit delay was $exp(0.01)$ seconds. We only simulated TCP traffic bound for port 80 (i.e. web traffic). This is a particularly hard case because legitimate traffic is also pretty diverse.

The simulated topology was flat: each outbound data packet from an internal network passed through exactly one IDS when bound for an external address and two IDSes when bound for a different internal network. We simulated three scenarios: one where the IDSes were inactive; one where they were autonomous; and one where they co-operated.

We introduced one copy of a fictitious worm into both internal subnets after the first four simulated hours had elapsed. The simulated worm behaved as a Poisson process with a parameter of 10 minutes; when active, it tried to infect $U[0; 20]$ randomly chosen addresses from a randomly chosen class C network in one go. It alternated between trying to infect external and internal networks (some real worms, e.g. Code Red 2 and Nimda, behaved in a similar – albeit not identical – manner[8]). It had an infection success probability of 20%. This means that each attacked computer stood a 20% chance of being up and running a vulnerable implementation of the attacked service at the time of attack.

The IDSes used an observation granularity of one minute (that is, they scrapped their observation data once each minute). Their "red alert" threshold was 1.1 times the maximum amount of "normal" traffic they saw during the first four hours (1.2 in the cooperative scenario). The "yellow alert" threshold was 0.6 times the "normal peak". The voting quorum for going to red alert was 0.5; that is, if more than half of the IDSes were at yellow alert, the system went to red alert.

We also simulated some legitimate traffic. Every computer in every internal network also ran a legitimate client that we modelled as an on-off source that was inactive for exp(1) hour. It then "browsed" for exp(5) minutes, during which it accessed U[0; 8] different remote webservers simultaneously (which happens when a new page is loaded) and then paused for exp(1) minute, which accounted for the time the user spent reading the content they had just fetched.

The simulation ended after eight hours of simulated time.

5.1 Simulation results

Figure 1 and 2 below show data gathered from the simulated internal network with 200 nodes. The seemingly random blue plot shows how many different webservers were contacted by nodes in this subnet during each minute. The grey line at the bottom shows the number of infected computers in the subnet. The dashed lines mark the computed threshold value for blocking traffic in Figure 1 and the threshold values for the yellow and red alert levels in Figure 2, where the IDSes worked in their distributed cooperative mode. The events used to "train" the IDSes in the beginning were the same in both cases; however, we can observe different behaviour after the worm has been introduced. Some data points that may be difficult to gather from the plots: red alert threshold: 149/163; yellow alert threshold: 98; Time of first infection: 4:28/4:27; time when traffic was blocked: 5:57 vs. 5:09 (the voting mechanism allowed the firewall to kick in earlier). Note that on Figure 1 traffic is strong even towards the end of the simulation, whereas on Figure 2 this is not the case, because the other IDSes/firewalls are also blocking traffic and because fewer total infections have taken place.

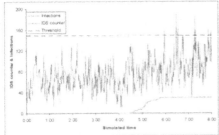 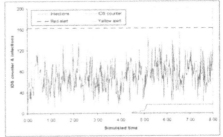

Fig. 1. Simulation results of the scenario where the IDSes worked in standalone mode

Fig. 2. Simulation results of the scenario where the IDSes worked in distributed mode

Figure 3 below shows how many computers were infected in each subnet at the end of the simulation. As you can see, the total number of infections is lowest when the IDSes work together: 3598 (all nodes) when no IDS was used; 370 when the IDSes worked in standalone mode; and only 238, less than 7% of the no-IDS case, when the IDSes co-operated.

There were no false positives; that is, no uninfected subnet was firewalled off, thanks to the automatic adjustment of the alert threshold.

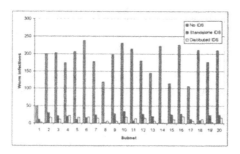

Fig. 3. Number of worms in each subnet

6 Summary

In this paper we presented WANDA, a novel algorithm for detecting and countering worm attacks and portscans. Based on a distributed traffic anomaly detection approach, we were able to reduce the number of successful infections a worm could carry out during an 8-hour period by up to 93% in a call-level simulation.

The resource usage of the algorithm is difficult to estimate in general as it will vary greatly from network to network; nonetheless, it can be said that as long as each IDS that runs it only monitors a network with at most a few hundred computers, both the memory footprint and the CPU usage should be very reasonable.

While WANDA certainly can't stamp out worms once and for all, it can help buy precious time during the early stages of the worm's lifetime; time that can be used to analyse the worm, to prepare signatures for antivirus products and to harden all instances of the service it tries to exploit.

References

[1] Kevin D. Mitnick, William L. Simon, Steve Wozniak: The Art of Deception: Controlling the Human Element of Security. John Wiley & Sons, 2002. ISBN 0471237124

[2] C. C. Zou, D. Towsley, and W. Gong: Email virus propagation modelling and analysis. Umass ECE Dept., Tech. Rep. TR-03-CSE-04, May 2003.

[3] Jack Koziol, David Litchfield, Dave Aitel, Chris Anley, Sinan Eren, Neel Mehta and Riley Hassel: The Shellcoder's Handbook: Discovering and Exploiting Security Holes. Wiley 2004. ISBN 0-7645-4468-3

[4] Thomer M. Gil, Massimiliano Poletto: MULTOPS: a data-structure for bandwidth attack detection. Proceedings of the 10th Usenix Security Symposium, pp. 23-38, August 2001.

[5] András Korn, Gábor Fehér: RESPIRE – A Novel Approach to Automatically Blocking SYN Flooding Attacks. Proceedings of Eunice 2004, pp. 181-187, June 2004

[6] Cheng Jin, Haining Wang, Kang G. Shin: Hop-Count Filtering: An Effective Defense Against Spoofed DDoS Traffic, Proceedings of the 10th ACM conference on Computer and communication security, pp. 30-41, 2003.

[7] Layer-7 Packet Classifier for Linux project homepage. http://l7-filter.sourceforge.net/

[8] Nicholas Weaver: A Brief History of the Worm. Online, http://www.securityfocus.com/infocus/1515, last modified November 26, 2001.

Mediating Hosts' Malicious Character

Mohammed Chihoub

LIRE Laboratory, Computer Science Department, University Mentouri of Constantine,
Route Ain El Bey, Constantine, 25000, Algeria

mchihoub@yahoo.com

Abstract. Right now there isn't any published solution to protect mobile agents against hosts' attack. This is known as the problem of malicious hosts. To solve this problem, Minsky proposed an approach based on replication and vote. Within this approach, vote diverging information hosts are considered to be malicious. We consider such distinctive qualification as simple, straightforward and not flexible. Our paper relates malicious property to a more elaborated process. We claim that our process is cautious and flexible. In this process we: (1) Explore how to attach a trust or suspicious quality with a host. This attachment must be temporal. (2) Perform Vote among agents handing out information from trusted hosts only. Suspicious hosts' information is dismissed. (3) Delegate the faculty to declare the malicious character to an adjudicator. The designation requires a dialogue and could be parameterized with a threshold. (4) Capture trusted hosts' bizarre behavior and disclose it.

1 Introduction

Right now there isn't any published solution to protect mobile agents against hosts' attack [1]. This is known as the problem of malicious hosts. To solve this problem, Minsky [2] proposed an approach based on replication and vote. Within this approach, vote diverging information hosts are considered to be malicious. We consider such distinctive qualification as simple, straightforward and not flexible. Our paper relates malicious property to a more elaborated process. We claim that our process is cautious and flexible. In this process we: (1) Explore how to attach a trust or suspicious quality with a host. This attachment must be temporal. (2) Perform Vote among agents handing out information from trusted hosts only. Suspicious hosts' information is dismissed. (3) Delegate the faculty to declare the malicious character to an adjudicator. The designation requires a dialogue and could be parameterized with a threshold. (4) Capture trusted hosts' bizarre behavior and disclose it. Our approach focuses on the way to determine if hosts' malicious acts have been attempted. Techniques that make tampering more difficult, such as mutating agents in the time limited black box approach are less viable. Although the importance of trust has long been recognized as paramount for the development of secure systems, the meaning associated with trust or trusted principal is seldom clearly defined [3]. Central to our approach is the technical reasoning, viewing trust as cooperation evidences. An agent-owner assesses host's trustworthiness by establishing a basis for believing that the host will behave correctly according to its published policy. In our approach we replace the hard problem of malicious hosts' detection by a simpler process for checking the suspicious host's explanation soundness. We believe that putting more burdens on host side will limit hosts temptation to tamper with mobile agents.

To achieve our goal, in one side the mobile-oo-action is enriched. Our extension provides two actions, one for cloning and, the other for moving clones onto different hosts at a time. Atomicity property is the main characteristic of these actions. This is quite important, since:

1. It is essential when performing verification as the traveling agents return home.
2. It will settle the basis of constructing clean, less verbose, and more expressive specifications.

The mobile-oo-action formal framework is the refinement calculus. Then, we can formally derive systems from their high level abstract specifications to detailed implementations.

Assuming the availability of such actions, we will develop a protocol for dismissing altered roving agents and for determining malicious hosts. The protocol is based on redundant computation. Trustworthiness assessment through redundant computation considers an agent as seemingly a "black-box agent" to its owner. What is valuable to the owner is the soundness of the agent's returned information. Therefore, providing effective protection to agents owners without the penalty of an overhead cost or reducing the flexibility of the agent-based systems. The remainder of the paper is divided as follows. In section two we will give an overview of mobile-oo-action. In section three we will describe our extension to mobile oo-action and its semantics. Section four surveys previous mobile agents' security approaches and then develops our proposal in details.

2 Mobile oo-action based Systems

Mobile oo-action system models an arbitrary number of agents, which can move freely, one place at a time in some domain and, in the same time, do whatever computation they desire. Lugia [4] extended oo-action systems formalism with a *move* action, *positioning* predicate, and a *coordination* class. The new *move* statement is:

$S := move(Olist, L_{exp})$ *(1).* $l := move(Olist, L_{exp})$ *(2).* Where:

1. *Oloc* denotes the domain of mobility.
2. L_{exp} is an expression yielding a place to move in.
3. *Olist* denotes the list of name objects to move.

The first statement evaluates the expression L_{exp} with a subsequent movement of the objects in *Olist* to this location. L_{exp} is an expression yielding as a result a location within the domain *Oloc*. The second statement stores the value of the evaluation in special attribute *l*. Also, present is the predicate *at(Olist, L_{exp})*, used to check whether the objects in *Olist* are in the location obtained by the evaluation of L_{exp}. When the list *Olist* is missing, the calling object is the target of the predicate evaluation. The L_{exp} gives a very general way to specify a location.

Unfortunately, using such *move* primitive to implement the verification protocol based on the parallel execution principle is awkward. In this protocol, it is required that, the agents *moving* process to different locations exhibits an atomicity property; assuming that the final stage of the process is a majority vote basis.

With Lugia [4] primitive, moving some agents to different locations requires an iterating loop where every move instance takes a different single location, standing for the instance of L_{exp}. The major problem with this schema consists of how to manage a *move* failure. We should point out that, a single *move* failure would bias the task of agents' verification protocol. Hence, the majority vote process should be aborted or a quorum lowering would take place. Both cases require a cleaning process generating a waste of efforts.

In our approach we propose a single *move* action. This action moves multiple agents to multiple locations at once. The new *move* is more powerful. It can handle Lugia's one easily. Even more characterizing this new *move* with all or nothing property is easier. The gathered code precludes the need to consider rather individual step actions. Analogically, *Cloning* is an atomic action too. In the next section we will give more details about the two actions.

3 Enriched Mobile object-based systems

Our perception of the move is somewhat different from Luigia's one. However, we will build upon the same background and syntax. We will keep, the concepts needed to model mobility within the same formalism. Also, the concept of mobility is kept abstract, leaving space for the designer to customize the concept to many different environments.

3.1 Principles

The idea is to provide various move actions as a library, implemented in the object context as an abstract class, providing that the language supports multiple dispatching. One of the moves is supplied to manage the presence of firewall, another to accommodate the presence of sandbox, and a third to confine interaction scope. Our main focus is on move encountering firewalls. The move action is made more general. By general we mean being able to move multiple agents to different places at once. Thus, we extend the mobile-oo-action systems formalism by the following new move statement:

$$Move(Olist, L_{exp}list)$$

This statement is more powerful than the one introduced by Lugia. In fact, it can easily achieve the semantics of the old mobile object-based systems. Making L_{exp}list a list of just one single location expression is enough. The new move will keep the same domain of mobility $Oloc$. The L_{exp} will also remain as an expression yielding as a result a location within the domain $Oloc$. Finally, $Olist$ will still stand for a list of objects names.

Our move statement evaluates the list of expressions L_{exp}list with a subsequent movement of the agents of Olist. Agents will be moved to the specified locations on one to one mapping rule. The mapping domain is the values of L_{exp}list with a co domain being the agents of $Olist$. Here, L_{exp} also gives a very general way to specify a location.

With respect to the clone operation, like the new move, cloning should create the agent extra-copies along the all or nothing property. We have decided to make the cloning process as a built-in capability for better security. One reason is precluding the miss use of such action (i.e., when it is not built-in operation). This capability can be supervised by a coordination action. Agents could enable and disable this capability at their wishes. Therefore, we extend the mobile-oo-action systems formalism with the statement:

Clone(NClone)

The cloning process must choose a *fresh* name for every clone. Even though, the extra-copies are denoting the same what is called a snapshot of the *behavior structure*. We must be careful to not just consider *aliasing*, where *OName* elements contain *references* to objects rather than the actual object value [5]. This allows two or more names to denote the same *reference* and thus refer to the same object. Cloning must attach different *ONames* to different values having the same snapshot of the *behaviour structure*. With respect to clones' cloning operations, the cloning agent could supervise the processes individually by a coordination action. The coordination action could enable and disable cloning capability on the fly. In order to make the idea more clear, the structure of an agent and its clone is given below:

```
Agent = Loc L:R
Attr x::=x₀  ∪ Nclone
Obj n:= n₀∪clone-id, ∀  i ∈ [1..Nclone]
Meth    m₁= M_I ... m_h= M_h
Proc p₁ = P₁ ... p_h = P_h∪Clone(Nclone : integer)
             Do
  ||cloneid[i].setCanclone (False)   /*line A:1)*/
  ||          od

Clone = Loc       L:R
Attr x::=x₀  ∪   Nclone ∪ canclone
Obj n: = n₀
Meth    m₁=M_I ... m_h=M_h ∪ SetCanClone(val   can: boolean)
                                   (canclone = can)
```

```
Proc p₁= P₁ ... pₕ = PₕᵁClone(Nclone : integer)
            Do
   ||canclone → Clone(Nclone) /* (line C:1)*/
   ||        od
```

Although, clone's cloning operation is inhibited (line A:1 & line C:1); clone computing is not altered in any way. Here, the agent is acting as a coordinator which can enable and disable the clones' cloning actions at different circumstances as he wishes and on the fly. The next section will define these statements semantics. To keep the same formal frame work of mobile-oo-action, the statements will be defined as weakest precondition transformers.

3.2 Extension semantics

Two aspects are distinguishing the new move statement:

> 1. Atomicity property
> 2. L_{exp}list parameter.

The atomicity is a shared property with the cloning statement. Whereas, the *list* notion is a concept, which is already present in the Lugia's move. Therefore, we will define the semantics of the cloning statement only. When treating the cloning action we are implicitly solving partially at the same time the move action. The one difference which will remain is the parameter L_{exp}list. This second parameter does not need a special care.

Cloning must attach different object names to different object values, denoting the same snapshot of *behavior structure*. The word different is standing for a property of freshness where a *behavior structure* is a fresh *store* and a fresh *stack*. Let's define formally now the freshness property:

```
fresh( φ ,E )          =   error
fresh( e , E )         =   e      if  e    ∉  E
fresh( e∪ E₁ , E )     =   e      if  e    ∉  E

                                  else    fresh( E₁ , E )
```

The clone statement is viewed as a predicate transformer, that is, a function from postcondition to precondition. Let StackVar, StoreVar be countable sets of variables of these particular structures. We are assuming some total ordering over StackVar and StoreVar, which gives a one-to-one correspondence between a set of pair variables (StackVar, StoreVar) and its ordered sequence. A naming is a mapping from the set of pairs (StackVar, StoreVar) to objects names *Onames*.

At the time of clone making, we select a fresh *behavior structure* (i.e., a pair of (StackVar, Store Var)) and attach it to a fresh name from *Oname* domain. Then, the calling agent core image is copied. However, to preserve the atomicity property when making more than one clone, no clone is made when just one clone can not be made.

In program *lattice*, a sequent statement of *magic* value evaluates to true, just if the statement has never been executed. To make our statement atomic, we make the selection of all fresh behavior structures as a *coercion* of the conjunction of all clones individual selection. The *coercion* would evaluate to *magic* if an individual selection were failed or otherwise to *skip*. The value *magic* will inhibit the subsequent action. However, in case of success a total sequence of substitution with agent core image in all fresh behavior structures is carried. Then, we map the fresh behavior structures to objects names. The more concrete description is:

```
Coercion(fresh₁(StackVar,StoreVar)∧.....∧)  ; Nam-
ing(([(StackVar,StoreVar)₁\AgentCoreImage]),.....,)
```

The ";" symbol represents a sequential composition operator, whereas, the "\" symbol denotes a substitution operator.

The extension is defined as predicate transformers. Therefore, it is fitting the same formal framework of mobile-oo-action formalism (i.e., the weakest precondition transformer). The next section will go into details of altered agents and malicious hosts' determination process.

4 Parallel execution Protocol

4.1 Mobile agents' protection background

The fact that the information returned by an agent to the agent owner cannot be validated by the owner is impeding the wide spread adoption of agent-based computing [6]. Recent research in mobile computing security contradicts the above statement by presenting a protocol that allows certain mobile code programs to execute in encrypted form except for the clear text instructions [7, 8]. Therefore, execution on a host system does not compromise an agent's privacy and it safeguards against agent tampering. However, it is impossible to prevent malicious or faulty sites from tampering with clear text agents [9].

We assume clear text agents in order to encompass all agent computations. Our approach assesses trust through redundant computation. Against tampering hosts, we use a protocol based on the parallel execution principle. Before going into further details in our protocol, we will first identify a few necessary characteristics of plausible security solutions that do not limit the potential and flexibility of the mobile agent-computing paradigm.

The most common approach for protecting agents and host systems has been simply to avoid migration to non-trusted hosts and not admit unknown code. This is commonly known as the "trust" approach. Techniques that make tampering more "difficult", such as mutating agents in the time limited black box approach [10] are less viable than focusing on ways to determine if hosts' malicious acts have been attempted. Mechanisms that detect occurrence of improper returned information improve the survivability of the agent owner. If the agent owner is being deliberately fooled by incorrect information from its agents, the former is almost certainly under some form of information assault. If the assaults can be thwarted, then the survivability of the agent owner is increased [6]. Vigna [11] has pointed out that tracking intermediate states created when mobile agents are executed is an important ingredient in producing secure, flexible distributed systems. Vigna's traces can be used to determine the possibility of agent tampering. Later, Kassab [6] introduces the assessment of trust through observability. Better observability is accomplished by inserting protective assertions inside the agent code.

4.2 Our approach

All information belonging to a mobile agent is completely available to its host system, then, it is difficult to apply traditional cryptographic techniques to detect tampering. Since, an agent cannot keep such cryptographic key secret from the system on which it is running; it cannot use cryptographic means to check whether or not it or the data that it has gathered to has been tampered with [5]. Like Minsky [2], our approach will assess trust through redundant computation. An agent is seemingly a "black-box agent" to its owner. What is valuable to the owner is the soundness of the agent's returned information, fooling information must be dismissed, and the correctness of computation should depend only on hosts that would be visited in malicious-free run.

Providing the agent-owner with a mechanism to check information validity will preclude the need to track intermediate agents' states. When the agent-owner is able to associate information with its source host, he can complain about suspicious hosts when fooled. To solve this problem, Minsky [2] proposed an approach based on replication and vote. Within the approach, vote diverging information hosts are considered to be malicious. We consider such distinctive qualification as simple, straightforward and not flexible. Our paper relates malicious property to a more elaborated process. We claim that our process is cautious and flexible. In this process we: (1) Explore how to attach a trust or suspicious quality with a host. This attachment must be temporal. (2) Perform Vote among agents handing out information from trusted hosts only. Suspicious hosts' information is dismissed. (3) Delegate the faculty to declare the malicious character to an adjudicator. The designation requires a dialogue and could be parameterized with a threshold. (4) Capture trusted hosts' bizarre behavior and disclose it.

Although the importance of trust has long been recognized as paramount for the development of secure systems, the meaning associated with trust or trusted principal is seldom clearly defined [3]. Central to our approach is the technical reasoning, viewing trust as cooperation evidences. An agent-owner assesses host's trustworthiness by establishing a basis for believing that the host will behave correctly according to its published policy. A crucial point left behind in approaches based on attack detection is when a host becomes suspicious. Esparza [12] proposed a solution based on limiting the agent's execution time, which can be used with vigna's traces protocol. One major drawback of the solution is that it can consider an honest host as suspicious if it spent more time than expected on execution. In our approach we overcome the problem by letting a host becomes suspicious when it fails to deliver its cooperation evidence and gives a vote's diverging information. Further negotiation with the host is necessary in order to declare the suspicious host as malicious one. Therefore, the hard problem of detecting malicious hosts is replaced by a simpler process for checking the suspicious host's explanation soundness. We believe that putting more burdens on host side will limit hosts temptation to tamper with mobile agents.

Our proposal executes a fair non-repudiation process to collect hosts' cooperation evidences. Therefore, mobile agents in the protocol may be distinguished asymmetrically with respect to hosts' trustworthiness. Since, potentially suspicious hosts are hosts which had failed to deliver evidences during the non-repudiation process. Then, the agents owner will maintain hosts classification, to enable a later complains. Redundant computation protocol success is due to two main reasons. Independent host organizations offering the same service are available. An opportunity of later complains exists. Hosts independence precludes collaborative attacks against roving agents, where as, the later complaining potential makes hosts' benevolent nature persistent (i.e., during visit time). Then we can assert that, a shared trusted hosts' common result is accurate.

Our protocol starts by hosts cooperation evidence collecting. An absence of a host's cooperation evidence is a necessary condition that characterizes a suspicion property, where as, a presence of such evidence is a symbol of trust qualifier. Even though, the agents (i.e., clones created) will move as planned at the first place, only agents handing out information from hosts with cooperation evidences participate in the vote process. Agents handing out information from potentially suspicious hosts not similar to the majority of the former class agents are simulated to be majority vote result equivalent (i.e., just dropped). Therefore, identical results from both agents' classes are strengthening only the vote result. The proposed protocol is a generic multiphase one and it is described as follows:

1. Making a number of clones
2. Performing a fair non repudiation protocol without trusted third party
3. Classify hosts by cooperation evidence availability
4. Moving all clones
5. Each stage's vote is among information of clones visiting cooperative hosts
6. Classifying clones upon return according to information handed out hosts' class
7. Performing a vote among agents handing out information of cooperative hosts.
8. Determining malicious hosts and trusted hosts with bizarre behavior.

This protocol will adapt a well-established realization in its second step. The evidences are usable to resolve possible future dispute (i.e., by presenting the evidences to an adjudicator). Non-repudiation protocols assume mutual suspicion between the parties involved. Many works deal with the non-repudiation problem. From ISO/IEC13888 models to the study carried in [13], a third trusted party is involved as soon as a problem occurs. The other category of protocols [14, 15] is hardware specific or participating parties computing power parameterized. In this paper we will adapt the proposed protocol in [16]. The protocol is a generic one. The generic protocol for evidences collection is as follows:

The agent owner determines the date D
1. Agent-owner → Host-Target: Sign$_{Agent-Owner}$(Move-Request, Agent-Owner, Host-Target, D)
   The Host-Target : Checks Date
                Chooses n

Computes the signed $f_1, \ldots, f_n$

2. Host-Target $\rightarrow$ Agent-Owner: $Sign_{Host\text{-}Target}(f_n(message), Host\text{-}Target, Agent\text{-}Owner, D)$
3. Agent-Owner $\rightarrow$ $Sign_{Agent\text{-}Owner}(ack1)$

.

.

.

2n. Host-Target $\rightarrow$ Agent-Owner: $Sign_{Host\text{-}Target}(f_1(message), Host\text{-}Target, Agent\text{-}Owner, D)$
2n+1. Agent-Owner $\rightarrow$ $Sign_{Agent\text{-}Owner}(ackn)$

Evidences Collection Protocol

The cooperation evidence is $Sign_{Host\text{-}Target} = \{ Sign_i \mid i=1,..,n$ with $Sign_i = Sign_{Host\text{-}Target}(f_i(message, Host\text{-}Target, Agent\text{-}Owner, D)$. The probability that the Agent-Owner does not send the acknowledgement and tries to compute precisely at the last transmission the composition (without being sure it is the last transmission) is according to the geometric distribution used to choose n. There, the host-target would have sent all the needed information to compute the cooperation evidence although the Agent-Owner does not send his evidence (i.e., ackn). This later case is worthwhile if the Agent-Owner is a familiar principle to the Host-Target.

Step7 is the vote process performed as agents return home. Although, the vote is the way of validating returned information, it settles down the basis for malicious hosts' detection. Only agents handing out information from hosts having delivered cooperation evidences (i.e., trusted) participate in the vote. Therefore, we can assert that their shared common result is accurate.

Agents handing out information from potentially suspicious hosts not similar to the majority vote result are ignored. However, the corresponding hosts are considered as tampering. These hosts are probably malicious. Such malicious behavior is checked with the collaboration of an adjudicator. Our generic complaining protocol, which determines malicious hosts, is described in the following section:

```
/* Agent-owner entering complaining state
     i.e., some hosts are characterized by
          1. Absence of cooperation evidence
          2. Diverging with vote result        */
1. Agent-owner → Adjudicator: Sign_Agent-Owner(move-time, move action, list suspicious
                              results, list suspicious hosts, vote result, list of hosts vote).
2. Adjudicator → A vote host: Sign_Adjudicator("give me: visiting Agent Identity & its
                              result but at move-time").
3. Compose a Check-list (i.e., creteria model), List MaliciousHosts:= ∅.
4. For each suspicious host :
          Adjudicator → Suspicious Host: Sign_Adjudicator(" Explain your misbehavior").
          If (no reply or explanation not sound) then  Add suspicious Host to List Maliciou-
sHosts.
5. For each Malicious Host :
          1. Send a warn , add warn to the Log if none
          2. Advance malicious host Log warn
          3. Threshold reached : Revoke malicious host.
```

Complaining Protocol

238

In the complaining stage, the agent-owner sends to the adjudicator a tampering proof ground. The proof ground is a signed message including *time-move, move-action, suspicious results, identities of potential malicious hosts, the majority vote result*, and *majority vote trusted hosts list*. Thereafter, the adjudicator builds the corresponding tampering proof (i.e., Check-List or criteria model). To do so, the adjudicator diligently examines non-repudiation protocol-underlying executing conditions. He can assert travels of supposed tampered with agents to supposed malicious hosts, by asking a trusted majority vote host. The assertion is true if the later confirms the arrival of the particular agent but at move time. This is convincing as move action exhibits an atomicity property. Meanwhile, the adjudicator can easily validate the vote result. He can do so by including in the same former request an acquirement to hand him the visiting agent result. Clearly, the vote result is valid in case of equality. After that, the adjudicator asks the malicious hosts to explain their misbehavior. A malicious host is one which is confirmed to be vote result diverging and not cooperation evidence holding. Later on, the adjudicator could decide to warn malicious hosts. He has enough information to decide about the soundness of suspicious hosts explanations. The adjudicator will declare hosts with non-sound explanations to be malicious. An explanation is not sound if its result is confirmed to be vote diverging and it has not also been able to confirm the claim of the cooperation evidence delivery. Even more, a suspicious host wishing to fool an adjudicator with old cooperation evidence can be soon disproved. Cooperation evidences are transient; expire as a new visit session of agents' starts. The fooling claims not sound an obtained trusted host cooperation evidence date is different.

The Adjudicator could gain a punishment skill when it maintains a warning Log. Whether a malicious host would tamper again with roving agents; the adjudicator can decide as in [1] to revoke the host. The watching out scenario could also be applied to minority vote hosts. The agent-owner can log the list of such hosts. Hosts occurring in the same list at many votes can at least be characterized by a bizarre behavior. The agent-owner can signal such hosts to the adjudicator and over the net.

5 Conclusion

This paper has defined the concepts needed to model cloning and multiple agents multiple places move. The concepts are characterized by the all or nothing property. The extension is established as weakest precondition transformer. Thereafter, Minsky protocol is extended to leave space for an adjudicator to determine malicious hosts and could decide to revoke recidivist ones. Yet bizarre trusted hosts' behavior could be disclosed to the net principles. This is feasible as long as hosts are known in advance. We are planning to extend the protocol by a mechanism for trust ant non-trust proliferation and addressing the vote convergence aspect.

References

1. Oscar Esparza, Miguel Soriano, Jose L Munoz, and Jordi Forné. Protocols for Malicious Host Revocation. "Information and Communications Security (ICICS'0303). Lecture Note in Computer Science Vol 2836, 2003, ISSN/ISBN 0302-9743.

2. Y. Minsky and Al. Cryptographic support for fault-Tolerant Distributed Computing, In seventh ACM SIGOPS European workshop 1996.

3. Uwe G. Wilhelm, Sebastian M. Staamann, and Levente Buttyan. A Pessimistic Approach to Trust in Mobile Agent Platforms 2000. CistSeer.IST. Scientific Literature Digital Library 2000.

4. Lugia perte and Kaisa Sere. Coordination among Mobile objects, Tucs Technical report N0 219, November 1998, ISBN 952-12-0332-3, ISSN 1239-1981.

5. Catherine Meadows. Detecting Attacks on Mobile Agents,1997. CistSeer.IST. Scientific Literature Digital Library 1997.

6. Lora L. Kassab and Jeffrey Voas. Agent Trustworthiness, Ecoop workshops 1998:300.

7. Tomas Sander and Christian F.Tschudin. On software protection via function Hiding, submitted to the 2 International workshop on information Hiding.

8. Tomas Sander and Christian F.Tshudin. Towards mobile cryptography, IEEE symposium on security and privacy May 1998.

9. David Chess and AL. Itinerant Agents for mobile computing, IEEE personal communications Magazine, 2(5):34-39, October 1995.

10. Fritz, Hohl. Time limited blackbox security: Protecting Mobile Agents from malicious Hosts, Springer verlag 1998. CistSeer.IST. Scientific Literature Digital Library.

11. Giovanni Vigna. Protecting Mobile Agents through Tracing, In proceeding of the 3rd ECOOP workshop on mobile objects systems, Jyvalskyla, Finland 1997.

12. O. Esparza, M Soriano, J.L, Munoz.and J.Forné. A protocol for detecting malicious hosts based on limiting the execution time of mobile agents. In IEEE symposium on computers and communications – ISCC'2003, 2003.

13. J. Zhou and D. Gollmann. An efficient non repudiation protocol. In proceeding of the 10th Computer Security fondations Workshop, pages 126-132. IEEE Computer Society Press, June 1997.

14. Y.Han. Investigation of non-repudiation protocols. In ACISP: Information security and privacy: Australasian Conference, Volume 1172 of lecture notes in Computer Science, pages 38-47 Springer-Verlag, 1996.

15. P. Syverson. Weakly secret bit commitment: Application to lotteries and fair exchande. In proceeding of the 1998 IEEE Computer Security foundations Work-Shop (CSFW11), June 1998.

16. Olivier Markowitch, Yves Roggman. Probabilistic non-repudiation without trusted third party. Second Conference on security in communication networks (SCN9°), Amalfi, Italy, September 1999.

Masquerade Detection by Using Activity Patterns

B. M. Reshmi [1], S.S. Manvi [2]

[1] Department of Information science and Engineering
[2] Department of Electronics and Communication Engineering
Basaveshwara Engineering College
Bagalkot, 587102, India
breshmi@yahoo.com,sunil@protocol.ece.iisc.ernet.in

Abstract. Masqueraders in computer intrusion detection are people who use somebody else's computer account. The typical approach is based on the idea that masquerader activity is unusual activity that will manifest as significant excursions from normal user profiles. When a deviation from normal behavior is observed, a masquerade attempt is suspected. This paper proposes a statistical approach for detecting masqueraders by tracing the activity patterns of the users. A probabilistic activity matrix is created for each user, which. will be used for detection of masquerading.

Key words   Anomaly, masquerading, computer security, intrusion detection, probability.

1 Introduction

Intrusion detection system (IDS) [1] serves as an alarm mechanism for a computer system. It detects the security compromises happened to computer system and then issues an alarm message to an entity, such as site security officer so that entity can take some actions against the intrusion. An IDS contains an audit data collector [2], which keeps track of the activities within the system, a detector which analyzes the audit data and issues an output report to the site security officer. IDS techniques [3] refer to the concepts such as *anomaly and misuse detection*. Anomaly detection refers to techniques that define and characterize normal or acceptable behaviors of the system (e.g., CPU usage, job execution time, system calls). Behaviors that deviate from the expected normal behavior are considered intrusions. Misuse detection refers to techniques that characterize known methods to penetrate a system. These penetrations are characterized as a 'pattern' or a signature' that the IDS looks for. The pattern/signature might be a static string or a set of sequence of actions.

In the field of computer security, one of the most damaging attack is masquerading. A masquerade attack in which one user impersonates another is among the most serious forms of computer abuse, largely because such attacks are often mounted by

241

insiders and can be very difficult to detect. Colloquially, masquerading is the act of substituting one self for another. The masquerade problem can be described in the following scenario [4]. The legitimate user takes a coffee break, leaving his/her terminal open and logged in. During the user's brief absence, an interloper assumes control of the keyboard and enters commands taking advantage of the legitimate user's password and access to programs and data. The interloper's commands may compromise read or write, installation of malicious software etc. Masquerade detection falls under the cover of anomaly detection. A masquerade may happen to similar behavioral patterns as the legitimate user of an account to which he or she is currently logged through escaping detection and successfully causing damage under the cover of seemingly normal behavior. Another problem caused by computer user's tendency toward concept drift- a change in activity that is not captured strongly in the original user signature. As a result legitimate user command sequence may differ enough from the signature to appear to be intrusion. Detecting anomalous behavior can be viewed as a binary valued classification problem in which measurements of system activity such as system log files, resource usage, command traces, and audit trails are used produce a classification of the state of the system as normal or abnormal. The problem of intrusion detection is inherently statistical because it is data driven.

Some of the related works on masquerade detection includes the following: (1) Du Mouchel [5] proposed a Bayes 1-Step Markov , this detector is based on single step transitions from one command to the next. The detector determines whether or not observed transition probabilities are consistent with historical probabilities. (2) The uniqueness approach [6] due to Schonlau and Theus is based on ideas about command frequencies. Commands not seen in the training data may indicate masquerade attempt, and the more infrequently command is issued by the user community as whole, the more indicative is that command is being masquerade. (3) The sequence match [7] approach due to Lane and Broadley, the method computes a similarity matches between the most resent commands user commands and a user profile. (4) The compression method [8] due to Karr and Schonlau, is based on the idea of compression approach is that new data from a given user compresses at about the same ratio as old data from that same user and that data from masquerading user will compress at a different ratio and there by be distinguishing from the legitimate user.

This paper is structured as follows: In section 2 we describe the proposed work. Section 3 provides simulation. Section 3 analyzes the results and section 5 concludes.

2 Proposed work

In order for the detection system to recognize anomalous behavior, it must form a user profile to characterize normal behavior. To form a user profile our approach learns characteristic sequences of actions generated by users. The underlying hypothesis is that a user responds in a similar manner to similar situations leading to repeated sequences of actions. It is the differences in characteristic sequences that we attempt to use to differentiate a valid user from an intruder masquerading as that user. An audit trail can be maintained for a variety of user activity types, logging, for example, operating system commands, database system interrogations and updates and the details of user interactions with specialized programs. The proposed model consists of three elements : audit data collector, profile builder and intrusion detector (see figure1).

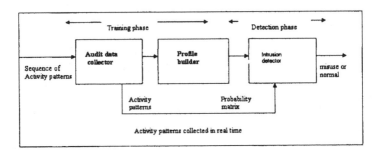

Fig. 1 Elements of the Masquerade detection .

(1) *Audit data collector*: This is responsible for collecting characteristic sequence of actions (i.e., activity patterns or sequence of commands executed), an ordered, fixed or variable set of temporarily adjacent actions for each user at different instances in regular basis. It translates the raw data stream of activity traces into a suitable format for storage and comparison. This translation suppresses activity arguments and preserves only the activity names. To define activity pattern for each user, first, we define an activity set, that contains all possible activities executed by the users (for example login, mail,..........) which is common for all the users i.e., A={a0,a1,a2,a3............................aK-1}, where, each element of the set represents a single command executed by a user and, K= total number of activities. Audit data collector collects different activity patterns for each user at different instances in training phase in regular basis and updates blackboard. Activity patterns collected for 'n' instances at different times, say, T = {t0, t1, ... , tn-1} is expressed as:

A(t0)={a1,a2,a3,a5,a6,a7,a8.,a7,a9.............,a5},
A(t1)={a3,a6,a4,a9,a6,a5,a3,a6,a4,a3.......,a2},

....
....
A(tn-1)={a2,a3,a8, ...,a10}.

Activity patterns collected for 'n' instances are represented as an activity matrix, in which row represents an activity pattern instance and column represents position of an activity in an activity pattern as given in figure 2.

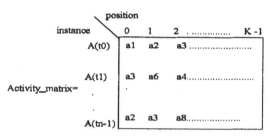

Fig. 2. Activity matrix

(2) *profile builder (training phase):* Masquerade detection (anomaly detection) consists of two phases: one is a training phase, in which normal profile for each user is constructed in regular basis as said above and, detection phase, in which anomaly detector monitors current user session to detect intrusions . The normal profile is used to learn the user normal behavior. In the training phase, profile builder computes a probability matrix for each user, which represents a user normal profile, based on activity patterns collected by audit data collector, by using statistical method. Probability matrix represents a normal behavior of a user in terms of probability of executing each activity in different positions. This normal profile is then used to detect intrusions in the detection phase. The probability matrix is as shown in figure 3.

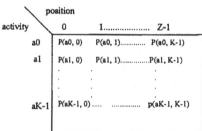

Fig. 3. Probability Matrix

In the probability matrix, row represents activity identity and column represents probability of an activity execution in that position (column numb); ·r), where Z= max number of sequence of activities traced in each instance, and K= maximum number of activities identified in the system.

For example, P(a0, 0) represents probability of executing an activity 0 (a0), in the position 0 (i.e., in the first position), P(a1, 0), probability of executing an activity 1 (a1), in the position 0. Computation of probability is done as follows given for P(a0,0).

$$P(a0,0) = \frac{\text{frequency of executing an activity 0 (a0) in position 0}}{n}$$

where, n = Total number of instances in the training data.

(3) Intrusion detector (detection phase): Once a user profile is formed, basic action of the intrusion detector is to compare the incoming sequences to the historical data and form an opinion as to whether or not they both represent the legitimate user. The fundamental unit of comparison in the anomaly detection is the activity sequences or patterns. For each activity pattern, intrusion detector computes a score, if this score exceeds or equal to some threshold value, it declares, that activity pattern is a misuse pattern. To compute a score for each activity pattern in observation, it considers each activity and its position. For each activity in the activity pattern, it starts searching a probability matrix to know a highest probability of executing an activity in that position and also the probability of executing an activity under consideration in the same position and the difference between these two results a deviation value for an activity. That is deviation is computed by subtracting the elements of the probability matrix determined from the test data from the probability matrix generated in learning phase. Product of all the deviation values gives a score for the single activity pattern.

Consider an example, to illustrate the intrusion detection, let us say, Activity set is: {a0,a1,a2,a3,a4}. Activity patterns collected at five instances (training data) for a user ' x ', are as follows :

$$A(t0) = \{a0,a1,a2,a3,a3\},$$
$$A(t1) = \{a0,a0,a2,a3,a3\},$$
$$A(t2) = \{a0,a0,a2,a3,a3\},$$
$$A(t3) = \{a0,a0,a2,a3,a3\},$$
$$A(t4) = \{a0,a0,a2,a3,a3\},$$

The activity matrix for user ' x ' is given in figure 4.

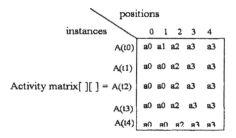

Fig. 4. Activity matrix

The probability matrix for user ' x ' is as shown in figure 5.

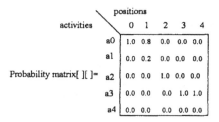

Fig. 5. Probability matrix

To illustrate the elements of probability matrix, let us consider one of the computations, P(a0,0). From the instances, we see that a0 occurs in the first position of all the 5 instances, hence P(a0,0)= 5/5 =1.0.

Consider each column in the probability matrix. Highest probability value for an activity a0 executing in the position 0, i.e., in the column 0 is 1.0; for an activity a0 executing in the position 1, i.e., in the column 1 is 0.8; for an activity a2 executing in the position 2 i.e., in the column 2 is 1.0; for an activity a3 executing in the position 3, i.e., in the column 3 is 1.0 ; for an activity a3 executing in the position 4, i.e., in the column 4 is 1.0.

Consider a test data for user ' x ' , at three different instances to check for intrusions as given below.

A(t0)={a0, a0, a2, a3, a3},
A(t1)={a1, a2, a1, a1, a1},
A(t2)={a3, a2, a1, a1, a2}.

The deviation value for each activity in the activity patterns and score for each activity pattern in different instances is calculated as given in figure 6.

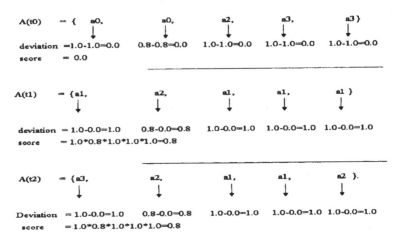

Fig. 6.. Deviation value and scores for activity patterns

Consider threshold score value to be maximum of three scores, which is 0.8.

The first activity pattern is not a misuse activity pattern. Since score < threshold.
The second activity pattern is a misuse activity pattern. Since score = threshold.
The third activity pattern is a misuse activity pattern. Since score = threshold.

The third activity pattern is not seen in the user's historical data (training data or normal user profile), i.e., anything not seen in the historical data represents a different user (intruder or masquerader).

3 Simulation model

To evaluate the proposed intrusion detection method presented, a training data set (user normal profile, historical data, and collection of activity patterns) for U users is randomly generated. Training data contains only normal activity patterns. An activity set defined for the user consists of K distinct activities i.e., A={a0, a1, a2, a3, a4,.....................aK-1}. Training data is collected at n instances, T={t0, t1, t2.............tn-1}. Test data consists of both normal activity patterns already generated in training and misuse activity patterns. Test data contains p activity patterns collected at different instances. In the evaluation process, some percentages of intrusions are added to the test data to check the detection rate. To raise an alarm for misuse activity in the test data, a score for each activity pattern is computed and that score is compared with the threshold value. If the score exceeds threshold value, an alarm is raised. The score is computed by cross validating the activity patterns in the test data and also considering the statistical values in the probability matrix. Based on these scores computed for each activity pattern, a threshold is fixed. We evaluate the system by taking three different threshold values (δ): minimum, average and maximum of the scores computed for each activity pattern and also by varying the size of the training data set (the total number of instances).

To illustrate some results of the simulation, we have taken, U= 5 users, K=25 activities , n=30, 40, and 50 instances, p= 10 instances, δ= minimum of scores, average of scores and maximum of scores .
The performance parameters measured are as follows.

- *Detection rate:* It is a ratio of attacks detected by the system to the attacks made on the system.
- *False positive and false negative*: False positive is a non intrusion activity pattern that the algorithm has labeled as containing an intrusion. False negative is an intrusion activity pattern that the algorithm has labeled as non-intrusion. Figure. 7 summarizes the calculation used to compute false positives, false negatives and detection rate.

---

f = number of false positives
x = number of non intrusion activity patterns
u = number of users

$$\text{false positives}_{(overall)} = ([\sum_{u}^{i} (f_i / x_i)]u)*100$$

f_n = number of false negatives
y = number of intrusion activity patterns
c = number of users who have at least one intrusion activity pattern

$$\text{false negatives}_{(overall)} = ([\sum_{u}^{i} (f_{ni}/y_i)] /c)*100$$

$$\text{detection rate}_{(overall)} = 100 - \text{false negatives}_{(overall)}$$

Fig 7. Computation of false positives and negatives

4 Results

Figure 8 illustrates Detection rate versus % of intrusions for 5 users (n=number of instances in the training data = 30, 40 and 50 and the threshold (δ) value is minimum of the scores computed for each activity pattern for the test data). It is observed that detection rate is 100% for all the samples. Even though the detection rate is 100%, it yields more number of false positives (false positive rate is very high).

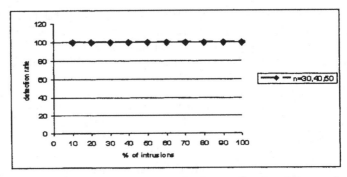

Fig. 8. Detection rate Vs. % of intrusions for 5 users (δ to be minimum of scores)

Figure 9 illustrates the Detection rate versus % of intrusions for 5 users (n=number of instances= 30, 40 and 50 and the threshold (δ) value is average of the scores computed for each activity pattern in the test data). It is observed that detection rate increases as the size of the training data set increases. It is also observed that, it results few false positives.

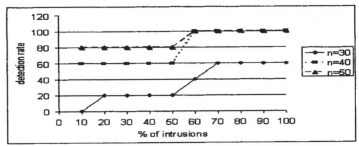

Fig. 9. Detection rate Vs % of intrusions for 5 users (δ to be average of scores)

Figure 10 illustrates the graph of Detection rate versus % of intrusions for 5 users (n=number of instances= 30, 40 and 50 and the threshold value is maximum of the scores computed for each activity pattern in the test data). It is observed that detection rate increases as the size of the training data set increases. It is also observed that, the detection rate reaches 100% slowly and but results in very few false positives compared to the results obtained in figure 9.

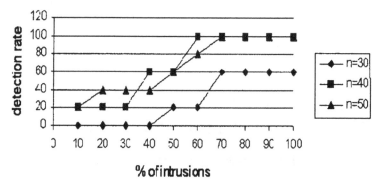

Fig. 10. Detection rate Vs % of intrusions for 5 users (δ to be maximum of scores)

5 Conclusion

The proposed work demonstrates that activity pattern learning can be a valuable technique in the domain of anomaly detection for user recognition in computer security. The performance of the algorithm can be improved to detect different types of exploits like privilege escalation, removable media, export via email, changing file extensions, encipher/decipher and unusual search by considering semantics and the arguments used for an activity.

6 References

[1]D. E. Denning, " An Intrusion Detection Model", *IEEE Transactions on Software Engineering,* vol. 13, no. 2, pp. 222-232, 1987.

[2]R. Bace, P. Mell, " NIST Special Publication on Intrusion Detection Systems", available at: http;//csrc.nist.gov/publications/nistpubs/800-31/sp800-31.pdf.

[3]   Theuns Verwoerd, Ray Hunt , " Intrusion Detection Techniques and Approaches", *Computer communications,* vol. 25, no. 15, pp.1356-1365, 2002.

[4] Roy A. Maxion and Tahlia N. Town send, " Masquerade Detection Using Truncated Commands Lines", *International Conference on Dependable Systems and Networks,* Washington, DC, pp. 23-26, 2002.

[5] W. DuMouchel, " Computer intrusion detection based on Bayes factors for comparing command transition probabilities," Technical Report 91, National Institute of Statistical Sciences, Research Triangle Park, North Carolina, 27709-4006, 1999.

[6] M. Schonlau and M. Theus, " Detecting Masqueraders in intrusion detection based on unpopular commands", *Information Processing letters,* vol. 76, no. 1, pp. 33-38, 2000.

[7] T. Lane. and E. E. Broadley: Temporal sequence Learning and data reduction for Anomaly Detection. *ACM Transactions on Information and system Security:* vol. 2, no. 3, pp. 295-331, 1999.

[8] M. Schonlau W. DuMouchel, W. H. Ju. A. F. Karr, M. Theus, and Y. Vardi, Computer Intrusion: Detecting Masqueraders, Statistical Sciences , vol.116, no. 1, pp 58-74, 2001.

SECTION V: Software for Security in Networked Environments

A Flexible, Open Source Software Architecture for Network-Based Forensic Computing & Intelligence Gathering

Christopher Meyler, Iain Sutherland

School of Computing,
University of Glamorgan, UK
{cpmeyle1, isutherl}@glam.ac.uk

Abstract. Currently real time support tracking and identifying files across networks is extremely limited. In this paper we propose a flexible, open source software architecture for real-time analysis of the Web and local area networks in order to identify and track images and other forms of illicit files or malware. A prototype architecture has been developed and was evaluated using a series of anonymous case studies. Calculating and storing their MD5 message digest identify the files. The results of this can be used in several different ways. For example, comparisons of message digest results on obtained from files on a user's machine against a database of known files may reveal certain malware, such as Trojans or unlicensed software. Additionally, an illicit image may be found in this way. If a file is found on more than one website or hard drive then a comparison of the modified, accessed, and created (MAC) times may give some idea as to the order in which a file has migrated across a network. Results showed that files could be tracked and identified in the majority of cases and that the prototype showed promise in a live case scenario.

Keywords: Network-based forensics, Open source, Intelligence Sharing, Digital Evidence.

1 Introduction

The proliferation of computer networks and electronic devices and the increased popularity of the World Wide Web have given rise to new challenges for computer forensic investigators, who are required to gather both intelligence and forensic evidence that is likely to be admissible in a court of law. It is now possible for crimes involving digital evidence from different sources to occur in real-time in different geographical locations.

1.1 Definitions

A broad definition of network forensics is taken for the purpose of this paper.
Network forensics to mean acquisition or analysis of any network or network-based
forensic evidence, or any remote acquisition and analysis that involves a network.
Remote analysis meaning any activity from a remote location e.g., SSh into a system
to run some commands or running a script to copy files across a network could both
be considered as remote analysis.

1.2 Aims of the Architecture

The architecture seeks to achieve three main goals:

- An open source method of identifying and tracking files, particularly
  illicit images, across local area networks both for the purpose of gathering
  intelligence and forensic evidence.
- An open source method of identifying and tracking files across the World
  Wide Web for the purpose of gathering forensic evidence and
  intelligence.
- A standard means of extending the functionality of the tool architecture so
  that other tools or databases can be developed in order to enhance the
  functionality.

2. Current Technology

A variety of proprietary and open source network forensic tools exist for the more
common operating systems, including Microsoft Windows and Linux. The following
section provides a summary of selected network-based forensic tools.

2.1 EnCase Forensic and Enterprise

The Guidance Software EnCase Enterprise tool is also capable of remote forensic
analysis, but like the MFP is not able to easily track the migration of files across the
network. A valuable way of facilitating extensibility of forensic tools is to support the
creation of scripts. Different functions may be grouped together and executed.
Guidance Software has incorporated such a facility with EnCase [6]. The language
allows the investigators to customize the tool's features and provide additional
functionality.

2.2 The Mobile Forensics Platform (MFP)

The MFP is intended to be a remote network forensic tool capable of acquiring and
analyzing forensic evidence. The investigator connects to the MFP via either a

Virtual Private Network (VPN) or a phone line [2]. The tool runs on the same subnet as the machine being investigated and is described as modular in design in order to facilitate tool extensibility [2]. Functions are available for a variety of analysis, including reading and parsing log files and checking their consistency.

2.3 The PyFlag Forensic Tool

The Forensic and Log Analysis (FLAG) is a web-based forensic tool that was intended to "simplify the process of log file analysis and forensic investigations", [9]. The tool has an HTML user interface and was designed to analyze a wide variety of areas, including the registry, Internet Explorer History and Microsoft Word documents. The tool is open source and makes extensive use of libraries to provide its functionality.

2.5 ODESSA

The Open Digital Evidence Search and Seizure Architecture (ODESSA) is an open source, extensible set of tools for extracting, analyzing and reporting digital evidence. The source code of which is freely available to download from the project website. The suite contains three forensic tools that are described as "highly modular and cross-platform" [8].

2.6 NetForensics

NetForensics have developed a tool, which, is claimed to be capable of real time forensic analysis [7]. The tool consists of three elements: - an event analyzer for analysis of events generated by network devices; an alarm console to provide a real time status of various devices; and a database system containing historical event data. The tool utilizes information such as intrusion detection logs on which to perform forensic analysis [7].

Gaining intelligence or potential evidence about the identification, source, or location of files, particularly illicit images are likely to progress an investigation. In addition, organizations gathering this information in a forensically sound measure are likely to be able to respond quicker in the event of an incident. The present suite of network forensic tool technology is not able to track and identify files in the manner proposed by this paper.

3. The Analysis Performed by the Tool

It is anticipated that the tool would have several different applications. Firstly, gathering intelligence or forensic evidence relating to files on the Web in order to identify illicit images or malware such as Trojans. Corporate intranet sites may also be analyzed in this way. In the same way investigators or system administrators should be able to monitor local area networks to identify illicit images, Trojans or possibly unlicensed software. Gathering forensically sound evidence over a continuous period of time is likely to enhance an organization's ability to respond to incidents once they occur and ultimately defend the network against misuse.

3.1 Investigating nodes on a Local Area Network

The network analyzer tool, implemented in C and C++ performs a similar function, but on a local network. The hard drive of each node is scanned and file attributes such as file name, size, and date created, accessed and modified, are extracted. In addition, the MD5 message digest of each file would be calculated. The investigator would be able to select an individual machine for acquisition by its IP address, or a series of machines by entering a range of IP numbers. Transfer of data between each computer and the forensic workstation is via Secure Shell (SSh). Any actions performed or errors generated would be written to the audit log in the same way as the web-based tool.

3.2 Monitoring the Web

The tool is implemented in Python and reuses code developed for the network analyzer. The purpose of this ODBC-compliant component is to trawl the Web, link by link, downloading files to a temporary area, and extracting various file attributes including the file size, and calculating a MD5 message digest. The data are written to a database for analysis. The tool starts at a specific web address and perform a scan for a given number of pages. All actions performed or errors generated as a result of using the tool would be written to the audit log. Figure One gives an overview of the tool architecture.

Fig. 1. An overview of the prototype software architecture

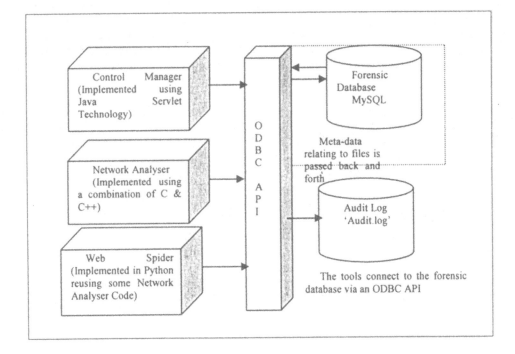

3.3 The Forensic Database

The meta-data gathered by the web spider and network analyzer are stored in a MySQL relational database. Logically, data is organized according to the their respective cases/investigations. However, there could be situations where an item of data belongs to more than one case. Therefore, this should be reflected in the tool design. A case is likely to have one or more investigators, so information about each investigator and the action they took during an investigation is also important. Progression in an investigation should generate a list of one or more suspects. Data about each suspect and how they fit into the case would need to be recorded. The network analyzer and web spider will produce meta-data relating to files. These could include the file name, location, the date that the file was modified, accessed, and created, the size of the file, and its MD5 message digest calculation.

3.4 Why have a Standard API?

Open source tools should be developed with a view to being able to add additional tools at later stages [5]. A standard interface would mean that developers could simply 'plug in' additional software once it has been developed. Therefore, a specific set of Application Programming Interfaces should be agreed and developed to allow as many tool developers as possible to achieve this aim.

3.4.1 Architectural Extensibility and ODBC

The Open Database Connectivity Standard (ODBC), devised by Microsoft, provides a standard way of interfacing with heterogeneous SQL databases [4]. Applications can access different databases via a common set of code. ODBC is key to providing extensibility to the architecture for three reasons: -

- Other developers would be able to develop tools for the current architecture without using a specific database management system, such as MySQL or Oracle.
- The architecture is not restricted to the DBMS with which the database was implemented and can be implemented with any other ODBC compliant relational database management system.
- Client-Server support for accessing databases over networks will mean that tools could potentially access the database from remote locations.

OBDC requires four layers or components to be set-up [4]. The first is the application/software program to submit SQL statements to insert or query the database. The second is a driver manager, which will load the required software drivers. The third is the driver and database agent, which process the ODBC function calls and submit SQL statements to the data source return the results to the original program [4]. The final part is the data source itself. According to [4] this consists of the data that are to be accessed, the associated database management system, the operating system and the network platform.

3.5 The Control Manager and User Interface

Implemented using a Java Servlet Technology so that the control manager can be run remotely on a machine other than the forensic database. This further demonstrates the flexibility of the software architecture. The Control Manager (CM) is the central part of the software architecture. It has several functions. Firstly, it allows the investigator to schedule the network analysis and web spider tools. The CM also allows investigators to query both the forensic database and the audit log. This would include predefined ODBC-compliant SQL queries and a facility for the user generate their own. Typical predefined queries would include comparing the message digest result of a recently downloaded file this those contained in the forensic database. This would allow investigators to determine if the file in question has appeared on machines other than the one visited. The database should be case-oriented and an overall administrator would be able to add investigators to cases in the database and manage the investigation in a later version of the prototype.

3.6 Accounting for the investigation with the Audit Log

All evidence acquired and processes undertaken by investigators need to be accounted for in order to maintain the evidential integrity. The Association of Chief Police Officers (ACPO) guidelines state, "An audit trail or other record of all processes should be created and preserved" [1]. The audit log is a plain text file containing recording every action or error that has occurred using the tool set. Its aim is to demonstrate a chain of evidence and account for every action the software or user has undertaken from running the network analyzer to error messages that have been reported. However, a live system is likely to generate far more data than the prototype evaluation, hence future work will involve developing the audit log as a relational database.

4. Evaluation & Results

The tool was evaluated using a series of three case studies. Each of the case studies has been made anonymous and was evaluated on a test network in a laboratory. Each of the case studies was run over a five-day period and files were placed on the network by a colleague, according to each of the facts devised in the case studies. The number of files found in the exercise measured the success of the experiment.

It would have been impractical to run the case studies on a live network or the Web itself. In addition to this it would have raised certain ethical, moral, and legal issues. It was for this reason that an isolated test network was created to run each of the case studies. There were three Pentium III PCs running either Windows 2000 service pack four or Windows XP, depending on the individual case study. In addition to this, there are three Sparc stations, each running Debian Linux. They were all networked via a 3-Com 100 Mega-bit network switch. Each of the PCs ran Internet Information Service (IIS) version five so that they could also be used as web servers. The three Sparc stations were configured as Apache web servers. The list of installed applications varied according to each case study. In addition to these, another PC, running Windows XP service pack one, was designated as the forensic server from which the tools were to be executed. The Forensic Database was also stored on this machine. The machines, including the Forensic workstation were wiped using EnCase version 4 and rebuild using the appropriate operating systems and software before each case study. Together, the three case studies evaluate attempt to evaluate the tool objectives set out earlier in this paper. A summary how the case studies and properties evaluated is given in Table 1.

Table 1. A summary of the tool objectives evaluated by each case study

Case 1 – The ABC College Case Study	Near real-time forensic analysis on a local area network Near real-time intelligence gathering on a local area network

Case 2 – Ad-Hoc IT Services Ltd Case Study	Near real-time forensic analysis on a local area network Near real-time intelligence gathering on a local area network Tool Extensibility
Case 3- The Trojan Defence Case Study	Near real-time forensic analysis on the web Near real-time intelligence gathering on the web

4.1 Case 1 – The ABC College Case Study

The first case study involved an investigation into a member of academic staff at a UK college of further education who, it had been alleged was sending emails with offensive images as file attachments over a period of some weeks. Several members of staff complained and an investigation was launched. The images were not of an illegal nature but were offensive and in breach of the college's Information Communications Technology (ICT) usage policy. The aim of the investigation was to identify the culprit and to ensure that no other member of staff was in breach of the policy.

4.2 Case 2 – Ad-Hoc IT Services Ltd Case Study

The second case study involved an employee at a small to medium sized (SME) IT Services Company, which was also based in the United Kingdom. The company offers a range of services to its clients, including software development, web development, network and desktop support, outsourcing, customer relationship management, and consultancy. The user in question was an employee of the company who specialises in desktop support so he was considered to be more knowledgeable than most users. A routine sweep of the network had uncovered suspicious activity and an MD5 hash of a file matched that of an illicit image. The images were found in several locations on the disk, some of which were found in unusual folder locations with renamed file extensions.

4.3 Case 3 – The Trojan Defence Case Study

The final case concerns a home user, based in the United Kingdom, whose personal computer has been seized by a local high-tech crime unit. The disk was imaged and analyzed using EnCase and was found to contain several illegal pornographic images. The defence team is claiming that the suspect was the unwitting the victim of a Trojan horse program, which placed the material on the disk. The defendant claims to have downloaded the software from the web. However, cannot remember when this occurred or the URL from where it was downloaded. The major difference between this case study and the previous two is that although it concerns the use of illicit or illegal images, the actual investigation involves searching for non-picture files. However, the principles remain the same.

4.4 Summary of Results

The evaluation process is still on going at the time of writing this paper. However, the results of the first case study are summarised in the below table (Table 2). While the network analyzer was able to locate the majority of images placed on the network, not all were found. Analysis of the audit log showed that some were did not appear in the forensic database, as the network analyzer was not able to open them. It is possible that they had been locked by the operating system at the point where the tool attempted to read the file. Re-running the test improved the hit-rate. However, further investigation is required to identify why not all the images were found. The remaining two case studies are on going and should produce results in the near future.

Table 2. A summary of results from the first case study

Total Number of Images Hidden	Total Number of Images Found	Percentage of Images Found
25	22	88

5. Summary and Conclusions

In this paper we have proposed flexible, open source architecture for identifying and tracking files across both local area networks and the Web. The architecture has been evaluated by a series of case studies and conclusions drawn as to its likely effectiveness in a live case.

The evaluation has shown that should be possible to track the migration of files across a local area network and the World Wide Web. It should also be possible to determine the source of a document by tracking the file and comparing the MAC date and times. Malware, such as Trojan horse programs are also likely to be identified in this way. The facilities have the potential for establishing normal behavior for network usage and patterns in criminal activity, and a Modus Operandi. Tracking files in this way should also be a routine for systems administrators. Organizations would benefit from continually gathering evidence in a forensically sound manner so that they are best placed to react and prosecute a crime as it occurs. The tool follows many of the principles of forensic readiness described by Rowlingson [10].

6. Future Work

At the time of writing this paper, the evaluation is on going and the first step is to ensure that all the main strands have been evaluated before final conclusions can be made. Secondly, the Development of tools to extend the architecture and perform similar functions on other devices such as mobile telephones, Personal Digital Assistants, and other portable devices. Integrating the forensic database with other databases, such as the National Software Reference Library (NSRL) would allow a more comprehensive system for identification of files.

References

1 ACPO, (2003), Good Practice Guide for Computer Based Electronic Evidence, The Association of Chief Police Officers.

2 Adelstein, F, (2003), "MFP: The Mobile Forensic Platform", International Journal of Digital Evidence, Vol. 2, No. 1, http://www.ijde.org/docs/03_spring_art2.pdf, (retrieved 27th August 2003).

3 Carrier, B (2002) "Open Source Digital Forensics Tools: The Legal Argument", @Stake, http://www.atstake.com (retrieved 4th November 2004).

4 Connolly, T; Begg, C; Strachan, A, (1998), "Database Systems: A Practical Approach to Design, Implementation, and Management", Addison-Wesley, pp496 -497.

5 Meyler, C; Sutherland, I, (2003), "A Generic Set of Requirements for Open Source Computer Forensic and Intelligence Gathering Tools", Proceedings of the 2nd European Conference on Information Warfare and Security, Reading, UK, pp225 - 233.

6 EnCase, (2005), "EnCase V5 Briefings", Available from Guidance Software.

7 "NetForensics 2.0 Technical Evaluation, NSS Group Report", (2000), NetForensics, http://www.netforensics.com, (retrieved November 2002).

8 ODESSA, (2003), http://www.odessa.sourceforge.net, (retrieved 3rd July 2003).

9 PyFlag, (2005), "Welcome to PyFlag.sourceforge.net", http://pyflag.sourceforge.net/, (retrieved 22nd July 2005).

10 Rowlingson, R, (2004), "A Ten Step Process for Forensic Readiness", The International Journal of Digital Evidence, Vol 2, No 3, http://www.ijde.org, (retrieved 4th November 2004).

Protecting Distributed Object Applications from Corruption of Class Bytecodes on Client Side*

Julian L. Rrushi

Joint Research Centre of the European Commission,
Institute for the Protection and Security of the Citizen,
Cyber-Security Group,
Via E. Fermi 1, I-21020 Ispra (Varese) - Italy

Abstract. In this paper are discussed cyber-attacks to Distributed Object Applications that originate from RMI client programs running on malicious hosts. These cyber-attacks may be performed by a cyber-attacker who has full control on his machine and intentionally uses debugging instrumentation, that potentially may be based on the Java Platform Debugging Architecture, to take full control over the RMI client bytecodes while they execute on the JVM of his machine, properly modify these bytecodes eventually adding new ones, and attack the RMI server through such a corrupted RMI client. The objective of the information reported in this paper is to raise the security awareness of distributed application developers and support them in protecting their applications from such a threat.

1 Introduction

Java Remote Method Invocation (RMI) is a distributed object model for the Java programming language that retains the semantics of the Java platform's object model, making distributed objects easy to implement and to use [1]. By supporting seemless remote invocations on objects that reside in different Java Virtual Machines (JVMs), the remote method invocation system of the Java platform makes it possible for Java programs running in different address spaces to communicate with each other, usually as a client-server configuration. The server program creates remote objects and the corresponding references, and makes those references accessible to clients, which in turn use them to invoke methods on those remote objects. Such applications are referred to as Distributed Object Applications [1].

* This research has been supported by $(ISC)^2$(International Information Systems Security Certification Consortium) through the "Year of the Security Professional 2005" program, and by the Joint Research Centre of the European Commission. Part of this research was carried out by the author at the Università degli Studi di Milano - Italy, while in the final year of his Master studies in Information and Communication Technology. Any findings, opinions, conclusions or any other kind of information expressed in this paper are those of the author and do not necessarily represent the official position of the aforementioned organizations.

The server registers its remote objects with the RMI's naming facility by calling the *bind* method of the *java.rmi.Naming* class. The RMI's naming facility is called registry and is in fact a remote object that maps simple names to remote objects. In order to be able to call a method on a remote object the client first obtains a stub for that remote object, i.e. a local representative for the remote object that implements the same interfaces as that remote object, by calling the *lookup* method of the *java.rmi.Naming* class.

Then the client invokes the method in question on the stub, which in turn performs all the necessary actions to carry out the call on the remote object. The remote JVM may have a skeleton for each one of its objects, although generic code could be used to carry out skeleton functionalities. The client is allowed to pass serializable objects, i.e. objects that implement the interface *java.io.Serializable*, as parameters of remote methods. If a remote object can't find locally the class definition for a serializable object, that remote object downloads the definition in question from the client. As it will be described in Section 2, under certain circumstances a cyber-attacker could take advantage of the dynamic nature of RMI.

The cyber-attacks discussed in this paper consist of making on-the-fly modifications to a running RMI client program. These cyber-attacks are carried out through debugging instrumentation, which could be thoroughly based on the Java Platform Debugger Architecture (JPDA) [2]. JPDA is a multi-tiered debugging architecture that provides the infrastructure needed by developers to build end-user tools for debugging Java programs. JPDA consists of three layers, namely Java Virtual Machine Tool Interface (JVMTI), Java Debug Interface (JDI) and Java Debug Wire Protocol (JDWP). JVMTI is a programming interface that defines the services that a JVM must provide for debugging bytecodes which run on it. These services allow for inspecting the state of bytecodes running on a JVM or even fully control their execution.

JDI is a high-level Java interface which allows easy construction of debugger applications and is implemented by a front-end. On the other hand, JDWP defines the format of the information exchanged between the debugger process and the target JVM, i.e. the JVM where the debuggee process runs. At JDWP start up there takes place a handshake between the debugger process and the target JVM consisting of the debugger process sending the 14 ASCII characters of the string "JDWP-Handshake" to the target JVM, and the target JVM responding with the same characters. There is also a back-end responsible for communicating requests from the front-end to the target JVM and responses from the target JVM back to the front-end.

The information reported in this paper represents an analysis worl . Java programming language, JVM and JPDA. Experiments were performed on a distributed object application where a user downloads from a HTTP server an applet, which runs in the Java Plugin of that user's machine and acts as a RMI client. So, the applet first gets an instance of the stub for a remote object whose methods it intends to invoke, downloads the stub class from the codebase of that remote object, in our case from the same HTTP server the applet itself was downloaded from, and then invokes remote methods of the remote object in question. To complete the view, the remote methods eventually execute queries on a database through Java Data Base Connectivity (JDBC).

The remaining of this document is organized as follows. Section 2 presents an analysis on threats to Distributed Object Applications deriving from the execution of RMI client programs in malicious environments. Section 3 discusses related research. Section 4 summarizes this paper and concludes it.

2   Threats to the RMI Server in a Distributed Object Application

RMI does not include any provisions for security, and it was developed under the expectation that the developer would augment the RMI application with Java security features [3]. While the infrastructure components are usually developed by experienced programmers with solid security skills, the application-specific code is often developed under strict time constraints by programmers with little security training [4]. The action that forms the basis for the cyber-attacks discussed in this document is malicious manipulation of a Java program that executes on the client JVM, consisting of operations such as tracing local or remote method invocations, replacement of method parameters, injection of new Java bytecodes into the address space of the target process or replacement of entire blocks of bytecodes with new ones, all these eventually combined with lack of ad-hoc and exhaustive security controls and verifications via Java intrusion prevention mechanisms and proper security configurations on the server side.

These malicious operations have demonstrated to be more dangerous to an RMI server when performed in run time on the Java bytecodes running on the JVM or Java Plugin of the client machine. This is because modifications to be performed on a RMI client program often depend on the state of the RMI client process in the moment of intervention, and on the actions that the RMI server has performed that far with respect to that RMI client. Preliminary static manipulation of the RMI client code, i.e. the RMI client source code is analyzed, modified to reflect cyber-attack attempts, compiled and then executed, may also be dangerous in some cases as well.

The first step taken by a cyber-attacker consists in connection and attachment to the target JVM, i.e. the JVM on his machine where the RMI client is running, through his debugging instrumentation. In the next step, that we call the bytecodes footprinting step, the cyber-attacker retrieves the bytecodes of the RMI client and studies its anatomy. Subjects of this study include the non-native classes that compose the RMI client under examination, the methods defined by each non-native class, global variables, local variables and parameters of a method, computational logic and execution flow.

The analysis of the RMI client code performed by a cyber-attacker in the previous step allows him to obtain information about the remote methods that may be invoked by the RMI client, the eventual parameters of those remote methods, the server's responses to remote method invocations performed by the RMI client, the employment of any Java security mechanism such as Authenticated Sockets, Java Authentication and Authorization Service, or Challenge-Response Authentication. This information is sufficient for the cyber-attacker to start stressing the server through modified versions of the RMI client.

A description of the malicious actions that a cyber-attacker can carry out against the server is given below:

1. During a Method Switching Attack a cyber-attacker manipulates in run-time the Java bytecodes running on his machine, so that to replace the JVM instructions that make invocations to remote methods the cyber-attacker can invoke, with JVM instructions that make invocations to remote methods that the cyber-attacker is not authorized to invoke, or directly inject new JVM instructions into the target process address space that make invocations to remote methods that the cyber-attacker is not authorized to invoke. The success of such a cyber-attack is thoroughly based on missing or flawed handling of authentication.

2. An RMI client may invoke remote methods passing them parameter values that are not directly input from the user, for example values that belong to the state of the RMI client or values that are result of some computation performed by the RMI client. There are real world examples where applets are downloaded on the client machine and locally perform a set of computations in order not to overload the server. Although this approach transfers the computational burden on the client machine and avoids creation of bottlenecks in the case too many clients interact with the server simultaneously, a blind trust on the client could allow it to cause dangerous affects on the server. A Parameter Spoofing Attack consists of the attacker manipulating in run-time the RMI client program so that to replace parameters of remote method invocations, of the kind defined above, in order to access server data in an unauthorized way or lead to incorrect computations performed by remote methods on the server.

3. In Distributed Object Applications a client is allowed to pass to the server objects as parameters of remote methods. References to objects are only useful within a single JVM, thus non-remote objects that are used as parameters of remote methods are passed by copy, i.e. the object is serialized and a copy of its actual implementation is sent to the server. During a Malicious Ob-

ject Injection Attack the attacker manipulates the RMI client code running on his machine and uses this modified code to pass to the server a hostile serializable object, in the form of a parameter of a remote method, which once executing in the remote machine returns computation results that aim at causing damage. The damage eventually caused by computations of such a malicious object has shown to be application specific.

4. A less probable, but still possible, attack could be performed by a malicious object in the case its methods interact in harmony with a remote method, which has that malicious object as a parameter, and return regular and expected results but additionally try to perform any kind of unauthorized operations. Such a malicious object could be called a backdoor object as it acts the same as traditional backdoor programs. The success of this kind of attack is strictly limited by default by the RMI Security Manager which is part of the remote method invocation system of the Java platform. As a matter of fact all programs using RMI must create and install an RMI Security Manager, otherwise the remote method invocation system will not download classes other than those available from the local classpath. The RMI Security Manager by default allows only minimal resources for execution of code loaded dynamically. But the eventual danger rises when policy files are used to grant additional permissions like file permissions, socket permissions, runtime permissions etc., and the cyber-attacker by modifying the code running on his machine can abuse with those permissions to perform malicious operations.

In order to figure out whether the server reflects any symptoms of weaknesses in the server exploitable by run-time modifications of RMI client bytecodes, the cyber-attacker will analyze the server's behavior in response to remote method invocations issued by exhaustively modified versions of the RMI client. If that is the case, the cyber-attacker will individualize the code modifications that caused a weakness symptom to appear, and will use this information to locate the eventual vulnerability itself. Furthermore, there are cases when the cyber-attacks in question depend on both weakness exploitation and interaction in harmony with the server. In those cases the cyber-attacker will also modify other parts of the RMI client and will change a part of its state so that to satisfy the conditions for a regular interaction with the server. Some interfaces that a cyber-attacker may use to corrupt the RMI client program are given in Table 1.

A final consideration on the malicious environment where a cyber-attacker is likely to operate. Although it is possible to build debugging instrumentation that uses directly either JVMTI or JDWP, the debugging instrumentation used for carrying out the cyber-attacks discussed in this paper is likely to be written in the Java language and operates through the JDI, as this interface has been built especially to allow for easy construction of debugging instrumentation. In fact all the experiments, whose results are reported here, have been performed through a debugging instrumentation that has operated on RMI client bytecodes through JDI. Furthermore, the cyber-attacker will use a JVM that supports all those features that are needed by the debugging instrumentation, that in this context serves as an attack tool, to enable himself to carry out these cyber-attacks. Examples of such features are support for addition of methods when performing class redefinition, support for any level of class redefinition, retrieval of a method's bytecodes, etc.

AttachingConnector	Virtual Machine	Method	StackFrame
Connects to the target JVM, attaches to the RMI client and then returns a mirror of the target JVM.	Lists all the classes loaded on JVM and redefines them.	Lists all variables and retrieves the bytecodes for each method.	Traverses individual stack frames and directly sets variables' values on it.

Table 1. *Some of the main interfaces that are likely to be used by a debugging tool so that to allow on-the-fly modifications to a running RMI client program.*

The cyber-attacks to Distributed Object Applications discussed here exploit flaws in the authentication management, lack of security controls and security misconfigurations. It is important to emphasize that the Java technology provides all the necessary mechanisms for protecting Distributed Object Applications from these cyber-attacks and other ones. By carefully using Authenticated Sockets, Java Authentication and Authorization Service, Challenge-Response Authentication for every method, combined with careful programming and strong controls, these attacks could be blocked. Unfortunately the reasons that could allow these cyber-attacks to occur are conceptually the same as those that expose computer systems to buffer overflows, format strings, first and second order SQL injections and many other cyber-attacks.

Experiments conducted during this work have shown that an efficient technique for finding weaknesses and lack of controls in a server program that potentially allow a misbehaving client program to cause harm, is software fault injection [10]. In our context such a testing technique focuses on the server program, therefore its main objectives are to test the server's resistance to malicious actions performed by any clients and locate the part of the server's code where a flaw eventually holds. Software fault injection for our purposes may be performed by instrumenting the client code, i.e. adding new instructions or modifying existing ones in the client program, compiling the modified version of that client program and then running it. Hence a non-intrusive instrumentation is used, since the additional code insertions or modifications are not performed on the program being analyzed, that is the server program, but on the client program whose actions have a direct impact on the state of the server program and allow for testing its defensive capabilities.

It is the author's hope that by identifying these cyber-attacks to Distributed Object Applications and by providing information about both how they are likely to be carried out and the instruments employed for that purpose, the threats deriving from client misbehaviors will be considered during development and testing of Distributed Object Applications, hence contribute to making these applications more secure. This wanted contribution is being extended actually by the development of data mining techniques that can recognize anomalies in client behaviors.

3 Related Work

The approach of using debugging instrumentation to control the execution of a client for attacking purposes has been used in [7] to demonstrate that programs running on insecure or malicious hosts are targets for security attacks. The dynamic instrumentation used in this work to carry out the attacks is the DynInst [5], which is an architecture independent library for making on-the-fly modifications to a running program

In [7] an attack was carried out to Condor, which is a specialized workload management system for compute-intensive jobs [6]. Condor allows a user to schedule and run his applications from his own machine, referred to as submitting machine, on a remote idle host, referred to as execution machine, in a widely-distributed environment. Condor links the application running on the execution machine with the Condor RPC library, which forwards all the system calls issued by that application to the submitting machine via remote procedure calls. Thus, system calls performed by an application on the execution machine are forwarded to that application's submitting machine, and actually execute on the submitting machine. The values returned by those system calls are then sent back to the application on the execution machine.

The attack strategy consists of the following steps:

1. The attacker prepares a malicious job and submits it to Condor.
2. Condor schedules the malicious job on an idle execution machine.
3. Once it starts executing on the execution machine with uid *nobody*, the malicious job forks a new process called *lurker*.
4. The malicious job completes or is migrated by Condor to another execution machine.
5. The lurker process waits till an honest Condor job arrives.
6. When an innocent Condor job arrives the lurker process uses DynInst to take control over that innocent Condor job as it also runs with uid *nobody*, and starts making system calls to the submitting machine of the innocent job in question.

Like the lurking Condor job attack, the attacks discussed in this paper use debugging instrumentation to take control over code interacting with a remote machine, and attack the remote machine by acting through the code in question. Furthermore, the hosts where the cyber-attacks are initiated are malicious in both cases. In the case of the lurking Condor job attack the host is not malicious by itself but was made such by Condor which was not providing any security mechanism for protecting Condor jobs running on execution machines. In the case of our attacks the host is malicious as it belongs to the cyber-attacker who has full control over it.

On the other hand, both the lurking Condor job attack and the attacks we discuss here are based on flaws on the serving side. The lurking Condor job attack exploits missing of security controls on the submitting machine like restricting access to the file system, restricting and controlling the system calls performed by the application running on the execution machine, etc. The attacks we discuss exploit improper authentication management, lack of security controls or misconfigurations on the server side. One of the attacks discussed in this document consists of replacing the parameters a Java client program passes to remote methods on a server. Well, such an attack technique has been used for evading an Intrusion Detection System (IDS).

The work in [8] describes an IDS that learns the normal behavior of applications by collecting system call traces during time intervals when the system is not under attack. This IDS extracts all possible subtraces containing six consecutive system calls and inserts them into a data base. This phase is referred to as the *learning phase*. A subtrace that does not match any of the entries of the database is tagged as abnormal. During an operational time interval, referred to as a *monitoring phase*, this IDS collects traces of the function calls executed by each application and measures the degree of abnormality of each individual call trace by computing the number of abnormal subtraces it contains.

In order to evade such an Intrusion Detection System the cyber-attacker replaces values of parameters of system calls that belong to the normal behavior of an application, with values that allow the attacker to perform unauthorized operations. As an instance, if the attacker wants to write to the shadow file and the open("/lib/libc.so", O_RDONLY) belongs to the normal execution of a program, the attacker replaces "/lib/libc.so" and "O_RDONLY" with "/etc/shadow" and "O_RDWR", respectively [9].

4 Conclusion

This paper has presented a discussion on threats deriving from the execution of RMI client code in hostile environments and that are reflected in Java security cyber-attacks to Distributed Object Applications. The reported information is the result of an analysis work on Java programming language, JVM and JPDA, and long practical experiments. It has been argued that a cyber-attacker, who has full control on his machine, by using debugging instrumentation based on the Java Platform Debugging Architecture could subvert the security of an RMI server that doesn't perform severe controls on clients' behavior.

This instrumentation enables the cyber-attacker to take full control over RMI client bytecodes and properly modify them on-the-fly so that to replace parameters of remote method invocations and try to access server data in an unauthorized way or lead to incorrect computations performed by remote methods on the server, replace JVM instructions and make invocations to remote methods that the cyber-attacker is not authorized to invoke, and pass to the server hostile serializable objects in the form of parameters of remote methods, which aim at causing harm to the remote server.

This work aimed at raising the security awareness of distributed application developers of the threats represented by the cyber-attacks discussed in this paper. It also gave information on those cyber-attacks and explained how they are likely to be carried out. Furthermore, software fault injection has been proposed as a testing technique for discovering the existence of flaws and lack of controls one a server program. All this was done so that to support developers in analyzing their Distributed Object Applications and finding eventual weaknesses that could allow these attacks to harm the server program, before those Distributed Object Applications are deployed at large and exposed to malicious crackers.

Acknowledgments

The author is very much grateful to Prof. Emilia Rosti from the Università degli Studi di Milano, and to the organizations which supported this work.

References

1. Sun Microsystems: Java Remote Method Invocation Specification, http://java.sun.com/j2se/1.5/pdf/rmi-spec-1.5.0.pdf
2. Sun Microsystems: Java Platform Debugger Architecture, http://java.sun.com/products/jpda/index.jsp
3. Taylor A., Buege B., Layman R.: Hacking Exposed J2EE & Java, Developing Secure Applications with Java Technology, (2002)
4. Valeur F., Mutz D., Vigna G.: A Learning-Based Approach to the Detection of SQL Attacks, In Proceedings of the Conference on Detection of Intrusions and Malware & Vulnerability Assessment, Vienna, Austria, (2005)
5. ParaDyn: An Application Program Interface (API) for Runtime Code Generation, http://www.paradyn.org/html/manuals.html
6. The Condor Team: Condor High Throughput Computing, http://www.cs.wisc.edu/condor/

7. Miller B.P., Christodorescu M., Iverson R., Kosar T., Mirgordskii A., Popovici F.: Playing inside the black box: Using dynamic instrumentation to create security holes, Parallel Processing Letters, (2001)
8. Hofmeyr S., Forrest S., Somayaji A.: Intrusion Detection Using Sequences of System Calls, Journal of Computer Security, (1998)
9. Wagner D., Soto P.: Mimicry Attacks on Host-based Intrusion Detection Systems, In Proceedings of the 9th ACM Conference on Computer and Communications Security, (2002)
10. Voas J., McGraw G., Kassab L., Voas L.: Fault Injection: A Crystal Ball for Software Quality, IEEE Computer, (1997)

Modeling and Construction of Web Services Security

Li-Guo Wang and Lyndon Lee

Security Research Center, BT
PP4 Admin2 B61, Adastral Park, Martlesham Heath,
Ipswich IP3 5RE UK
li-guo.wang@bt.com

Abstract. In the paper we present a model and a construction mechanism of web service security. The model defines a set of security properties of web services including secure message, secure communication, security policy, and secure service federation in terms of abstract concepts. The construction mechanism then shows how these generic high-level conceptual models can be translated into abstract implementations through stepwise refinement.

Key words: web services, security, modeling, refinement

1 Introduction

Web service security is one of the most crucial aspects in enterprise-class Internet applications. However, security is usually designed in a bottom-up manner and is implemented in an ad-hoc and application-specific way. There would be no high-level view of how security is constructed and hence systems may not be fully compatible with each other, resulting in unintentional vulnerabilities. We argued that web service security would be better understood and designed by developing high-level generic models that encapsulate the essence of enterprise application architectures. To achieve that, we set out two goals in this paper.

First, we need to develop a high-level model that can capture common properties of secure web service precisely. Secondly, we need to specify a mechanism that can translate these models into low-level computational models. Architects would be benefited from the use of high-level models which can describe crucial common security properties of various enterprise systems; while developers can use the construction mechanism to help building secure software following a common computational model.

Our models are building on current web service technologies [1, 2, 3], and the set of web service specification standards [4, 5, 6, 7, 8, 9]. The models attempt to generalize the web services security techniques in term of their characteristics using concise ontological concepts represented in UML [10]. Moreover, we will discuss the construction mechanisms that map high level descriptive models to computation models by means of case studies and examples.

In Section 2 we introduce basic concepts about web services, security and modeling. Then a model of secure messages, secure communications, security policy, and secure web service federation will be discussed in Sections 3, 4, 5, and 6 respectively. In each of these sections, concrete examples will be used to illustrate the application of these models. We summarize the approach and discuss further work in Section 7.

2 Web Service, Security and Modeling

From the point of view of information exchange, a web service can be regarded as a simple mechanism by a node uses to send and receive messages. Hence web services can be seen as a set of nodes interacted with each other based on messages. Since web services are usually used to provide business functions on the Internet, they are essentially an Internet interface to an organization's core business systems. Complex business processes or applications can be realized by invoking web services in some meaningful sequences. Moreover, the very nature of the Internet gives web services such a global reach that the source of invocation is no longer confined geographically. As a result, web service security has become a major concern because of its dynamic and open architecture.

Security relates to each aspect of web services and at different levels. It may concern individual parts, contents of message or whole message, the entity (person or service) which operates on the message or the relationship between entities regarding their integrity, confidentiality, authentication and authorization. It may work at transport level (such as SSL), message level or business application level.

Fig. 1. Model 1: elementary link of web services   **Fig. 2.** Model 1.1: challenge-response

As the figure 1 shows, for web services the basic link is the pair of services communicating via a message flowing between them. In the form of UML the message is an association class. The model 1.1 is a special case of the model 1.

At the high level of a modeling language what concerns us is how the language can describe the essential content of web services while ignoring implementation-specific details to enable the language to catch the generality of web services. Meanwhile, we will demonstrate how the high level description can be refined to get low level computational implementations, especially how they can be mapped into current popular specification standards.

3 Modeling Secure Messages

With current web service techniques, a message is expressed in the form of XML, typically the envelope of a SOAP message [11]. In our language, by using UML we can express messages at a more abstract level. To catch the essence of message security we merely need to focus on the basic structure of message: whole-part structure. This is as in model 2. In UML the star "*" means any number of message contents can be selected from the message. When current security techniques [4] deal with message security they just manipulate the security of the message content. Such a whole-part structure has brought generality as security concerns can be put onto *any* part of a message including whole message as a special case.

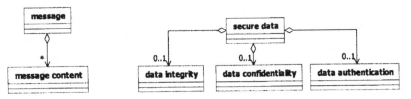

Fig. 3. Model 2: whole-part structure   **Fig. 4.** Model 3: secure data

To introduce security concepts to messages we define the model 3. The model implies that the secure data may be any one selection among data integrity, confidentiality and authentication or their arbitrary combinations. In UML we use aggregation relationships with number 0 or 1 on each selection. With models 2 and 3 we can infer that at high-behavioral level, the secure message is realized by ensuring any selected content (individual part) of the message to be secure and the security can be integrity, confidentiality, authentication or any of their combinations.

We first consider refining the model 2. For this we need to introduce the SOAP envelope which has two parts: header and body. The header can contains a number of security blocks to hold security-related information, as in the figure 5.

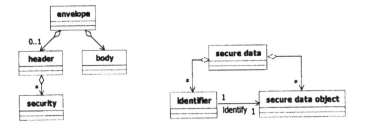

Fig. 5. Model 4: structure of envelope   **Fig. 6.** Model 5: reference structure

In addition to introducing SOAP envelope we also need to introduce a very useful reference structure to describe a secure data object. This is represented in the model 5.

276

With the model 5, secure data is constituted from one type of identifier and another type of referred secure data object. They are one-to-one and the secure data can contain any number of pairs of identifier and secure data object.

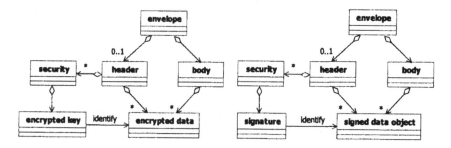

Fig. 7. Model 6: high-level data encryption   **Fig. 8.** Model 7: high-level data signature

Using the reference structure model 5 to the envelope model 4, then using the secure data model 3 with its data confidentiality and data integrity selections, we can get the models 6 and 7 respectively.

In the figure 9 we show how an envelope can hold the secure message. In the example only high level and key components are given. The confidentiality of the message is implemented by encrypting the "encrypted data" part of the body of the envelope. The integrity of the message is implemented by signing the "time stamp" part of the header and the whole body part of the envelope.

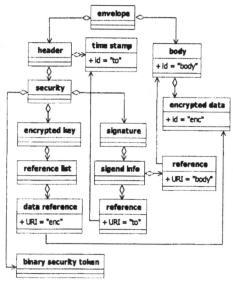

Fig. 9. A secure envelope

4   Secure Communication

4.1. Secure Web Service Interaction

The modeling of the secure message defines the basic model for the security of a message. Based on the modeling we can discuss the models for secure communication. First, we need to set up a model for web service.

WSDL [14] specifies the interface of a web service. It concerns the external behaviors of web services. In order to study the security of web services we need to further concentrate on the security aspect of the external behaviors. For this we have a model as in the figure 10.

In model 9 a web service has a policy component and a security token component. The security of the two components themselves is covered by secure message as discussed in section 3. What we are discussing in this section is the security of web services communicating with each other. When acting as service provider, a web service uses its policy to indicate its requests to service requestors. When acting as service requestor a web service uses its security token to demonstrate its credentials to service providers. Secure interaction between web services is the successful match between the incoming message of the service requestor (which includes the credentials of the requestor) and the requests described in the policy of the service provider.

Fig. 10. Model 9: toke-concern structure   **Fig. 11.** Model 1.2: service supply link

A security token represent a collection of claims and the claim is a statement about a client, service or other resource [5].

To deal with service issues the model 1.1 in the section 2 should be further specialized to model 1.2 as in figure 11 where web services are specialized to two types: service requestor and service provider and message is specialized to "request service" and "provide service".

To securely realize the model 1.2 we need to use model 9 with model 1.2. The target is to set up a token-based trust relationship in the service supply link. This leads to the model 10.

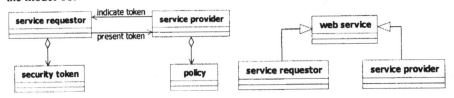

Fig. 12. Model 10: token for trust   **Fig. 13.** Model 11: inheritance of web service

In model 10 the service provider indicates its requested token with its policy component and the service requestor presents its token with its security token component.

Model 10 is based on the assumption that both service requestor and service provider are special cases of generic web service model 9. This is as in model 11.

4.2. Security Token Service

To secure a communication between two web services, the two web services must exchange security credentials and each web service needs to determine whether they can trust the asserted credentials of the other web service. For web services the security token is just such a credential.

As a security token becomes the key factor of secure communications a special web service is reasonably introduced. For the service its issuance is a special resource – security token. The special web service is called "security token service".

A security token service is a web service that can issue, renew, or validate security tokens. This is as the model 12 shown in figure 14.

Fig. 14. Model 12: exchange security token

There are two special cases of model 12, models 12.1 and 12.2 as below. The model 12.1 defines the behaviors of the issuance of a security token service to a service requestor. Model 12.2 defines the behaviors of validation of a security token service to service provider.

Fig. 15. Model 12.1: token issuance   **Fig. 16.** Model 12.2: token validation

During security token acquisition a more general situation can be the process of multi-message exchange. Namely, there is a dialogue between the service requestor and service provider. The challenge-response model 1.1 has set up a generic basis to describe the process. We assume that such a case has already been considered, so we have omitted them from further discussions.

For current web service techniques, the security token and security token service have become the foundation for trusted interoperation.

4.3. Trust Triangle Model

A security token service forms the basis of trust by issuing and validating security tokens that can be used to broker trust relationships between service requestors and service providers of different trust domains

Combining models 1.2, 10, 12.1 and 12.2 we can obtain a trust triangle (model 13) as shown in the figure 17.

By applying the model 9 to model 13 we can obtain model 14 which considers the token treatment.

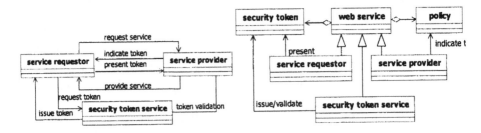

Fig. 17. Model 13: trust triangle model   **Fig. 18.** Model 14: token treatment

"Trust is the characteristic that one entity is willing to rely upon a second entity to execute a set of actions and/or to make set of assertions about a set of subjects and/or scopes" [5].

Fig. 19. Model 15: trust root and chain

For web service trust models the fundamental is their trust root. The security token message should provide not only a claims token but also the trust to the token. The trust is proved by the possession of that token. It is the security token service issuing the tokens. So, the trust chain is reduced to the security token service chain. When applying such a trust model, the trust chain cannot be broken. So, the trust chain will certainly lead to a root. The root is a trust axiom. Given the current level of technology, the typical trust roots might be the Kerberos tokens from a special realm or an X.509 tokens from a specific CA or tokens from some authentication service. Here, the Kerberos token issuer, CA and the authentication service can all be considered as special security token services. All trusts on token come from these roots. For this we define the trust root and chain model as figure 19.

5. Security Policy

Web service security policy provides a general purpose model and corresponding syntax to describe and communicate the policies of a web service. Web service security policy defines a base set of constructs that can be used and extended by other web service specifications to describe a broad range of service requirements, preference, and capabilities.

As shown by figure 20 at a high level of abstraction, a security policy is a collection of policy assertions and their combination via policy operators. The policy operators are recursive. This means the model can cover complex policy combinations.

As a more detailed model we have model 17. As shown by figure 21 there are three types of policy operations: "all", "exactly one" and "one or more". The policy by itself can be an operator that has the same semantics as "all". Just as their names

280

imply, the operator "all" requires that all of its child elements be satisfied. The operator "exactly one" requires that exactly one of its child elements be satisfied. The operator "one or more" requires that at least one of its child elements be satisfied.

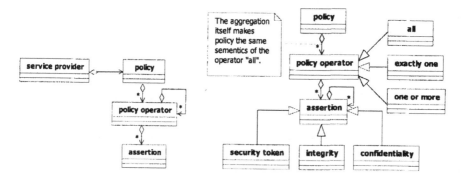

Fig. 20. Model 16: high structure of policy **Fig. 21.** Model 17: general structure of policy

The recursive structure of the policy operator can help to create a complex policy. This means the policy can be widely used. However, for web service, the main aspect is that policy is taken as a set of conditions. The service provider generally has conditions under which it provides the service. A requestor might use this information to decide whether or not to use the service.

6. Modeling Secure Service Federation

6.1. Extension of Trust Triangle Model

For complex applications the security token based trust model should be extend to provide more sophisticated means. A typical example is detailed access control on any information that may be considered personal or subject to privacy governance. Another example is obfuscation of identity information from an identity provider to prevent unwanted correlation and the automatic mapping of identities. For this, identity provider, attribute service and pseudonym service are introduced by current web service technologies.

Identity provider is a special type of security token service. It acts as an authentication service to an end requestor and data origin authentication service to service provider. Attribute service is a web service that maintains the information (attributes) about a principal (service requestor) within a trust realm or federation. Pseudonym service is a special type of attribute service that maintains alternate identity information about a principal (service requestor) within a trust realm or federation. This is as in model 20.

With identity provider, attribute service and pseudonym service the trust triangle model can be developed as shown by model 21.

As in model 21, an attribute service can store information (attributes) of service requestors. The information can be accessed by a service provider or its security token service. The service provider can set or register its pseudonym by itself or through a security token service to a pseudonym service. A trust relationship between security token services and attribute service should have been set up prior to the event as a basis for the above operations. Although attribute service is not required for "the organization of the data" by current web services technologies, page 17 [8], we assume that the service requestor should associate information with the attribute service.

As a composition of the model 13, 14 and 21 we have an extended trust triangle (model 22).

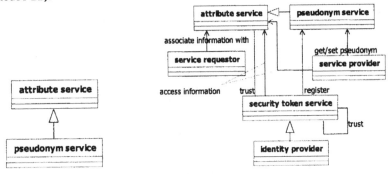

Fig. 22. Model 20: attribute/pseudonym service   **Fig. 23.** Model 21: addition for trust model

6.2. Application of Federation Model

In an example to illustrate the application of the extended trust models discussed above, we describe a behavioral sequence detailed for a general application scheme, but not only for a concrete application. This is shown by figure 25.

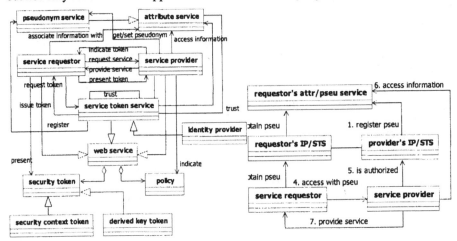

Fig. 24. Model 22: extended trust triangle model   **Fig. 25.** An example of applying models

The behavior sequence shown by the figure is a general process where advanced services, such as attribute service and pseudonym service, can be used to enhance secure communication of web service to higher performance level.

Step 1: for many reasons a service provider may use its identity provider (IP) or security token service (STS) to register a pseudonym with a requestor's pseudonym service. Step 2: the pseudonym can be obtained by the requestor's IP/STS. Step 3: the pseudonym is passed to the service requestor. Step 4: the service requestor uses the pseudonym to access the service provider. Step 5: the service provider needs more information to further confirm the service requestor. For this it needs to be authorized with its IP/STS for accessing the requestor's attribute service. Step 6: the service provider accesses information from the requestor's attribute service. Step 7: finally, the service provider provides service to the service requestor.

Model 22 has synthesized the main means provided by current web services technologies.

7. Conclusion and Further Work

In this paper we presented a series of models to generalize the security techniques used in current web services. Our approach attempts to represent the common security characteristics underpinning these techniques in a number of concise and intuitive *elements*. We then demonstrate how to combine these basic elements to obtain a complicated composition.

The generality should be expressed in both aspects of the fundamental elements and their combination. In so doing we emphasize the inherent logical essence behind current web services technologies. As further work we will try to find a general composition mechanism to explain the existing web service techniques and to direct their further development.

8. References

[1]. Brown A, Johnston S and Kelly K, Using Service-Oriented Architecture and Component-based Development to Building Web Service Applications, Rational Software While Paper [online]
[2]. Web service essentials, Ethan Cerami, pub. O'Reilly.
[3]. OMG, MDA, An Introduction, OMG [online]
[4]. Web Services Security: SOAP Message Security 1.0 (WS-Security 2004), OASIS Standard 200401, March 2004.
[5]. Web Services Trust Language (WS-Trust), Version 1.1, May 2004.
[6]. Web Services Policy Framework (WS-Policy), Version 1.1, 28 May 2003.
[7]. Web Services Security Policy Language (WS-SecurityPolicy), Version 1.0 December 18 2002.
[8]. Web Services Federation (WS-Federation), Version 1.0 July 8 2003.
[9]. Web Services Secure Conversation Language (WS-SecureConversation), Version 1.1 May 2004.
[10]. Sinan Si Albir, UML In A Nutshell, O'Relly, 1998.
[11]. W3C Note, Simple Object Access Protocol (SOAP) 1.1, 08 May 2000.
[12]. XML Encryption Syntax and Processing, W3C Recommendation 10 December 2002. Authors: Takeshi Imamura, Blair Dillaway, Ed Simon.
[13]. XML Signature Syntax and Processing, W3C Recommendation 12 February 2002. Authors: Mark Bartel, John Boyer, Barb Fox, Brian LaMacchia, Ed Simon.
[14]. Web Service Description Language (WSDL) 1.1, W3C Note 15 March 2001. Authors: Eric Christensen, Francisco Curbera, Greg Meredith, Sanjiva Weerawarana.

Normalising Events into Incidents Using Unified Intrusion Detection-Related Data

Nikolaos Avourdiadis, Dr. Andrew Blyth
School of Computing, University of Glamorgan, Pontypridd,
Wales-UK
{navourdi, ajcblyth}@glam.ac.uk

Abstract: In heterogeneous and distributed networked environments, the unification of intrusion related events from various and desperate sensors under a single database schema can provide a level of multiplicity not only towards the identification of security events but also for the minimisation of false positive alarms. Furthermore, the identification of the steps an attacker performs towards the exploitation of host and network based vulnerabilities can be captured in detail, and an incident classification can be used, using information from logged events.

In this paper, we present a method for normalising/classifying events into incidents, using the SoapSy database schema. This method aims to provide a level of abstraction for the captured events, and present them in a format that can be compatible with the IODEF and INCH standards.

Keywords: *unification, SoapSy, events, abstraction, incident, intrusion detection.*

1. Introduction

Over the few years, the rapid growth of the Internet was accompanied by the equal growth of computer security incidents(Allen, Christie et al. 2000; Anderson, Brackney et al. 2000). New threats and vulnerabilities are discovered day by day, and the number of attacks is growing geometrically(Allen, Christie et al. 2000). Computer and network security have become mission-critical functions for businesses and organizations, and a number of differentiate Intrusion Detection technologies have been introduced for strengthening the line of defence(Denning 1987; Escamilla 1998; Allen, Christie et al. 2000; Fyodor 2000; Almgren and Lindqvist 2001; Uppuluri and Sekar 2001; Debar and Morin 2002; Verwoerd and Hunt 2002). The vast increase of such systems, capable of detecting and logging attacks, counter measured such computer security incidents, but additionally resulted to an enormous increase of intrusion related data(Frincke, Tobin et al. 1998; Bass 2000; Flack and Atallah 2000; Debar and Wespi 2001; Valdes and Skinner 2001). However, such an increase in logged data has generated the need not only to store them in data repositories for further analysis and processing, but furthermore, to unify them under composite databases, due to their homogeneous and/or heterogeneous sources(Frincke, Tobin et al. 1998; Avourdiadis and Blyth 2005; Avourdiadis, Blyth et al. 2005).

In the field of Intrusion Detection Systems (IDS), the aspect of data integration has been initially proposed by means of collecting information from multiple homogeneous IDSs to a centralised server, and practical examples can be found in the field of Distributed Intrusion Detection Systems (Allen, Christie et al. 2000). Recently however, attempts are been made towards the incorporation of heterogeneous IDSs through data integration (Avourdiadis and Blyth 2005; Avourdiadis, Blyth et al. 2005). The need of using a common format for representing intrusion related logged data was identified by various bodies, such as the Internet Engineering Task Force (IETF), the World Wide Web Consortium (W3C), the Intrusion Detection Working Group (IDWG), the Computer Emergency Response Team (CERT), and the Computer Security Incident Response Teams (CSIRT), while other teams such as the Incident Object Description and Exchange Format Working Group (IDMEF WG) and the Extended Incident Handling Working Group (INCH WG) were introduced for developing such standards (Arvidsson, Cormack et al. 2001; Rose 2001; Feinstein, Mathews et al. 2002; Corner 2003; Harold 2003; Debar, Curry et al. 2004). Nowadays, the Intrusion Detection Message Exchange Format (IDMEF) (Corner 2003; Debar, Curry et al. 2004), the Incident Object Description Data Exchange Format (IODEF) (Arvidsson, Cormack et al. 2001; Demchenko 2003) and the Extended Incident Handling (FINE) (Demchenko 2003; Demchenko, Ohno et al. 2004) can be used as basic standards for representing incident related data (still in draft mode), and provide a framework for data sharing and interchange. Both IODEF/FINE and IDMEF incorporate the eXtensible Mark-up Language (XML) (Bates 2003; Bray, Paoli et al. 2004) using either a Document Type Definition (DTD) document or XML based Namespaces for structuring and encoding data.

The aforementioned standards attempt to identify data formats for the exchange of security related incidents against information systems between CSIRTs. Yet, in differentiate and distributed environments where intrusion related data is captured and logged from various types of sensors and loggers, the unification and fusion of logged data is a vital requirement for providing not only a universal picture of coincided security events, but furthermore, for identifying incidents and performing threat assessment and threat management. This can be advantageous in many ways towards the identification of actual security incidents, but a vital requirement towards this direction is the normalisation of logged events into actual security incidents.

This paper attempts to describe a method for normalising/classifying events captured and logged into the **SoapSy** database (Avourdiadis and Blyth 2005), using abstraction. The proposed method attempts to provide a level of compliance with the proposed IODEF, IDMEF, and FINE, by incorporating entities supported by these standards.

2. Unifying Intrusion Detection Events

In order to unify homogeneous and heterogeneous intrusion detection data (Avourdiadis and Blyth 2005; Avourdiadis, Blyth et al. 2005) we need a mechanism that will not only provide a framework for the incorporation of various sensors, but furthermore allow the storage of logged data under a single data schema. **SoapSy** (Avourdiadis and Blyth 2005; Avourdiadis, Blyth et al. 2005), has been introduced as a model system that provides such a framework and attempts to unify logged events from various heterogeneous sensors. In addition, SoapSy attempts to describe incidents using the proposed event-based database schema and abstraction (Avourdiadis and Blyth 2005; Avourdiadis, Blyth et al. 2005).

2.1. The SoapSy Architecture

SoapSy is a system conceptually based on the idea that various, heterogeneous event monitoring mechanisms can simultaneously report to a centralized database, if they are capable to use a common way to report data. XML(Bates 2003; Bray, Paoli et al. 2004) and SOAP(Box, Ehnebuske et al. 2000; Scribner 2000) can provide such a framework by providing semantics to raw data, and a mechanism for transferring such data accordingly.

The role and function of the system architecture is to provide a lightweight secure access mechanism through which information from a number of heterogeneous distributed sources can be logged to a single database via a SOAP (Box, Ehnebuske et al.; Scribner 2000), front end. The SOAP front end functions as the light-weight data access mechanism through which it is ensured that data is transferred from the source to the destination in a reliable and verifiable manner. The basic architecture is illustrated in Figure 1. The front end of this system the SOAP Handler that received SOAP requests from a set of sensors.

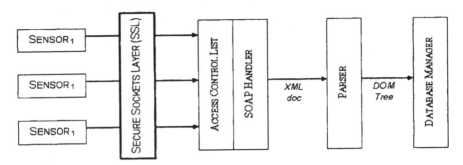

Figure 1 – The SoapSy Architecture

Due to the nature of the proposed system, the behavior of the system is event-based, i.e. it is changing state (e.g. data insertion) only when an event has occurred. This is an important aspect of the functionality for the proposed system, as it affects fundamentally its architecture and design.

2.2. SoapSy Database Design

The proposed database architecture for SoapSy(Avourdiadis and Blyth 2005; Avourdiadis, Blyth et al. 2005), presented a partitioned database design that would involve three different but co-existing, interrelated, and co-operating sub-schemas: the **Core**, the **Extensible**, and the **Abstraction**. Various types of sensors are able to log captured data on a single database in a dynamic way that allows the aggregation of captured data under a single database schema. Furthermore, the database schema is comprised of relations that describe fundamental concepts for occurring events that always exist, and thus are static with regard to the description of events (i.e. attacker, victim, timestamp, etc.).

The Core sub-schema is static, and incorporates those entities of the database that describe fundamental information with regard to a captured event. Practically, this means that for reported events, information regarding the origin and the target for that event can be traced and thus, available (in terms of Intrusion Detection Systems or Event Loggers), together with information describing the observer and the reporter for the occurred event (Avourdiadis and Blyth 2005; Avourdiadis, Blyth et al. 2005).

The Extensible database sub-schema is dynamic and constitutes the evolving component of the database schema. It comprises of the multiple relations/objects that describe the various types of sensors that report to the database. Such systems are dynamically added to the database, and are connected to the Core via the *Event* relation (Avourdiadis and Blyth 2005; Avourdiadis, Blyth et al. 2005).

Finally, the Abstraction sub-schema is static and is used for the aggregation of events into incidents. The fusion of event data is performed using a management mechanism, as this subschema attempts to describe incidents in an abstraction level, by describing those characteristics of logged events that would comprise incidents based on the IODEF specification draft.

2.3. Unifying Events

Events describe actions that have been observed and reported to the SoapSy database. Events logged on the SoapSy database have specific sets of attributes that can uniquely identify them. More specifically, an event describes an action that originated by a specific source, against a specific destination, and has been observed by a specific observer and been reported by a specific reporter. A specific action (originating from the same source against the same destination) can be observed by multiple observers and reported by multiple reporters (depending on the system specification); thus a number of events logged into the database may describe the same action although having different attributes (observer and/ or reporter).

SoapSy boosts the unification of data derived from various types of intrusion detection and logging mechanisms using the aforementioned (§2.2.) database sub-schemas (Avourdiadis and Blyth 2005; Avourdiadis, Blyth et al. 2005). The **Event** relation is the mediator between the sub-schemas and interconnects them by integrating them into a single, compound schema in a way that allows the unification of data from the various sensors (Avourdiadis and Blyth 2005; Avourdiadis, Blyth et al. 2005). Such an integration of the two sub-schemas not only provides a solution for the dynamic expansion and evolvement of the database schema with minimal affect to the optimisation and performance of the database, but furthermore, allows the continuous unification of data stored into the database, by allowing various types of sensors to be added, removed or updated.

3. Normalising Events into Incidents

Unifying events from heterogeneous sensors can result to the generation of an enormous amount of records within the database and data mining techniques are required for knowledge management. Events describe actions that have originated by specific sources, targeting specific destinations, observed by specific sensors, and finally reported by specific reporters, in a precise time frame. Furthermore, they represent actions that may or may not interrelate to each other. An event describes a specific action that has taken place against a protected entity (a computer, a process, or a user) within the defended computer or network perimeter, and has been identified and reported by a number of systems. Additionally, a sequence or a scattered set of events may also describe a set of actions against a defended entity within a computer or a network perimeter.

The tables in Figure 2 demonstrate a simplified scenario of attacks that have been captured and logged into the Core subschema of the SoapSy database.

EVENT

event_id	timestamp	obsrv_id	rptr_id	src_id	dstn_id
1	01/09/05 20:03:12	1	1	1	1
2	01/09/05 20:03:12	2	1	1	1
3	01/09/05 20:15:44	3	2	1	2
4	02/09/05 20:15:45	4	1	1	2
5	02/09/05 21:17:00	2	1	2	1
6	05/09/05 21:34:00	4	1	2	2
7	05/09/05 23:12:00	2	1	3	1
8	05/09/05 23:12:00	4	1	3	2
9	05/09/05 23:59:44	1	1	2	1
10	06/09/05 00:00:01	2	1	1	1

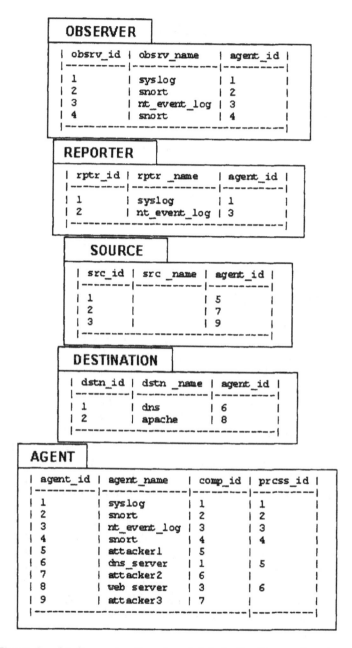

Figure 2 – An Example of captured data in the Core sub-schema

```
COMPUTER

| comp_id | hostname           | os | ip             | mac              | domain     | comp_type_id |
|---------|--------------------|----|----------------|------------------|------------|--------------|
| 1       | j4-itr1-01         |    | 193.63.148.198 | 00-05-B5-9F-D1-3C | glam.ac.uk |              |
| 2       | j4-itr1-02         |    | 193.63.148.199 | 00-01-A5-1A-D7-3A | glam.ac.uk |              |
| 3       | j130-ma            |    | 193.63.148.230 | 00-07-E9-9E-C8-3A | glam.ac.uk |              |
| 4       | snort              |    | 193.63.148.200 | 00-04-E1-8B-C8-3C | glam.ac.uk |              |
| 5       | cpc1-trefi-4-0-cust112 |  | 81.106.241.172 |                 | ntl.com    |              |
| 6       | cpc1-trefi-5-0-cust192 |  | 81.106.240.192 |                 | ntl.com    |              |
| 7       |                    |    | 61.10.108.189  |                  |            |              |
```

```
PROCESS

| prcss_id | prcss _name  | prcss _pid | usr_id |
|----------|--------------|------------|--------|
| 1        | syslog       | 3131       |        |
| 2        | snort        | 4487       |        |
| 3        | nt_event_log | 4064       |        |
| 4        | snort        | 2927       |        |
| 5        | bind         | 2998       |        |
| 6        | apache       | 2998       |        |
```

Figure 2 (Continued...) – An Example of captured data in the Core sub-schema

In this example a number of attacks have been identified by agents against a DNS (BIND) and a Web server (Apache). These attacks have been identified by different systems (syslog, snort, NT event logger) and have been reported to the database through the configured reporters (syslog and NT event logger). The challenge now is to identify patterns within the database that would allow the identification of those groups of actions, which have been performed for the accomplishment of a single purpose. Such groups of actions are characterised by sets of attributes that allow their categorisation under the same grouping. For example, a single attribute for a number of logged events could be the source or the destination for those events, or even the combination of both as attributes. Furthermore, the timestamp could also be added as an attribute for the categorisation of these events.

The process used for the identification and classification of events that share common sets of attributes is defined as **event normalisation**. Various sets of attributes can be defined for the categorisation/classification of events, and each categorisation could also be used in combination with others. Event normalisation allows the creation of an entity that will be defined as an **Incident**. Grouping events into incidents allows the fusion of logged data into entities that provide a more meaningful way for providing a level of semantics to large amounts of logged data.

3.1. Defining Incidents

In order to describe such groups of events, the **Incident** object is introduced as a mean of aggregation of events that share common sets of attributes. An incident is defined as *"the aggregation of a set of (sequential or scattered) events across a given event space, using abstraction"*.

For example, across an event space Ω, a number (v) of events (e) can share one or more attributes (α_i); this can be any generic information that is logged into the database with regard to the possible identification of various events on a higher level. Thus, an Incident can be represented using the following equation: $I = \sum\limits_{\alpha 1,...,\alpha i}^{\Omega}\{e1,e2,...,ev\}, v, i \geq 0.$

This practically means that an incident is the aggregation (or set) of (v) events (e) that belong in an event space Ω and have αi number of attributes, where $v, i > 0$. For example, a time frameset could be used as an attribute $\alpha 1$ (or a defining signature) for normalising events into groups and thus, creating incidents. In addition, the destination computer IP address could also be used as a second attribute $\alpha 2$ for normalising events into incidents. In the example presented in figure 2, $\alpha 1$ could be defined as $\alpha 1=$ **01/09/05 00:00:00 – 01/09/05 23:59:59** and $\alpha 2$ as $\alpha 2=193.63.148.199$. Finally, Ω is equivalent to: $\Omega = e1 \rightarrow e10$

Attributes correspond pragmatically to relations that exist within the SoapSy database schema; these relations can belong to either the Core or the Extensible sub schemas, and can widely be used for the normalisation of events into incidents. Consequently, an attribute α_i can be used for the *event normalisation* of a large set of events into an Incident I_i. This can result to the grouping of a single event into a number of different incidents. Since an incident is a subset of events that derives from a larger set of events Ω, two or more incidents may include into their subset one or more events e_v, i.e. $e_v \in \{I_1, I_2,..., I_i\}$. Practically, this may furthermore mean that an incident I may also include subsets of events which may also be incidents, and thus the following condition may also be true: $I_A = \{I_B, I_C, e_i\}$.

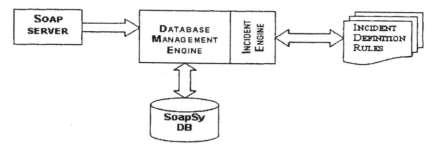

Figure 3 – The Database Management Engine

Figure 3 describes this case by presenting three sets of events (Ae, Be, Ce) that belong to an event space Ω, and comprise a number of different incidents.

Relational algebra could very well describe the process of event normalisation, as incidents are comprised by the selection σ of events that satisfy a condition ∂. This condition can very well describe a single or more set of attributes that describe events e that belong to Ω. Thus, an incident could be also described as $\sigma_\partial\Omega$. Thus, using the aforementioned example, event normalisation could be performed as:

$$\sigma_{\text{timestamp}>=01/09/05\ 00:00:00\ \text{AND}\ \text{timestamp}<=01/09/05\ 23:59:59}\ (Event)$$

An incident, as defined in this paper, is an aggregated group of events that derives from a larger set of events. The attributes used for the normalisation of the set of events is the factor that can provide a level of semantics to the Incident relation. Incidents attempt to project events that interrelate, and describe a number of actions that have been taken towards the accomplishment of a specific result. For example, this can practically mean the port scanning of a network or a single computer, or the attempt to exploit vulnerabilities within the defended network perimeter.

3.2. Normalising Events into Incidents – The Incident Management Engine

Normalising events into incidents is a mechanism that takes place separately from the logging process of events into the database. The Database Management Engine is the system responsible for the management of the SoapSy database (including the parsing of logged data into the database), while the Incident Engine is on of its subsystems, responsible for the normalisation of events into incidents, by directly inserting them into the Abstraction subschema (Avourdiadis, Blyth et al. 2005). A set of Incident Definition Rules exist that describe incidents and how they are derived from a set of events that exists within the database. These rules are actual projections of events (using relational algebra) π_σ (Event) that exist already within the SoapSy database. Figure 4 presents in a high level, the interaction between the various components of the proposed system; the Soap server passes captured data to the Database Management Engine which is responsible for the parsing of data into the database (XML to SQL transformation (Avourdiadis, Blyth et al. 2005)) while the Incident Engine, acting as a subsystem of the Database Management Engine normalises the events into incidents using the Incident Definition Rules.

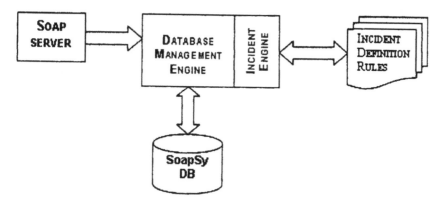

Figure 4 – The Database Engine

4. Specifying the Incident Database schema

4.1. The Incident database schema Design

The Abstraction sub-schema[1] of the proposed SoapSy architecture includes a number of entities (relations) that attempt to describe an Incident in the same manner that IODEF manages to.

As presented in figure 5, there an incident consists of a number of different entities that may uniquely identify it. These are its history, its report, and its notes. As described before, an incident is the abstraction of a number of events that have common sets of attributes. The many-to-many relation that exists between the event and the incident relations is overcome through the use of the attack relation. It can be clearly seen that an event may belong to one or more incidents, and also, an incident may be consisted by one or more events. Thus, an incident relates to an event (and vice-versa) through the attack relation.

As mentioned before, the **Attack** relation acts as the mediator between the event and the incident relations. An attack is described by an attack name and is associated with the incident using the incident_id as a foreign key. The attack_id is is also used as a foreign key in the event relation.

---

[1] → defines a one-to-many relation

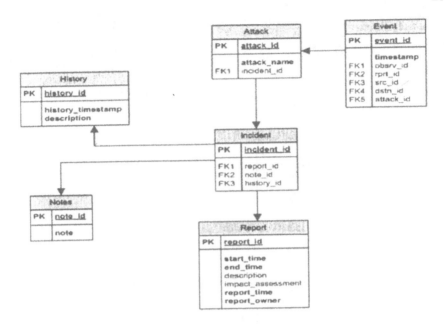

Figure 5 – The Abstraction sub-schema

```
CREATE TABLE attack (
attack_id   bigserial NOT NULL,
attack_name text NOT NULL,
incident_id bigserial NOT NULL REFERENCES incident,

PRIMARY KEY (attack_id),
FOREIGN KEY (incident_id) REFERENCES incident);
```

The **Incident** relation is comprised of a number of foreign keys that belong to relations that are associated with an incident. An incident will always have a report associated with it, together with an attack id; optionally, a note may also be associated with it.

```
CREATE TABLE incident (
incident_id bigserial NOT NULL,
report_id   bigserial NOT NULL,
note_id     bigserial NOT NULL,
history_id  bigserial NOT NULL,

PRIMARY KEY (incident_id),
FOREIGN KEY (report_id) REFERENCES report,
FOREIGN KEY (note_id) REFERENCES notes,
FOREIGN KEY (history_id) REFERENCES history);
```

The **History** relation describes the history of an incident, in a similar way as it is used by IODEF[2]. A history is described by a timestamp amd a description and relates to the incident relation through the use of the history_id as a foreign key in the incident table.

```
CREATE TABLE history (
history_id          bigserial NOT NULL,
history_timestamp   timestamp NOT NULL,
history_description text NOT NULL,

PRIMARY KEY (history_id));
```

The **Report** relation describes a report that can be created regarding an incident. A report describes the impact assessment for the associated incidents, and has a number of attributes, such as a start and end time for the described incident, a description, and the impact assessment. A report has an owner and a time associated with it that describes the creation time of the report. An incident may have more than one reports associated with it.

```
CREATE TABLE report (
report_id          bigserial NOT NULL,
start_time         timestamp NOT NULL,
end_time           timestamp NOT NULL,
description        text,
impact_assessment  text,
report_time        timestamp NOT NULL,
report_owner       text NOT NULL

PRIMARY KEY (report_id));
```

The **Notes** relation describes notes that can be attached to an incident, in order to provide more information for a single incident.

```
CREATE TABLE notes (
note_id bigserial NOT NULL,
note    text NOT NULL,

PRIMARY KEY (note_id));
```

5. Conclusions

Normalising events into incidents is a process that allows the fusion of unified data by providing a level of semantics to large amounts of data. Our attempt is definitely not to reinvent the wheel, as various technologies and techniques already exist for performing data mining into large amounts of data for intelligence and knowledge gathering and management. The purpose of the proposed work is to attempt to describe security-based events as incidents

---

[2] http://www.cert.org/ietf/inch/docs/draft-ietf-inch-iodef-04.txt

while they are logged into the SoapSy database (Avourdiadis, Blyth et al. 2005), in order to identify events that correspond to specified sets of actions that have been captured by a number of incorporated systems (IDSs, event loggers, etc). By providing a level of abstraction to captured data, it is possible to have a clearer picture of the events that have been reported to the system, and be possible to identify threats against the defended perimeter.

References

Allen, J., A. Christie, et al. (2000). State of the Practice of Intrusion Detection Technologies. Pittsburgh, Carnegie Mellon Software Engineering Institute.

Almgren, M. and U. Lindqvist (2001). Application-Integrated Data Collection for Security Monitoring. Proceedings of the 4th International Symposium on Recent Advances in Intrusion Detection (RAID 2001), University of California at Davis, CA, USA, Springer-Verlag.

Anderson, R. H., R. Brackney, et al. (2000). Advanced Network Defense Research: Proceedings of a Workshop. RAND, RAND.

Arvidsson, J., A. Cormack, et al. (2001). "TERENA's Incident Object Description and Exchange Format Requirements (RFC 3067)." RFC 3067. Retrieved September 2003, 2003, from http://www.ietf.org/rfc/rfc3067.txt.

Avourdiadis, N. and A. Blyth (2005). Data Unification and Data Fusion of Intrusion Detection Logs in a Network Centric Environment. The 4th European Conference on Information Warfare and Security, University of Glamorgan, UK, Academic Conferences International.

Avourdiadis, N., A. Blyth, et al. (2005). "SoapSy - Unifying Security Data from Various Heterogeneous Distributed Systems into a Single Database Architecture." The Journal of Information Systems Security 2(1).

Bass, T. (2000). Intrusion Detection Systems & Multisensor Data Fusion: Creating Cyberspace Situational Awareness. Communications of the ACM, ACM Press.

Bates, C. (2003). XML in theory and Practice, Wiley.

Box, D., D. Ehnebuske, et al. (2000). "Simple Object Access Protocol (SOAP) 1.1." Retrieved March 2002, 2002, from http://www.w3.org/TR/SOAP.

Bray, T., J. Paoli, et al. (2004, 04 February 2004). "Extensible Markup Language (XML) 1.0 (Third Edition), W3C Recommendation." 3. Retrieved 20 February 2004, 2004, from http://www.w3.org/TR/REC-xml/.

Corner, D. S. (2003). IDMEF – "Lingua Franca" for Security Incident Management Tutorial and Review of Standards Development, SANS Institute.

Debar, H., D. Curry, et al. (2004). "The Intrusion Detection Message Exchange Format (draft-ietf-idwg-idmef-xml-12)." Internet Draft. Retrieved August 2004, 2004, from http://www.ietf.org/internet-drafts/draft-ietf-idwg-idmef-xml-12.txt.

Debar, H. and B. Morin (2002). Evaluation of the Diagnostic Capabilities of Commercial Intrusion Detection Systems. Proceedings of the 5th symposium on Recent Advances in Intrusion Detection (RAID 2002), Zurich, Switzerland, Springer - Verlag.

Debar, H. and A. Wespi (2001). Aggregation and Correlation of Intrusion Detection Alerts. Proceedings of the 4th International Symposium on Recent Advances

296

in Intrusion Detection (RAID 2001), University of California at Davis, CA, USA, Springer-Verlag.

Demchenko, Y. (2003). "Requirements for Format for INcident Report Exchange (FINE) (draft-ietf-inch-requirements-02.txt)." Internet Draft. Retrieved November 2003, 2003, from http://www.ietf.org/internet-drafts/draft-ietf-inch-requirements-02.txt.

Demchenko, Y., H. Ohno, et al. (2004, June 2004). "Requirements for Format for INcident information Exchange (FINE) <draft-ietf-inch-requirements-03.txt>." Internet Draft. Retrieved July 2004, 2004, from http://www.cert.org/ietf/inch/docs/draft-ietf-inch-requirements-03.txt.

Denning, D. E. (1987). An Intrusion Detection Model. IEEE Transactions on Software Engineering, IEEE Press.

Escamilla, T. (1998). Intrusion Detection - Network Security Beyond the Firewall, Wiley.

Feinstein, B., G. Mathews, et al. (2002, October 22, 2002). "The Intrusion Detection Exchange Protocol (IDXP) (draft-ietf-idwg-beep-idxp-07)." Internet Draft. Retrieved March 2003, 2003, from http://www.ietf.org/internet-drafts/draft-ietf-idwg-beep-idxp-07.txt.

Flack, C. and M. J. Atallah (2000). Better Logging through Formality. Recent Advances in Intrusion Detection: Third International Workshop, RAID 2000, Toulouse, France, October 2000. Proceedings, Toulouse, France, Springer-Verlag.

Frincke, D., D. Tobin, et al. (1998). A Framework for Cooperative Intrusion Detection. Proceedings of the 21st NIST-NCSC National Information Systems Security Conference, Arlington, VA, www.securityfocus.com.

Fyodor, Y. (2000). SNORTNET - A distributed Intrusion Detection System. Bishkek, Kyrgyzstan, Kyrgyz Russian Slavic University. August 2003.

Harold, W. (2003). "Using Extensible Markup Language-Remote Procedure Calling (XML-RPC) in Blocks Extensible Exchange Protocol (BEEP) (RFC 3529)." RFC 3529. Retrieved April 2003, 2003, from http://www.ietf.org/rfc/rfc3529.txt.

Rose, M. (2001, March 2001). "The Blocks Extensible Exchange Protocol Core (RFC 3080)." RFC. Retrieved March 2003, 2002, from http://www.ietf.org/rfc/rfc3080.txt.

Scribner, K. (2000). Understanding SOAP, SAMS.

Uppuluri, P. and R. Sekar (2001). Experiences with Specification-Based Intrusion Detection. Proceedings of the 4th International Symposium on Recent Advances in Intrusion Detection (RAID 2001), University of California at Davis, CA, USA, Springer-Verlag.

Valdes, A. and K. Skinner (2001). Probabilistic Alert Correlation. Proceedings of the 4th International Symposium on Recent Advances in Intrusion Detection (RAID 2001), University of California at Davis, CA, USA, Springer - Verlag.

Verwoerd, T. and R. Hunt (2002). "Intrusion Detection Techniques and Approaches." Computer Communications 25(15): 1356-1365.